TRACES OF LIGHT

Absence and Presence in the Work of Loïe Fuller

Ann Cooper Albright

WESLEYAN UNIVERSITY PRESS | MIDDLETOWN, CONNECTICUT

Published by Wesleyan University Press,
Middletown, CT 06459
www.wesleyan.edu/wespress

Printed in China

5 4 3 2 1

Design and composition by Chris Crochetière,
BW&A Books, Inc., Durham, N.C.

Library of Congress Cataloging-in-Publication Data
Albright, Ann Cooper.
    Traces of Light : absence and presence in the work
  of Loie Fuller / by Ann Cooper Albright.
      p. cm.
    ISBN 978-0-8195-6842-7 (cloth : alk. paper)—
    ISBN 978-0-8195-6843-4 (pbk. : alk. paper)
   1. Fuller, Loie, 1862–1928—Criticism and
  interpretation. 2. Dancers—United States.
  3. Modern dance—History. I. Title.
      GV1785.F8A42   2007
      792.8'028092—dc22
                        2006052802

For Tom,
who understands the pleasures
of reading history with soul

CONTENTS

Illustrations

ACKNOWLEDGMENTS

Without the artistic support and practical knowledge of lighting designer Jen Groseth, this book could not have been written. Her professional interest in Fuller's innovative lighting and her imaginative use of modern technology to re-envision its effects helped me see what I might have otherwise passed over. From the moment when I casually asked whether she knew anything about nineteenth-century magic lanterns (whereupon she proceeded to buy one on eBay), to our wonderful collaboration on *Dancing with Light*, Jen has sustained my work on Loïe Fuller in many ways. I also want to acknowledge costume designer, Chris Flaherty, who first recreated Fuller's costume from a patent in 1990 and who helped me with *Dancing with Light* by creating a Fuller-inspired costume for a contemporary work.

The actual book you are holding is also a result of a creative collaboration. I showed Chris Crochetière, the book's designer, my favorite richly colored posters and prints of Fuller well before I actually began writing the chapters. Her enthusiasm for these images helped me envision the finished product as I was writing the text. Chris designed the striking layout of "Matters of Tact" (*Dance Research Journal* [Fall 2004]), which threaded layers of textual analysis with photos of my dancing and images of Fuller's motion. Although we decided not to pursue this direction in the final book, her work helped me integrate the book's design into the writing process. I thank the copy editor, Barbara Norton, as well as my student assistant, Beth Rogers, for their help in preparing the manuscript. Also helpful was my Mc-Nair Scholar student, Baccilio Mendez, who several years ago spent a week at the Jerome Robbins Dance Collection helping me gather initial materials on Fuller's legacy. One of the pleasures of publishing with Wesleyan University Press is working with my editor, Suzanna Tamminen. Our collaboration has continued to grow over the last decade's worth of projects, and I am deeply appreciative of her support not only of my work, but of the field of dance studies in general.

I started this project with a desire to write an academic book that would let me integrate my dancing into the thinking and create a pleasurable and sustainable process of working. I am happy to report that it is possible; this book has been a joy from start to finish. Part of this very real pleasure is due to the fact that much of my archival research took place in Paris. When I was in my early twenties, I went to Paris and decided to become a dancer. My teacher at that time was Françoise Morandière. When I entered her studio one autumn afternoon, she told me that, for her, dancing was a way of life. Over the course of working on this book, I was able to reconnect with Françoise, who helped me find an apartment to sublet and was wonderful company when I was in town. I am indebted to many other scholars and friends for sustaining the French part of my life over these past years. I thank Isabel Ginot, Claire Rousier, and Sarah Cordova for welcoming me into their homes and helping me navigate the complexities of the French archival system. I also want to thank Hélène Pinet of the Rodin Museum for giving me one of her last copies of *Ornement de la durée* and for supporting my research. Thanks also go to the staff at the Bibliothèque Nationale, division of Arts et Spectacles, and the Bibliothèque de l'Opéra, as well as the Cinemathèque de la Danse in Paris. Philippe and Brigitte Guillot were always wonderfully hospitable whenever these research trips to France allowed me to visit them in Dordogne.

In the United States, I am indebted to many, many people, some of whom I will no doubt forget to mention. To begin with, I remember a conversation with Susan Foster in which I was questioning whether this was the right project for me. She encouraged me to write this book as both a dancer and a scholar, and for that little kick in the ass, I will always be grateful. Ann Dils, as always, provided interesting perspectives in our ongoing conversation about writing dance history, and as editor of *Dance Research Journal*, she was very supportive of my first attempts to write about Fuller. She also arranged a residency at the University of North Carolina at Greensboro where I was able to try out my performative lecture on Loïe Fuller. I appreciate similar opportunities at the University of Minnesota, York University, and the University of Virginia. The members of the International Federation of Theatre Researchers (FIRT) "Corporealities and Choreographies" working groups of 2000 and 2002, as well as Susan Manning, David Gere, Ellen Graff, Yopie Prins, and, more recently, Deidre Sklar, have been generous with their intellectual companionship, and for that wonderful mix of thought and fun I am deeply grateful. I want to also acknowledge Candace Feck, my partner in *Accelerated Motion*, for helping me think through the connections between bodies and machines. Participants in the 2006 Screendance conference organized by Doug Rosenberg at the American Dance Festival were wonderfully generous with their ideas and encouragement of the direction of my final chapter.

In New York, I was always welcomed into the home of my oldest friend, Katherine Bourbeau, whose support of my life over these past thirty years is rooted deep in our mutual histories of school, work, and family. I want to acknowledge the help of Charles Perrier, Madeline Nichols, and Pat Rader at the Jerome Robbins Dance Collection at Lincoln Center Library. Jody Sperling met with me over lunch one day to share her insights about dancing with Fuller's legacy.

More locally, I want to thank Allison Gallaher, a librarian at Oberlin College, for being enthusiastic about Loïe Fuller more than fifteen years ago, when I first started teaching dance history there. The deans and administration at Oberlin College have supported my work on Loïe Fuller in many ways over the years, from giving me a scholar's study in the library, to granting me a year of research status at a critical time, to helping fund the color images in this book. This support from an institution where I have based my scholarly career is much appreciated. Recent grants from the Ohio Arts Council and the National Endowment for the Humanities were crucial in giving me the time I needed to write this book, and a spring 2006 fellowship at the Camargo Foundation in Cassis, France, was an extraordinary blessing, especially because they allowed me to come with my children. My warm thanks go to my co-fellows as well as the wonderful staff there.

Last, but most certainly not least, I want to thank my family, Cyrus, Isabel, and Tom Newlin. Over the past five years, my children have grown up hearing about Loïe Fuller, traveling and living in France with me, and accepting with a great deal of patience and good humor my borderline obsession with this early-twentieth-century dancer. During that time, they have matured into amazing and inspiring individuals who seem not the least daunted by my periodic absences from their lives. To my husband, to whom this book is dedicated, I owe a tremendous amount of gratitude for his willingness to imagine a life in which kids, animals, friends, artistic and scholarly projects, houses, and countries weave their way through the landscape of our mutual and independent passions.

In this final gesture of the book, I want to thank Loïe Fuller for inspiring me to write a dancing history.

Author's Note

Over the course of this book, I move from an analysis of the expressive dynamics at the core of Loïe Fuller's dancing to an examination of her integrated use of lighting technologies to discussions of her role as an American artist in Paris. I present the historical progression of her solo choreography from her original *Serpentine Dance* through its various transformations, such as her celebrated *Fire Dance* and her infamous staging of *Salomé*. I also trace her group choreography as it evolved from a collection of individual dances to the atmospheric presentation of abstract movement, sound, and lighting effects, creating a total visual palette that marked her contributions to the early development of cinema. This scholarly journey has included my own physical practice of moving in a reconstruction of Fuller's serpentine costume and staging similar lighting effects (most memorably her underlighting), as well as a selective engagement with a variety of cultural discourses and historical comparisons. My intellectual curiosity about Fuller's work focuses in particular on the theoretical questions concerning what constitutes a choreographic signature. I find these especially relevant as we enter the twenty-first century, a period of increasingly mediated dance.

The initial impetus for this study was my desire to engage with the physical experience of Fuller's dancing body. I wanted to insert the dynamic of her expressive movement into discussions about her artistry. I was convinced that it was her control of a specific movement vocabulary, and not simply the sum of her magical lighting effects, that was largely responsible for her incredible success in Paris at the cusp of a new century. What I soon realized, and what I articulate in chapter 2, is how completely interconnected her dancing was with her use of lighting technology. Unlike so much of our contemporary experience in dance production, where the movement is set in rehearsal studios and the costumes and lighting are included only in the last week or so of production in the actual theater, Fuller's choreography was created in the midst of her swirling costumes and multicolored lighting. This integrated and interactive aspect of Fuller's work has helped me, in turn, to see her oeuvre as part of a larger continuum of bodies and machines. Fuller's imagistic evocations of a bird or lily or forces of nature taught her audiences how to see continuity in movement, how not only to see the pose at the end of a phrase, but to follow her ongoing transformations of figure and ground. This new way of seeing moving light helped establish a visual literacy that paved the way for watching early experiments in film, including Fuller's own *Le lys de la vie*.

More than any other early modern dancer, Loïe Fuller can help us recognize the historical lineage of dance and technology and the way that bodies and machines have long been in conversation with one another. My hope is not only that this book will introduce various overlooked facets of Fuller's long career, but that it might also help us consider contemporary mediated dance in a different light. When I first started this book, I decided to create a dance along with each chapter in order to explore with my body an aspect of the ideas I was presenting. Last summer, as I was researching my final chapter, my editor suggested I might want to think about a Web site for the book. Breathing deeply and refusing the tightness of my first, admittedly knee-jerk, reaction (a resounding NO WAY!), I decided that this new project might just be the perfect "dance" to accompany my final chapter on image, the body, and technology. In talking with the IT (information technology) people responsible for producing Web sites for the press, I became inspired to think of the possibilities of a space where voice, text, body, and image could intersect. I love books, and in conjunction with the production crew for this book, I have worked hard to create a text that would give the reader a visual and kinesthetic, as well as an intellectual, experience. While I am still a bit reluctant to give up the primacy of that medium, I am increasingly curious about the possibilities of this new forum of exchange. Intrigued by how a Web site can make present aspects that are usually absent in a finished book, I invite you to visit www.wesleyan.edu/wespress/tracesoflight and experience for yourself some of the physical research embedded in the spine of *Traces of Light*.

TRACES OF LIGHT

Tracing the Light

Let's begin with traces. Traces of the past. Traces of a dance. Traces of light . . . and color and fabric. Traces of a body, animating all these sources of movement. Traces of a life, spent spinning across nations, across centuries, across identities. How do we trace the past? Reconfigure what is lost? Are traces always even visible?

Perhaps we should lose the noun, which renders us nostalgic, maybe even melancholic at the extreme. Replace our ambition to find out what happened with a curiosity about how it came to be that it was happening. Replace traces with tracing—the past with the passion. Tracing the contours of fabric that spiral upward and outward, we spill over beyond any one historical or aesthetic discourse. This act of tracing can help us become aware not only of what's visible, but also what is, has been, will always be, less clearly visible. Beyond the image into the motion.

ong before I became a committed academic, long before I was a college professor teaching dance history, long before terminal degrees and professional titles, I chanced upon an exhibition of early dance photographs at the Rodin Museum in Paris. I bought the small catalog, and from time to time I would page through the striking black-and-white images searching for dancing inspiration. I always paused at a certain picture of Loïe Fuller. There she is, radiant in the sunlight of Rodin's garden, chest open, arms spread like great wings, running full force towards the camera. It is an image of a strong, mature woman, one who exudes a joyful yet earthy energy. A copy of this photograph, taken in 1900 by Eugène Druet, hangs above my desk. Throughout the process of writing this book, I have referred to this photograph, taking in not simply the visual image of this early-twentieth-century Nike of Samothrace, but also its somatic reality. Using my kinesthetic imagination to embody images of Loïe Fuller (sometimes literally, sometimes figuratively) has fueled much of the intellectual work in these pages. It has also given me one of the most satisfying experiences of researching, dancing, and writing that I have had to date in my academic career. It is my hope that some of this pleasure in doing history translates into the reading experience. For, as Gertrude Stein once asserted, "In the midst of writing there is merriment."[1]

Figure 1. "Loïe Fuller dansant." Photograph by Eugène Druet. Musée Rodin, Paris

Loïe Fuller is one of the most interesting and paradoxical figures in early modern dance. Born in 1862 in Chicago, Fuller began performing in her teens, first as a temperance speaker and later as a member of the Buffalo Bill troupe, touring America on the vaudeville circuit. Her various dramatic roles included cross-dressed ones, such as the lead in the fast-paced melodrama *Little Jack Sheppard*, but it is as a "serpentine" or skirt dancer that she became well-known. In the 1890s Fuller created an extraordinary sensation in Paris with her manipulations of hundreds of yards of silk, swirling high above her and lit dramatically from below. She embodied the fin-de-siècle images of woman as flower, woman as bird, woman as fire, woman as nature. One of the most famous dancers of her time, Fuller starred as the main act at the Folies Bergère, inspiring a host of contemporary fashions and imitators. Fuller's serpentine motif is also visible in much of the decorative imagery of Art Nouveau, and she was the subject of many works by such renowned figures as the artists Auguste Rodin and Henri de Toulouse-Lautrec and the poet Stéphane Mallarmé, among others. Yet despite the importance of her artistic legacy, Fuller's theatrical work fits uneasily within the dominant narratives of early modern dance. Most historians don't see Fuller in light of the development of expressive movement, but rather relegate her to discussions concerning dance and lighting, or dance and technology.

With a nod to the meanings embedded in historical study, Walter Benjamin once wrote, "To dwell means to leave traces."[2] Indeed, traces are the material artifacts that constitute the stuff of historical inquiry, the bits and pieces of a life that scholars follow, gather up, and survey. The word itself suggests the actual imprint of a figure that has passed, the footprint, mark, or impression of a person or event. These kinds of traces are omnipresent in the case of Loïe Fuller. Some traces are more visible than others, some more easily located. But all traces—once noticed—draw us into another reality. *Someone passed this way before.*

I had been thinking about writing a book on Loïe Fuller for some time, but it took me a while to come to terms with how I wanted to respond to the less visible traces of her work. My book project began with a question: why do so many critics and historians dismiss the bodily experience of her dancing in their discussions of Loïe Fuller's theatrical work? The question grew into a dance. The dance, in turn, taught me how to write history from inside the vibrations of its ongoing motion. This book carries the story of an intellectual approach to the past that not only recognizes the corporeal effects of the historian's vantage point, but also mobilizes her body within the process of research and writing. It is the story of a dance shared across a century of time and two continents, a dance that takes place at the meeting point of physical empathy and historical difference.

I am engaged in writing on Loïe Fuller. I use this term engaged very consciously, for I want to highlight both the sense of binding oneself to another person and the word's etymological meaning as "interlocking," a literal as well as a figurative meshing with someone or something. I have chosen to work on this book in a way that integrates conceptual and somatic knowledges, engaging my physical as well as my intellectual and analytic facilities. Dancing amidst clouds of fabric in elaborate lighting effects, I try to understand something of Fuller's experience from the inside out. I also dance with words, moving with my writing to see how ideas resonate in my body. Then too, as I weave my way through archival materials and historical accounts of cultural milieus, I practice staying attentive to what I have learned through that dancing experience. This research process challenges traditional separations between academic scholarship and artistic creation, between criticism and autobiography—in short, between dancing and writing. More than just another layer of historical excavation, my dancing creates a strand of physical thinking that weaves back and forth between the presence of historical artifacts (posters, reviews, photos, memoirs, and paintings) and the absence of Fuller's physical motion.

This introduction is an attempt to articulate the theoretical implications of my embodied approach to this book, an attempt to understand the very conditions of its possibilities. In what follows, I identify two strategies—two practices, if you will—that guide my scholarship on Loïe Fuller. While one is primarily intellectual and the other is based in physical study, both practices refuse the conventional separation of scholarship and the studio, folding themselves into a mix of dancing and writing that houses a certain physical receptiveness at its core. These strands of embodied study create a textured fabric in which aspects of Fuller's work are made visible through my body as well as my writing.

> In all writing, a body is traced, is the tracing and the trace—is the letter, yet never the letter, a literality or rather a lettericity that is no longer legible. A body is what cannot be read in a writing.
>
> (Or one has to understand reading as something other than decipherment. Rather, as touching, as being touched. Writing, reading: matters of tact.)[3]

Despite its linguistic unwieldiness (an effect, no doubt, of the difficulties of translation), this quotation from Jean-Luc Nancy's "Corpus" signals what is for me a profound difference in my current approach to historical work from that of others. Moving from traces to tracing incorporates the tactile and thereby refuses the traditional separation of object from subject. Reaching across time and space to touch Fuller's dancing means that I allow myself, in turn, to be touched, for it is impossible to touch anything in a way that does not also implicate one's own body. (Ask any kid who has just been burned.) Touching, then, becomes the space of our interaction, a mutual engagement. As I touch Loïe Fuller through my historical research, both textual and physical, I am touched in return.

This metaphysical conundrum—how is one touched by history?—has, in my case, a very physical complement. Much of my dance experience over the past two decades has been generated by a form of contemporary dance called contact improvisation. In contact, the actual point of contact (defined, usually, in terms of physical touching, although it can be defined as rhythmic, visual, or kinesthetic touching) creates an improvisational space in which assumptions as to what the dance will be like (future tense) are eschewed in favor of a curiosity about what is happening now (present tense). The meeting point of contact creates an interconnectedness of weight, momentum, and energy that channels a common physical destiny. The partnering in contact is not simply an addition of one movement to another, but rather a realization that both movements will change in the midst of the improvisational duet. In addition to learning how to meet others in a dance, contact dancers train in extreme spatial disorientation. Releasing the uprightness of the body and learning how to be comfortable upside down, rolling and spiraling in and out of the floor, falling without fear—these are all aspects of a training that redirects visual orientation into a kinesthetic grounding.

In a variety of ways, I think of the physical aspects of my research on Fuller in terms of a contact duet. My body is influenced by her dancing as I imagine how she must have used her spine, her head, her chest. Suddenly, historical descriptions of Fuller laid up in bed with excruciating pain and ice packs on her upper back make sense to me. Spinning with my arms raised high and my head thrown back, I realize that Fuller must have slipped a disc in her cervical spine. These kinds of biographical details begin to make sense as I literally incorporate some aspects of the physical tolls her nightly performances must have incurred. Even on an intellectual or metaphysical level, I think of our interaction as a contact duet, a somatic meeting set up by the traces of history. I believe that envisioning this relation in terms of an improvisational duet usefully redefines the traditional separation of a historical subject (treated as the "object" of study) and the omniscient writer of history. When, for instance, I review the enormous variety of images of "La Loïe"—the posters, photographs, paintings, prints, and program covers—I try not only to analyze the visual representation of her work, but also to imagine the kind of dancing that inspired such visions. That is to say, I allow myself to be touched (these "matters of tact") by what remains only partially visible.

In her introduction to *Choreographing History*, Susan Foster also sees the interaction of historian and the bodies of history as a dynamic tango between traces and tracing, between artifacts and the language that reanimates their cultural significance. Her notion of "bodily theorics" engages with similar metaphors of writing history as a tactile duet, an improvisational connection between past and present bodies. But, she reminds us:

> This affiliation, based on a kind of kinesthetic empathy between living and dead but imagined bodies, enjoys no primal status outside the world of writing. It possesses no organic authority; it offers no ultimate validation for sentiment. But it is redolent with physical vitality and embraces a concern for beings that live and have lived. Once the historian's body recognizes value and meaning in kinesthesia, it cannot dis-animate the physical action of past bodies it has begun to sense.[4]

Loïe Fuller's work embodies a central paradox of dance as a representation of both abstract movement and a physical body. Her dancing epitomizes the intriguing insubstantiality of movement caught in the process of tracing itself. Surrounded by a funnel of swirling fabric spiraling upward into the space around her and bathed in colored lights of her own invention, Fuller's body seems to evaporate in the midst of her spectacle. Nonetheless, Fuller's body is undeniably present, and discussions of her sartorial style and physical girth break through these romantic representations of her ethereality and femininity in interesting ways. Splayed across history and geography, Fuller's dancing takes place at the crossroads of diverse languages, two centuries, and many cultural changes.

Intellectually, the material is fascinating. But there is something even more compelling for me in this subject. It's a gut thing. I feel that many scholars cover over the kinesthetic and material experience of Fuller's body in favor of the image, rather than reading that image as an extension of her dancing. Descriptions of her work get so entangled with artistic images or poetic renderings that they easily forget the physical labor involved. Then too, there are all those apologies and side notes about how Loïe Fuller didn't have a dancer's body, or any dance training really, as if the movement images were solely dependent on the lighting, as if it were all technologically rendered. (One typical example: "The influence of Loïe Fuller upon the theater will always be felt, particularly in the lighting of the scene and in the disposition of draperies. *But she was never a great dancer. She was an apparition*" [emphasis added].)[5] There is an odd urgency in my responses to these commentaries: my whole body revolts with the kinesthetic knowledge that something else was going on. *My body tells me this.*

In 1990 I made a dance called *Traces of Light*. It was the first time I incorporated light as a source of movement and stillness within the choreography, the first time I experienced what it was like to dance in, with, through, and next to light. The following year I traced another dance that used light as a partner for movement. I recreated Loïe Fuller's dance "Le lys" (1895), or, at least something approximating it. It was part of an evening-length choreographic work, and although we meticulously reconstructed Fuller's patented design for costume and curved wands, I thought about this dance not as a historical reconstruction, but rather as more of an interesting effect plundered from the abundant resources of early modern dance. Because of budget constraints, we used parachute material, not silk. Purple, not white.

I remember the first time I danced in her costume. It felt odd to be cloaked in yards of fabric, me, who was so used to dancing in pants and a top, with nothing in my way, every movement and each direction easily accessible. Within her costume, I have to prepare each step in order not to trip on the extra fabric. Twisting first to one side, then to the other, I gather my strength and then launch the spiral, catching the air underneath the fabric and opening my arms and reaching towards the sky. Two minutes later, I collapse, exhausted and dizzy. I am awed by the upper-body strength and aerobic stamina Fuller must have had to keep the fabric aloft and swirling for up to forty-five minutes a night. How odd that some historians insist that she wasn't a dancer.[6] Was it that she didn't look like a dancer? That she didn't act the way they thought a dancer should? Clearly she had a trained body and specific movement techniques in her body. In order to make a mere twelve-minute solo with much less fabric than she used, I had to train intensively in my upper body for several months. *In motion, my body talks back to historical representation and teaches me to look again, to read beyond the visual evidence and into its source.* Ironically, then, where others savored the image of her disappearance (into the dark, into the folds of cloth, into the ideal symbol), I have come to appreciate the dynamic of her vital presence, those moments of becoming, and becoming again.

In the ensuing decade I returned to the costume and her dancing each time I taught early-twentieth-century dance history. Taking history from the classroom to the studio, my students would try on Fuller's costume. But nothing happens until you begin to move and spin. Some students would get caught up in Fuller's whirl, the mystique of her dancing. Their enthusiasm inspired me. Eventually I became aware of a need to write on Fuller. Part physical, part intellectual, this desire was fueled by the intriguing complexities of a cultural moment in which a short, stocky lesbian from Chicago arrives in Paris to inspire a famous poet's evocation of the dancer as at once feminized and yet also decorporealized into a vision of pure movement. I began to conceive of this twisted relationship between dance and image as a Möbius strip, one in which the interconnectedness of figure and body would never entirely line up, but always exist just across the fold.

What is so fascinating for me about dance as a historical phenomenon is the many different kinds of layers and information we need to excavate in order to understand that kinetic and artistic experience. What constitutes the dance as staged in Western theaters? Is it the movement? The dancers embodying the movement? The narrative plot or libretto? The entire theatrical apparatus, including sets, costumes, music, choreographer, technicians, and company managers? The social and cultural context in which it was created? All of the above? In other words, what do we need in order to know the dancer and the dance?

In the introduction to their collection of essays *Acting on the Past*, Mark Franko and Annette Richards describe this process of culling many different kinds of historical sources: "Absent performative events have conceptual, imaginary, and evidential, as well as actively reproductive bases. They are especially characterized by movement between present and past, one in which archive and act, fragment and body, text and sounding, subject and practice, work in provocative interaction."[7]

I see my work as taking place in the midst of this "provocative interaction"— right at the imaginative intersection of the past and the present. I visualize this (double) crossing spatially, marked in the center of a vast, cavernous space—much like the old wooden dance studio where I teach and work. At one end is the stage of the Folies Bergère. My view is from backstage, with all the workings of its magical effects revealed. Programs, posters, and images of Loïe Fuller, as well as pages from her autobiography and countless other articles about her, dot the floor, creating a historical landscape and defining various pathways through the space. I improvise my way through these artifacts to the opposite end of the room, where I also envision a backstage. This time, however, it is backstage of the theater where I work. There is a new Plexiglas floor in the middle, underneath which we will project lights in multiple colors, reinventing Fuller's lighting designs within a contemporary context. It is the motion between these two backstage spaces (one in the past, the other in the present) as well as the dancing pathways I construct from source to source that inform my research methodology.

A major attraction in Paris at the end of the nineteenth century, Fuller left her mark on the imaginations of many poets and artists of her time. My scholar's cubicle in the library is filled with images of Fuller's dancing: posters, sculptures, photographs, articles about her. How do I respond to these traces? Looking at the reproductions, reading texts, I am fascinated—and moved. What would happen if I took these images, these ideas, into the studio? *I grab my notebook and sprint out of the library.* Inspired to move as well as to write, I take the plunge back into the physical, using my body both as a point of departure and as a moving vehicle, a method of transportation into history.

In an early essay entitled "Rereading as a Woman: The Body in Practice," the feminist scholar Nancy Miller discusses the ways in which readings of literary texts are very much affected by the cultural experience of the reader. She writes: "To reread as a woman is at least to imagine the lady's place; to imagine while reading the place of a woman's body; to read reminded that her identity is also re-membered in stories of the body."[8] My studies in feminist theory, inspired by the work of scholars such as Nancy Miller, have taught me to be aware of how I produce a double reading—as a scholar, as a woman. These days, I am challenging myself to push the implications of Miller's essay even further, that is to say, to read (and, by extension, to write) as a dancer, allowing my body to be present even in the midst of a scholarly project.

Because I have decided to posit my dancing body as a research tool or guide (perhaps assistant is a more apt expression, for my body certainly has a mind of its own and doesn't always follow my instructions), I feel compelled to grapple with the relationship of my body to history. In the dance field, there often seems to be a split between researchers who focus primarily on reconstructing a dance from the past on bodies from the present and those scholars who use dance as the hook into a broader cultural study of modes of production, representation, and reception of artistic endeavors. Of course, we all might quickly assert that we do both, but it is rare that I read an essay in which I feel that the writer's bodily knowledge was a crucial part of the scholarly process. Indeed, although *theoretically* we might be interested and excited by the possibilities of a dialogue between the dancing body of the researcher and that of the subject they are researching, we are rarely willing to confront that methodologically murky territory for ourselves. With this work on Loïe Fuller, I am asking what it would mean to research a historical body, a dancing body, a desiring body precisely through the intertext of an "other" body—my own. How can I use my embodied knowledge to move beyond the traces of artistic and literary representations of Fuller's dancing into the physicality at their core?

Over the past few years, I have developed a series of solo performances inspired by my work on Loïe Fuller. These dances take place at the intersection of historical research and choreographic expression. Although they do delineate a movement vocabulary that references Fuller's work, these choreographies are not reconstructions of her works. Spinning, spirals circling out of the upper body, and large expansive gestures of the arms with an upward gaze of the face—these motifs constitute much of the dancing. My first solo, "Searching for Loïe," was a structured improvisation that used my earliest writings on Fuller as a sound score. Playing with the juxtaposition of poetic and expository prose, the read text created an open field (semi-serious, semi-playful) in which to explore my physical response to Fuller's historical legacy. Later, the dance morphed into a performative lecture entitled "Acts of Passion: Tracing History through the Body." In this more recent incarnation, I interrupt an academic discussion with dancing that pairs my movement with slide images of Fuller's dancing. Moving back and forth across the stage, my body interrupts the projections, flashing my shadow onto the screen. In these moments, Fuller's image is joined by my image, creating a complex duet involving interpretation, interconnection, and reflection. Bringing myself into the dancing in this manner forces me to reflect on my own intellectual position and physical experience as I ask myself, "So what does this embodied experience tell me about history?" My answers to this question encompass both specific details about her movement, staging, and lighting techniques and a more general sense of her performance energy and the role light played within Fuller's own personal cosmology.

Loïe Fuller thought of her theater spaces as laboratories in which to combine lights and movement in increasingly sophisticated ways. Fortunately, I have a wonderful collaborator and lighting designer in my colleague Jen Groseth, who also became quite interested in Loïe Fuller's work and legacy. One year our university situation gave us the luxury of a significant amount of time to spend experimenting with lighting in the theater, creating the lights and movement both simultaneously and interactively. Although we were not attempting to reconstruct her dances per se, we did use Fuller's original design patents and depictions of her staging (with live lighting technicians above, below, and to the sides of her specially raised platform) to inform our updated use of her lighting inventions. For instance, we created a floor out of Plexiglas, with intelligent lights revolving above and below its surface. The result was a twelve-minute performance entitled "Dancing with Light."

Collaborating with a lighting designer for days on end brought me closer, I believe, to the reality of Fuller's working environment. Not only did I begin to understand the physical labor involved, I understood why she is always pictured wearing shoes (the stage floors of variety theaters being notoriously dirty and riddled with nails and bits of this and that). I also realized that the reason she never mentions using haze to intensify the rays of light (an effect every critic comments on) was because the theaters were already so dusty and smoky, one didn't need any additional stuff in the air. It seems so simple and obvious, but the physical experience of making a dance in the middle of a busy theater jerked me out of the modern-dance paradigm of solo artist working alone in the studio, waiting for inspiration, and brought me headlong into the gritty realities of popular theater. Although it is true that at the beginning of her career, Loïe Fuller was mostly known as a soloist, she never performed anything without the committed assistance of a whole crew of technicians. Both an artist and a craftsperson in the theater, she transcended a deep and still omnipresent division between artists and technicians, directors and stage hands, dancers and electricians.

One of the most important aspects of "Dancing with Light," for me, was a new appreciation of the experience of moving in strongly defined lights. Unlike lighting whose sole purpose is to illuminate the dancers, the lighting we created was an equal partner in the dance. Sometimes the light obscured me, sometimes it revealed my dancing, and sometimes I was simply a screen onto which a variety of moving lights were projected. At various times I felt sheltered and enclosed, inspired, even disoriented (especially when dancing on clear glass with lights shining from underneath). The palpable presence of these lights reminded me of otherworldly spirits.

Returning to my study, I began to understand more concretely the spiritual role that light played for Loïe Fuller. I believe that Fuller experienced a certain kind of euphoria when dancing that was intensified by her dramatic approach to lighting. Her dances generally followed a classic creation narrative. They began in a total blackout (highly unusual for that time), with the first strands of music calling forth a dim illumination of the small motions of her hands and fabric. The lights, movements, and music would generally crescendo into a final frenzy of color and motion that faded abruptly back into a primordial darkness. The idea that light had spiritual overtones for Fuller is confirmed by her own writing—both her published autobiography and unpublished letters and fragments of a book she was writing later in her life. Although I don't always know what to make of this visionary aspect of Fuller's work and life, I do know that I would never have understood its significance without having danced in a light so defined, I could pierce it with my body.

In her essay "The Concept of Intertextuality and Its Application in Dance Research," Janet Adshead-Lansdale identifies the imaginative possibilities of an approach to dance research that resonates with my own:

> These methodological shifts of position are sometimes in harmony and often not, but they can be tolerated and made to function by seeing that it is in the spaces created between a multiplicity of texts and traces [that] there is the opportunity, indeed, more strongly, the demand, that each reader should engage in this process of constructing meaning by unraveling what seems to be implied by the work, or the method, or the discipline, while simultaneously creating their own threads from their own experience.[9]

This layering of texts forms a web of signifying practices that merge and emerge depending upon the historical or methodological lens one chooses to use. Yet these intertexts can also produce a misleading sense that we have captured the thing itself—the *presence* of a dancing body.

I want to introduce the concept of intertextuality, not in order simply to add another historical layer or methodological option, but rather to point out the space between these texts. Although this space may figure as an absence, it is not necessarily a loss. Rather, I see it as a distance (both historical and cultural) across which desire always pulls interpretation. At once opportunity and demand (which I sometimes experience as an internal command, an urgency that compels action or speaks to a particular direction of thought), this intertextuality marks the space of improvisation possible within historical work. It recognizes the gap between myself and the subject of my inquiry—that historical distance—while simultaneously foregrounding the desire to close that gap, to build bridges and cross over from one period to another. Not every subject would necessarily elicit such mobile strategies. But given the elusive quality of Fuller's work and reception in combination with the unpredictable edge of my physical commitment to exploring her dances, this methodological fluidity seems right at the moment.

Writing a scholarly book on Loïe Fuller while making a series of dances incorporating aspects of her oeuvre opens up an intertextual space that can become the site of a negotiation between past and present bodies, between history and desire. More than a poststructuralist ploy (one in which movement is simply a slippery strategy of evasive criticism), however, this approach stretches the seams of traditional historical inquiry. My research uses these subjective perspectives as points of entry to a variety of intellectual trends and physical experiences critical to understanding the transition from the nineteenth to the twentieth century.

Although at times I have been daunted by its complexity, Loïe Fuller's work reflects many of the key social and aesthetic issues embedded in this shift into a modern, industrial, and increasingly global world. Documenting the creation and reception of Fuller's choreography has led me to grapple with a plethora of intriguing contradictions: Fuller was one of the most famous dancers of her time, but was later marginalized by modern dance history. Her dancing evoked visions of nature, yet her spectacles were renowned for their elaborate use of electrical lighting and theatrical artifice. She was lauded as the epitome of the symbolist ideal (ethereal, mysterious, poetic), yet she was also embraced by the futurists as an industrial engineer of the theater. Fuller was seen by her public as quintessentially American, yet she lived most of her adult life in Paris and was always associated with the particularly French style of art nouveau. She was celebrated by the most important artists, scientists, and literary figures of her time, yet she performed mostly in working-class venues and music halls. These are just a few of the many contradictions that animate the intellectual trajectory of this book.

The six chapters here progress from solo dancing to group choreography, from discussions of Fuller's physical technique to analysis of her staged productions, and finally to explorations of her work within the larger milieus of early-twentieth-century theater and film. Chapter 1, "Serpentine Signatures: Inscription and Representation in Loïe Fuller's Early Dances," traces the creation and reception of Fuller's wildly successful serpentine dance. I discuss the development of her physical technique and explore how she led the audience to focus on the motion of her draperies instead of the pose at the end of a musical phrase. I also look at the strategies she used to create a recognizable signature, even though she was unable to copyright her dances. Finally, I take up Stéphane Mallarmé's evocations of her dancing, including his reading of her dancing as a hieroglyph-like script, to talk about dancing as writing.

The second chapter, "Becoming Light: Engaging the Dynamics of Color and Space," analyzes the elements of light, space, and color at work in Fuller's spectacles. I argue that Fuller engaged the expressive possibilities of electricity by dancing with, instead of merely in the middle of, her theatrical lighting. Finally, I look at one of her most famous dances, "Fire Dance," to articulate how Fuller's dancing staged a "dramaturgy of darkness," using light to create an emotional narrative even in the midst of ever changing patterns and abstract design.

Chapter 3, "Born in America, Made in Paris: Loïe Fuller and the Exposition Universelle of 1900," focuses on Fuller's involvement in this world's fair in Paris and on her image as the poster child of art nouveau. Here, I utilize Patrice Higonnet's concept of phantasmagoria to develop a trajectory of Fuller's work as it moves from nineteenth-century spectacle to twentieth-century trope. The chapter reflects on how the complicated networks of nationalism, aesthetic ideology, and global marketing involved in this extravagant festival had an impact on the reception and future directions of Fuller's career, in terms of her work both as an artist and as a director and producer.

Chapter 4, "Femininity with a Vengeance: Strategies of Veiling and Unveiling in Loïe Fuller's Performances of *Salomé*," compares Fuller's 1895 and 1907 performances of *Salomé*, works that have been given little sustained critical attention. Dance historians writing on Fuller's career tend to focus on the innovations of her serpentine dance, rarely considering her *Salomé* performances except as precursors to Fuller's famous "Fire Dance." Many critics consider these two "lyric pantomimes," in which Fuller returns to her melodramatic roots, artistic failures. Certainly the critical reception was mixed, and some of Fuller's most avid supporters panned her 1895 version of the Salomé legend. But when placed in the cultural frame of fin-de-siècle Salomania, Fuller's two productions of *Salomé* reveal intriguing feminist approaches to this infamous femme fatale. By staging herself as this hypersexualized decadent icon, Fuller was, I argue, resisting the conventional reading of her dancing as "chaste."

The fifth chapter, "Staging the Self: Expressive Bodies and Autobiographical Acts," places Fuller alongside three other well-known women acting and dancing in Paris during the early years of the twentieth century. I compare the performance work of Colette, Eva Palmer, and Isadora Duncan with the group choreography of

Fuller's later career, analyzing how all four women challenged nineteenth-century gendered hierarchies to stage and then write about their visions of the "new" woman. Despite their very different interests and aesthetics, these four women were connected by their belief that women's bodies could be agents of self-expression and by an equally fervent desire to share their ideas in autobiographical writings that doubled as aesthetic and social manifestos.

My final chapter, "Resurrecting the Future: Body, Image, and Technology," addresses the integration of dance and technology (the body and machine) throughout Fuller's long, multifaceted career. Beginning with her original patents of the 1890s and ending with the avant-garde legacy of her 1921 film *Le lys de la vie*, I argue that unlike many modern dancers who set their dancing in opposition to modern machinery, Fuller was able to conceive of technology as a way to connect to her body, a way to highlight, rather than hide, the physical expressivity of her movement. Developing some of the theoretical discussions that arose during the 2006 Screendance conference at the American Dance Festival, I draw some parallels between Fuller's later group dance spectacles (her use of shadows, images projected on a large backdrop, etc.) and more recent adventures of dance on screens. Reviewing how critics wrote about Fuller's absence of body and presence of figure at the beginning of the twentieth century can be an enlightening introduction to discussions of mediated dance at the beginning of the twenty-first century. I use the contemporary example of *Ghostcatching*, the digital dance collaboration between Bill T. Jones, Paul Kaiser, and Shelley Eshkar, to articulate how both Fuller's work and this more recent exploration of virtual dancing can teach us to see movement with a more active, kinesthetic perception. At the core of this discussion lies the complex relationship between physical expression and visual abstraction, between body and image in dance.

Loïe Fuller has fascinated me for a long time now. I offer *Traces of Light: Absence and Presence in the work of Loïe Fuller* as one dancer-scholar's critical reflections on her choreographic oeuvre and artistic legacy. I point out this obvious fact because I am deeply and humbly aware of the paucity of book-length studies on Fuller. With the exception of Lista's work in French, the Currents' book in English, and several exhibition catalogs, there are few works devoted entirely to investigating Fuller's dancing. Fortunately, there are many shorter pieces, including several interesting essays and smart chapters in books, that explore different aspects of Fuller's performances as well as her role in the fin-de-siècle Parisian environment. In particular, I was inspired by the interdisciplinary scholarship of Rhonda Garelick, Felicia McCarren, and Julie Ann Townsend, and by the writing of the dance scholars Sally Sommer, Jody Sperling, and Amy Koritz.

In France, where I wrote most of the second half of this book, servers in restaurants wish you "Bon appétit" at the beginning of a meal. Because most French dinners extend through multiple courses, however, they often wish their guests "Bonne continuation" as they serve the next dish. I am amused by thinking of this study as one course within a feast of work on Loïe Fuller. My appetite was whetted by other scholars' contributions. I have prepared a main course for people to digest, but I also look forward to the next course that someone else will create. My hope is that rather than being the definitive study, this book will inspire others to write about Loïe Fuller. *Bonne continuation!*

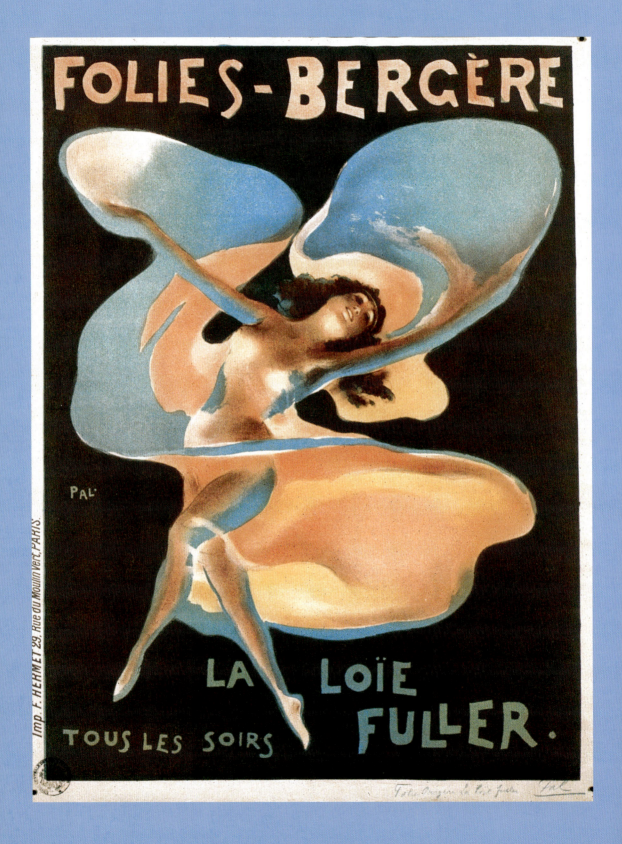

CHAPTER 1

Serpentine Signatures

Inscription and Representation
in Loïe Fuller's Early Dances

The preparation is crucial. Once inside the costume, I must lightly lift the fabric all around, so that it spills away from my body. Otherwise, I run the risk of getting the extra fabric caught between my feet and tripping, a rather ignominious beginning to a dance famous for its graceful fluidity. Pressing my feet deep into the ground, I begin to twist my upper body from side to side, catching a bit of air under the fabric. After a few passes back and forth, I bend my knees and lean forward to trace a slight under-curve with the wands in my hands before swooping to one side to launch the fabric high into the air. If I initiate the movement with the right amount of percussive twist in my torso, I can create a loft in the fabric and sustain the serpentine swirl for quite some time, continuing the spiraling image long enough for it to crystallize in the audience's mind.

This serpentine spiral was Loïe Fuller's signature. Almost every representation of Fuller's dancing refers in some way to this figurative motion. It is iconic, doubling as an image of Fuller's dancing as well as a quintessential motif of art nouveau, a major decorative influence of her time. But it is doubly significant. Although most critics focus on the traces of Fuller's work left by other artists, documenting the visual effects of her motion, I want to consider the implications of tracing the inside action, the central torque and its sequential expansion into the periphery. As I will propose over the course of this chapter, it was the combination of these two forces—the outside visual effect and the inside torque—that propelled Fuller into international celebrity at the end of the nineteenth century and separated her performances from those of her many imitators. Rather than dismissing Fuller's dancing as simply a means to the end of her sophisticated visual spectacle, I suggest that it was, in fact, a fundamentally innovative and modern way of moving, one that also precipitated a radical new way of seeing bodies in motion.

This chapter traces the creation and reception of Fuller's wildly successful and widely imitated serpentine dance. Writing from the dual perspective of a dance historian exploring a cultural moment and a dancer spinning inside the spiraling fabric that produced Fuller's signature swirl, I explore both the visual and the kinesthetic im-

Figure 2. "La Loïe Fuller." Folies Bergère poster by PAL, 1895. Musée de la Publicité, Paris

plications of this work. As the dance evolved from its first incarnation in a regional theater to its signature status as the main attraction at the Folies Bergère in Paris, it acquired a variegated mantle of cultural significance. Some people saw the dance as the latest and most spectacular innovation of skirt dancing, the staple of music-hall entertainment. Others saw the work as a cleansing of that tradition, placing onstage in its stead an abstract vision of motion that appealed to a more modernist sensibility. Yet others saw it as an archetypal rendering of a creation myth or the magical metamorphosis of natural forms.

In 1892, the same year Loïe Fuller won acclaim in New York City and Paris for her serpentine dance, she also set a legal precedent by suing for copyright infringement (*Fuller v. Bemis*). Unfortunately, she lost her case, creating a judicial precedent that kept choreography out of the realm of copyright protection until the 1970s.[1] The story of her "invention" of the serpentine dance, its critical reception, and the subsequent dismissal of the expressive value of that dance in the eyes of a U.S. district court judge, gives us a great deal of insight into how popular dancing was viewed at that time. By tracking the issues of artistic innovation, popular imitation, and the development of a choreographic signature, we can chart the ways in which Fuller's performances changed how people came to perceive female dancing bodies on turn-of-the-century theatrical stages in Europe and America.

One of the most intriguing aspects of Fuller's oeuvre to me is the enormous range of artistic and critical responses to her serpentine dance, each one contributing a different perspective on this seminal choreography. Because an exhaustive survey of these responses would most likely end up being a compilation of written reviews and works of art dedicated to Loïe Fuller, I have chosen instead to tease out various aspects of a critical question for dance—what constitutes a movement signature? The first section of this chapter will explore the transformation of Fuller's serpentine dance from its origins as a new rendition of the classic skirt dance to the abstract vision of moving fabric presented to critical acclaim in Paris. Over the course of this discussion, I will review how Fuller's work fit into the emergence of an ideology of individually "expressive" movement and its role in defining the development of early modern dance. I then chart how Fuller's dancing moved beyond the tropes of expressivity to enact what Hillel Schwartz calls a "new kinaesthesia." The second section will consider the question of artistic signatures within popular entertainment. Here I explore how within the frame of the various music halls, such as the Folies Bergère, where her works were often produced, Fuller's dance was at once seen as completely her own and imitated by hundreds of other dancers. The third section will use Stéphane Mallarmé's writings on Fuller's performances to situate her work within the context of an emerging discourse about meaning and visual abstraction in aesthetic dancing at the beginning of the twentieth century. In a final section, I will weave these various strands into a discussion of morphology, linking the themes suggested by the title of this chapter—the connections between writing and dancing—to a discussion of desire.

In her autobiography, *Fifteen Years of a Dancer's Life*, Loïe Fuller describes the discovery of her famous dance in an early chapter entitled "How I Created the Serpentine Dance." Her narrative of her accidental discovery of the effects of light on gauzy fabric and her subsequent honing of different methods for manipulating that fabric in light is reiterated practically verbatim in virtually every historical account written about Fuller's early career. As she recounts the events in her autobiography, it was while touring in a new play called *Quack M.D.* that Fuller was called upon to add a scene in which she would be "hypnotized." Finding a long skirt from India sent to her by acquaintances, she raised the waist up to her chest to fashion an empire-waist gown made of a very light and transparent fabric. Always quick to point out the irony of such situations, Fuller comments: "The robe looked thoroughly original, perhaps even a little ridiculous."[2] She continues, describing what was, in effect, a classic staple of nineteenth-century theater, the Pygmalion scene.

> The stage scenery, representing a garden, was flooded with pale green light. Dr. Quack made a mysterious entrance and then began his work of suggestion. The orchestra played a melancholy air very softly, and I endeavoured to make myself as light as possible, in order to give the impression of a fluttering figure obedient to the doctor's orders.
>
> He raised his arms. I raised mine. Under the influence of suggestion, entranced—so, at least, it looked—with my gaze held by his, I followed his every motion. My robe was so long that I was continually stepping upon it, and mechanically I held it up with both hands and raised my arms aloft, all the while that I continued to flit around the stage like a winged spirit.
>
> There was a sudden exclamation from the house: "It's a butterfly! A butterfly!"
>
> I turned on my steps, running from one end of the stage to the other, and a second exclamation followed: "It's an orchid!"
>
> To my great astonishment sustained applause burst forth.[3]

Although Fuller promoted the notion that her serpentine dance spontaneously arose from a fortuitous combination of lack and luck—that is to say, from a combination of her resourcefulness in finding a costume quickly and her willingness to follow the audience's excitement for the images that gauzy skirt created—her dancing that evening was not without precedent. It was clearly indebted to the skirt-dancing craze that had crossed the Atlantic Ocean from England to the United States. Although Fuller was known to claim at times that she had never danced before, in fact, her multifaceted career had brought her more than once to the stage in a movement-based role.[4] In 1889, for instance, she traveled to London to perform in a dramatic play entitled *Caprice*. Once there, she ended up performing with the Gaiety Company first as a replacement for Florence Saint John, and then later for Letty Lind in *Carmen Up to Date*. At that time, Lind was the star of the Gaiety Theatre, a London music hall famous for the "Gaiety Girls," a nineteenth-century British version of the Radio City Music Hall Rockettes (see Figure 2).

In his *Modern Dancing and Dancers* (1912), J. E. Crawford Flitch describes the skirt dance as a compromise between the overly academic ballet of the time and the more outrageous step-kick dancing, such as the can-can (*le chahut*) or its English derivative, the "ta-ra-ra-boom-de-ay."

> The Skirt Dance broadened the scope of dancing. In itself never a performance of very great artistic merit, it had all the value of a revolt. It broke down the dominion of a tradition which had become too narrow. It opened up new vistas. It contained the seeds of future movements. In particular it recalled the forgotten dances of antiquity. Though essentially modern, and notably so in its lapses into vulgarity, it nevertheless suggested new possibilities in the grace of flowing drapery, the value of line, the simplicity and naturalness that were characteristic of Greek Dance.[5]

Skirt dancing quickly became the latest novelty item within the popular variety entertainment circuit. It demanded only the simplest foundation in folk (clogging) or waltzing steps, and the long, billowing skirts could make up for a variety of skill levels. In an interview Letty Lind discussed the dance for which she became well-known. When asked, "What do you say to 'X.X.'s' assertion that 'voluminous petticoats cover a multitude of careless steps?'" Lind replied: "That is quite true in many instances, and that many girls acquire a knowledge of singing and skirt manipulation enough to be merely pleasing and graceful, but in no sense can they be called dancers in the highest and most thorough meaning" ("The Length of a Petticoat," *Daily Graphic*, February 13, 1891). As it evolved, skirt dancing became increasingly associated with burlesque, an excuse to flaunt what was hidden underneath the skirt. Nonetheless, some dancers continued to elaborate on the basic ripple effects of the undulating fabric. Alice Lethbridge, another Gaiety Girl, developed a variation in which she bent her body backward until it was almost horizontal and then proceeded to revolve around her own axis as she circled the stage.[6] This spectacular move may well have been the source of Fuller's extravagant back-arch, memorialized in the famous Jules Chéret poster advertising her early performances at the Folies Bergère.

Returning from London, Fuller was hired first in *Quack M.D.* ("discovering" her own variation on the skirt dance) and then as a specialty act (in "The Serpentine Dance") in *Uncle Celestine*. On March 19, 1892, the *New York Blade* reported on her dancing in terms that made its origins clear.

> She held the skirt out to either side. It looked like a big white fan inverted. She went at the active business of dancing. Her dance might have been a failure if it hadn't been for the soft footfalls and the wonderful skirt. She made no more noise than a cat, and in the limelight it seemed as though the great skirt had a million folds and every one a yard. . . . When she came back . . . she wound it up and her figure showed out clear through the white. That was a bit of the Nautch dance. Then she dropped it all and began gath-

Figure 4. "Skirt Dancing: Mlle. Loïe Fuller and Her Transformations." Picture Magazine. *Jerome Robbins Dance Division, The New York Public Library for the Performing Arts, Astor, Lenox and Tilden Foundations*

ering it fast on the sides. . . . After the second recall, she gathered the skirt at the same funny angle and twirled and pirouetted until the white silk took the form of a gigantic screw.[7]

Although the plebeian choice of words is rather jarring, this article does give us a sense of Fuller's growing movement vocabulary.

In the Jerome Robbins Dance Division at the New York Public Library for the Performing Arts is a series of black-and-white sketches, originally published in the French magazine *L'illustration* and reprinted in *Picture Magazine*, that depict Loïe Fuller in various traditional skirt-dancing poses (see Figures 4 and 5). Entitled "Skirt-Dancing—Mlle. Loïe Fuller and Her Transformations," the series presents eight different images of Fuller performing, each with a caption classifying the movement motif and/or the costume. Numbers such as "The Serpent Dance," "The Spiral," and "The Butterfly Dance" represent Fuller classics and match the various souvenir postcards produced during her early career. In these posed studio shots, it is clear that Fuller is marketing herself within the conventional frames of variety entertainment. In a literal (if potentially ironic) twist on later-twentieth-century genres of pin-up shots, a London publicity card shows Fuller standing

Figure 5. "Skirt Dancing: Mlle. Loïe Fuller and Her Transformations." Picture Magazine. *Jerome Robbins Dance Division, The New York Public Library for the Performing Arts, Astor, Lenox and Tilden Foundations*

against a backdrop with her butterfly dress "pinned up" in a circle around her (see Figure 6). Although the sketches in *Picture Magazine* clearly reflect the showgirl aspects of skirt dancing (that is to say, skirts as decorative frames for female bodies), the studio photograph provocatively hints at Fuller's eventual disappearance into her costume. The vivid contrast of light and dark allows her torso to blend into the light background and her hair to merge with the dark butterfly figures, leaving only her face and arms to stand out. Eventually, even these parts of her body would become obscured by her increasingly voluminous costume.

In her paper "Loïe Fuller's Serpentine Dance: A Discussion of Its Origins in Skirt Dancing and a Creative Reconstruction," Jody Sperling, a self-described "Loïe Fuller imitator," makes an important distinction between Fuller's work and the standard approaches to skirt dancing: "Hitherto, the skirt dance consisted of the graceful manipulation of a full skirt by the dancer. By adding substantially more fabric to the width of the skirt and introducing novel lighting effects, Fuller shifted the skirt dancer's emphasis from displays of pretty refinement or leg-revealing suggestion, instead concentrating on creating abstract visual imagery."[8] Whereas skirt dancing tended to present a display of physical attributes (and occasionally physical skills), Fuller's performances focused on a transformation of the dancer into the

Figure 6. "Loïe Fuller." Studio shot by Rotary Photo. Jerome Robbins Dance Division, The New York Public Library for the Performing Arts, Astor, Lenox and Tilden Foundations

image. Sperling's point is an important one and leads to an interpretation of Fuller as an early abstractionist. The problem with dubbing Fuller's work abstract is that it can easily reinforce a perspective on modern dance that pits expression against abstraction when really Fuller's early work bridged the two.

The *Picture Magazine* sketches of Fuller dancing are bookended by two depictions of Fuller "At Rest." The second one particularly intrigues me, for it shows a woman in street clothes, her head drooping over her right shoulder, her arms hanging in the center of her body. This position could come directly from a nineteenth-century Delsarte manual. More than simply the artist's attempt at closure, this final posture, I believe, indicates the liminal status of Fuller's early dancing—that it took place somewhere in between the variety-hall genre of skirt dancing and the gestural vocabulary of Delsarte. Although she drew on her experience in popular entertainment as well as her exposure to the expressive principles of dramatic gesture and persona, Fuller never committed herself to either the flesh-market mentality of the one or the middle-class aestheticism of the other. Instead, she played across these genres while developing an approach to movement that was truly her own.

In an article praising her performances at the Boston Theatre in Boston in 1896, a reviewer makes an interesting distinction between skirt dancing and Fuller's serpentine dance. Although the article collapses the four distinct pieces, "La nuit," "Le feu," "Le firmament," and "Le lys du Nil," into one genre, the description of how to watch the serpentine dance reveals how successful Fuller was in teaching the audience to attend to different priorities.

> In the skirt dance, the artistic value of the skirt lies less in its graceful swing
> per se than in its swing seconding, emphasizing and throwing into relief the
> graceful bodily movement of the dancer. In the serpentine dance, on the
> other hand, the drapery—for it is too voluminous to be called a skirt—and
> the movements imparted to it by the dancer are all in all of themselves;
> what the dancer does with her body and limbs is of quite vanishing impor-
> tance for you do not see it; the main matter is what she does to her drapery
> and how it is illuminated by the many-colored electric lights. . . . One of the
> most striking features of the whole performance is its absolute perfection
> in every smallest detail; it leaves nothing whatever to be desired . . . it is a
> spectacle for the most poetically and artistically inclined, for the imagina-
> tive and sensuously luxurious; in a word, for the élite of humankind.[9]

In the section of her autobiographical narrative subtitled "A Great Discovery," Fuller elaborates on how she "studied" the effects of the fabric in various kinds of light, in order to "make sure of what I had done the evening before."

> The mirror was placed just opposite the windows. The long yellow curtains
> were drawn and through them the sun shed into the room an amber light,
> which enveloped me completely and illumined my gown, giving a translu-

cent effect. Golden reflection played in the folds of the sparkling silk, and in this light my body was vaguely revealed in shadowy contour. This was a moment of intense emotion. Unconsciously I realized that I was in the presence of a great discovery, one which was destined to open the path which I have since followed.

Gently, almost religiously, I set the silk in motion, and I saw that I had obtained undulations of a character heretofore unknown. I had created a new dance.[10]

What I want to emphasize in this story of the genesis of her serpentine dance is the intriguing mixture of study and impulse—that is to say, of artistic creation and scientific invention. Unfortunately, the social position of women and the cultural representation of dance in music halls and regional theaters ideologically separated aesthetic creation from scientific study (along with the usual binaries of body/ mind, rational/irrational, male/female, and so forth). As a result, Fuller's complex interweaving of expression ("This was a moment of intense emotion") and study ("A play of colours in the draperies that could be mathematically and systematically calculated") has generally been oversimplified, relegating her work to only one side of the equation. Evolving in the public's imagination from a nineteenth-century variety-hall performer to a leading artist at the cusp of a new century, Fuller becomes associated with electrical lighting, theatrical acumen, scientific inquiry, and, eventually, entrepreneurship, thus fashioning her in their eye as an extraordinary woman—but not quite a dancer.

Mark Franko begins his chapter "The Invention of Modern Dance" with that quintessential moment of the "birth" of modern dance—Isadora Duncan's spiritual revelation of the wellspring for authentic movement in her bosom. *For hours I would stand quite still, my two hands folded between my breasts, covering the solar plexus. . . . I was seeking and finally discovered the central spring of all movement.* Unlike those euphoric histories of early modern dance written in the middle of the twentieth century, Franko's chapter, written at that century's close, attempts to delineate the underlying ideologies of Duncan's dancing, what he quite rightly refers to as the "foundational narrative of modern dance, its myth of origin": "Expressivity, then, is inseparable from an idealist perspective in which the body acts as a 'medium' giving the spectator access to an extra-corporeal self of which the body's movement furnishes traces."[11]

For Duncan, inspiration was the quasi-religious energy (some call it soul) that emanated from the core of the body out through expressive gesture into the world to awaken a degenerate public to the "truth" of movement. Although it is easy these days to make fun of Duncan's romantic, overwrought rhetoric, the fact still remains that much modern dance throughout the twentieth century was committed (despite stylistic differences) to a similar vision of the dance artist as a vehicle for the expression of inner forces. Franko reads this myth of original expression as a gendered paradigm:

The dancer "responding" to herself or reveling in her own dance repro-
duces the patriarchal myth of the feminine body's closeness-to-itself. It is
not productive, but reproductive. The dancer does not, therefore, partici-
pate in the public sphere of productive labor, but typifies instead bourgeois
privacy-as-subjectivity already firmly established by late-nineteenth-
century capitalism. The dancer moves in the "natural realm of the self,"
having no public, impersonal language.[12]

For a variety of reasons, Loïe Fuller's work was never tied to such a model of
feminine expression. Right from the beginning of her career as a dance artist, she
was framed as an inventor, someone who crafted the theatrical experience from the
resources at hand, rather than divining it. Writing in 1912, J. E. Crawford Flitch
describes Fuller's creative process in decidedly nonprivate, nonnaturalistic, indeed,
practically impersonal terms: "The invention of the Serpentine Dance coincided
with the discovery of electricity as a method of lighting the stage. . . . Loïe Fuller
immediately saw the possibilities of the new scientific illumination, and with the aid
of a few friends she devised a means by which the effect of vivid sunshine could be
obtained through the use of powerful electric lights placed in front of reflectors."[13] If
Duncan is mythologized standing, waiting for divine inspiration, Fuller is pictured
with her sleeves rolled up, ready to experiment with the next interesting variation
on a theme. What is interesting about this juxtaposition between the internal creative process and the external awareness of theatrical effects is that they are always
interpreted as mutually exclusive. What would it mean to allow Fuller both a sensate connection to her physical body as well as an acute visual sensibility? That is
to say, what if we posit a correspondence between the inside and the outside of her
serpentine swirl? Perhaps then we could follow it, like a Möbius strip, from physical motion to visual image and back again, deconstructing, en route, the accepted
notions of expressivity in modern dance.

"Upon the whole, one may doubt whether the exercise really deserves to be
called dancing."[14] The press coverage of Fuller's early American appearances is
filled with comments such as this one from a Boston paper. Indeed, Flitch echoes
popular sentiment when he writes in the section of his book on the serpentine
dance: "It is doubtful whether this invention of Loïe Fuller comes within the sphere
of dancing in the proper sense of the word at all. The Serpentine Dance has no steps,
no gestures, no poses, none of the *usual criteria* by which dancing can be judged.
The function of the limbs is merely to put measureless lengths of drapery in motion. . . . Loïe Fuller's chief merit was her faculty of invention" (emphasis added).[15]
Flitch is quick to emphasize Fuller's professionalism and her theatrical acumen but
can't quite bring himself to call her a dancer. Ironically, just two pages prior to this
pronouncement, Flitch had elaborated on the physical and technical difficulties of
the serpentine dance:

When the enormous dimensions of the skirt are taken into account, the achievement of managing it with grace is not altogether to be despised. The strain on the arms is severe. To wave them in such a manner that the folds of the skirt do not become entangled with one another, and that the whole of it is in motion at the same time, is a feat of dexterity difficult of accomplishment.[16]

To prove his point, Flitch goes on to relate an anecdote about an embarrassed lady who, "[became] so enveloped in her hundred yards of drapery that she had at last to be carried ignominiously from the stage in the arms of an attendant and unraveled behind the scenes like a twisted ball of string."[17] Although he will admit that Fuller had fashioned a specific technique in order to manipulate her fabric so beautifully, Flitch was not willing to label this physical dexterity as dancing, nor was he able to imagine that these ever changing patterns could be emotionally expressive.

Unable to imagine anything outside of "the usual criteria," Flitch insists on defining dance as the aesthetic placement of the limbs in steps and gestures. Like many of his contemporaries, he sees dance as a series of poses linked together by graceful transitions. Not only did Fuller's work eliminate the poses (until the very end of the dance), but it also used the body sequentially, constantly initiating the movement with her spiraling torso, flowing out through the arms into the wands and fabric, then looping back into the center in order to start the cycle all over again. Fuller's serpentine dance confused the conventional ways of looking at dance. In an attempt to prove his point about Fuller's non-dancerliness, Flitch quotes Fuller. While she admits to not following the "laws of dancing schools," Fuller obliquely suggests another way of looking at her performances: "I have never studied, and I don't believe the ancient Greek dancers ever studied how to move their feet, but danced with their whole bodies—with their head and arms and trunk and feet. I believe that they studied more the *impression* that they wished to convey by their dancing than the actual way of dancing."[18]

> *Suddenly the stage is darkened and Loïe Fuller appears in a white light which makes her radiant and a white robe that surrounds her like a cloud. She floats around the stage, now revealed, now concealed by the exquisite drapery which takes forms of its own. . . . She is Diana dancing in the moonlight with a cloud to veil her from Acteon. She is a fairy flitting about with a cloak of thistledown. The surprised and delighted spectators do not know what to call her performance. It is not a skirt dance, although she dances and waves a skirt. It is unique, ethereal, delicious. As she vanishes, leaving only a flutter of her white robe on the stage, the theater resounds with thunders of applause.*[19]

By focusing on the "impression" made by her innovative combinations of fabric and lights, Fuller created a dance that clearly affected her increasingly enthusiastic audiences, even as it bewildered those attempting to categorize it. Of course, her early success was complicated by the variety-show format in which she developed her work. In that environment, the choreographic contributions of the (mostly) female performers were rarely given artistic credit. Because she was not a big star in the beginning, she could not command star billing, effectively limiting her ability to authorize her production—to sign her name to the dance she invented. In her autobiography, Fuller relates the difficulties she had trying claim ownership of the serpentine dance: "Next day the whole city was plastered with lithographs, reproduced from one of my photographs, representing me larger than life, with letters a foot high announcing: 'The Serpentine Dance! The Serpentine Dance!' But there was one circumstance came near giving me heart failure. My name was nowhere mentioned."[20] Running to the theater manager, Fuller insisted on being a featured act in the publicity, only to be told that he had another dancer ready to take her place, thus initiating the first of many, many Loïe Fuller imitators.

Thirty years old and dependent on her theatrical career for financial stability, Fuller turned to the legal system and filed suit against that dancer for copyright infringement. As the *New York Times* reported the story: "Loïe Fuller asked for an injunction against Minnie Renwood Bemis to restrain her from dancing the 'serpentine' dance during the summer on the roof of Madison Square Garden. Miss Fuller asserted that she originated the dance, and having had it copyrighted, it was her exclusive property." In terms that demonstrated a clear sophistication in compositional savvy and stage design and asserted her artistic authority, Fuller had submitted a description of her serpentine dance. A certain Judge Lacombe of the New York Circuit Court, however, saw her work in a radically different light. His opinion reads:

> It is essential to such a composition that it should tell some story. The plot may be simple, it may be but narrative, or a representation of a single transaction, but it must repeat or mimic some action, speech, emotion, passion, or character, real or imaginary. When it does, its ideas thus expressed become subject of copyright.
>
> An examination of the description of the complainant's dance, as filed for copyright, shows that the end sought for and accomplished was the illustrating and devising of a series of graceful movements combined with an attractive arrangement of draperies, lights, and shadows, telling no story, portraying no character, depicting no emotion. The mere, mechanical movements by which effects are produced on the stage are not subjects of copyright. Surely this dance described here conveyed and was devised to convey to the spectator no other idea than that of a comely woman illustrating the poetry of motion in a singularly graceful fashion, and, while such an idea may be pleasing, it can hardly be called dramatic. Motion . . . denied. ("Dancing and Copyright," *New York Times*, June 19, 1892)

The basis of Judge Lacombe's decision is the expressive paradigm that Franko describes as the foundational narrative of modern dance, where the (feminine) body translates interior and transcendent "ideas" into physical forms. This ideology insists on a "natural" body. Fuller's work, I would argue, was just as expressive of "ideas" (indeed, we will soon turn to the avalanche of expressive [French] metaphors inspired by her performances at the Folies Bergère), but its expressivity refused the "natural" interiority of a feminine body. Thus, Fuller's dancing required a new way of seeing, one that would take some time and critical dialogue to crystallize. In her paper on the origins of Fuller's serpentine dance, Sperling suggests that Fuller had created the first truly "abstract" dance: "The implications of the ruling are enormous. Fuller had created an abstract art. One in which the visual effect was primary. By insisting that a 'dramatic composition' had to have character, emotion, and story, the judge failed to comprehend the development of an expression that was visually based."[21] Because Fuller was so aware of the visual aspects of her performances and because she has been repeatedly written out of the history of modern dance as an expressive discourse, it would be easy to fall into oppositional distinctions between the visual and the kinesthetic, between the practice of dancing and the visual images that evolve from that practice. But a nuanced exploration of her work demonstrates how these two experiences are always already interconnected in her moving body.

For instance, an early Taber studio photograph of the serpentine dance provides a striking example of the blend of abstraction and expression in Fuller's movement (see Figure 7). By the time this was taken, Fuller had eschewed any figurative decoration on her costume, choosing instead plain white silk in order to reflect more effectively the colored lighting that was an essential element of her performances. She has also added short wands (one can see her left hand grasping a wooden dowel). The photo shows her just as she has switched directions, reversing the counterclockwise rotation to produce a serpentine swirl on the right side. Unlike many of her imitators, whose symmetrical maneuvers quickly became visually static, Fuller had mastered the complex rhythms of asymmetrical soaring, in which one side is ready to take off as the other side descends. In this photo we can see that the right side is just beginning to descend as she prepares the left wand to sweep up and over. Her upper body both reflects and extends the spiral in her torso, reaching through space in a manner that remains integrated with her center.

At the beginning of his essay "Mediators," Gilles Deleuze draws an intriguing connection between philosophical inquiry and late-twentieth-century movement habits, calling for a philosophy that focuses less on the problem of origins and more on what he terms the "in between." For the physical equivalent to this paradigm, Deleuze looks to popular sports such as surfing or hang gliding, where what is important is less a matter of individual force or impact on an outside object (either running or throwing a ball, for instance) than the ability to join a flow (of air, water, snow, or momentum) that is already in motion: "Many of the new sports . . . take the form of entry into an existing wave. There's no longer an origin as start-

Figure 7. "Loïe Fuller." Photograph by Isaiah W. Taber. Jerome Robbins Dance Division, The New York Public Library for the Performing Arts, Astor, Lenox and Tilden Foundations

ing point, but a sort of putting-into-orbit. The basic thing is how to get taken up in the movement of a big wave, a column of rising air, to 'come between' rather than to be the origin of an effort."[22] By focusing on the moments of the glide, the surf, or the flow, Deleuze elides the often effortful preparation (the furious paddling out to meet or catch up with the right part of the wave, for example). Nevertheless, his comments resonate with my analysis of a crucial aspect of Fuller's dancing, which is the balance between the intense effort needed to launch her fabrics into the air and the riding of that motion, knowing exactly which positions of the body offer enough resistance to catch more air and lift up with a minimum of effort. Of course, like any movement practice, these skills take time to develop.

When I was first working with a replica of Fuller's serpentine costume, it took all my energy just to keep the fabric aloft for a minute or two. Constantly holding my arms above my head as I raised the wands and the fabric was exhausting. With time and repetition, however, my movements became more efficient as I experimented with using my whole torso to sustain the work of my upper body. I also learned how to exploit the diagonals such that my movements were not simply to the front, the sides, or above, but included powerful figure-eight sweeps that went from up to down and looped back behind my body as well. Eventually, I realized that rather than focusing on lifting my arms, I needed to release my weight and accelerate into the downswing, after which I could let go of the effort and ride the upswing into a loft. It was just like riding the crest of a wave. The key ingredient here is the torque in the body, that quick twist of the torso, which functions much like the handle of a whip to send the peripheral extensions of fabric up into the air. Learning to coordinate first the left and then the right side, playing with torque and momentum, and banking the fabric in ever larger loops was both physically challenging and thrilling, and I felt the dual satisfaction that comes from both powering the rollercoaster and getting a chance to ride it.

In his essay "Torque: The New Kinaesthetic of the Twentieth Century," Hillel Schwartz surveys a myriad of cultural discourses to show how many aspects of twentieth-century life were influenced by new ideas about movement. In addition to looking at modern dance and physical comportment, he discusses the influences of psychology, fashion, child rearing, physical education, pedagogy, and even graphology: "Over the next century, between 1840 and 1940, children and adults would slowly be rehearsed into a habit of gesturing and a repertoire of 'streamlined' gestures central to the new kinaesthetic—clean, fluid, curvilinear gestures moving from the center of the body outward through uninterrupted but muscularly well-controlled rhythmic impulses."[23] Although Schwartz never mentions Loïe Fuller in his catalog of early modern dancers, his analysis of their movement innovations describes the physical basis of her dancing as well:

> Indeed, Laban with his Effort/Shape studies, St. Denis with the sensuous pulsing/writhing of her bare midriff, Duncan with her earthward stamping, spinning gestures, and Graham with her contractions and releases

together *established a model of motion as a spiral at whose radiant center was a mystical solar plexus and at whose physical axis was the preternaturally flexible spine, bound link by vertebral link to the earth as to the heavens.*" (Emphasis added)[24]

As I mentioned in the introduction, most cultural historians and dance scholars elide Fuller's movement contributions to early modern dance, preferring (if they mention her at all) to elaborate on her innovations in lighting and scene design. Schwartz is no exception. Nonetheless, if we keep in mind his description of motion "as a spiral at whose radiant center was a mystical solar plexus and at whose physical axis was the preternaturally flexible spine" as we look at two photographs of Fuller taken in Rodin's garden by Eugène Druet, we see immediately that Schwartz could be talking about Fuller as well (see Figures 8 and 9). Even though she tilts her face toward the photographer and smiles, the overall impression of her dancing in this action shot revolves around the force and momentum of her torso's movements. The fabric becomes the afterimage, the traces of her motion as it ripples out into space. Indeed, in many ways, Fuller's dancing prefigures Schwartz's notion of the "new kinaesthetic." Certainly, as the serpentine dance evolved from its premiere in 1892 to its more elaborate manifestations as "Le feu" or "Le lys du Nil" (with more fabric added to make her costumes longer and wider, as well as increasingly sophisticated lighting effects), Fuller had to use more and more torque to send her silks rising farther into the space around her. Arching and spiraling, her whole torso was involved in a movement task that was both expressive and functional.

Like any innovation in art, this new way of moving required a new method of perceiving. As Schwartz suggests near the end of his essay:

> Motion pictures, like modern dance, corporeal mime and, soon, the schools of naturalistic or Stanislavskian acting, demanded much more than a simple reading of one discrete attitude after another. They demanded a reading of the body in motion and an appreciation of the full impulse of that motion. As directors learned the tricks of the close-up and the dissolve, the quick cut and the wipe, movie audiences learned to presume continuity between positions, to require more than mere "attitudinizing," to watch for those subtler motions of the face, shoulder, ribcage and pelvis that reflected inner states but had been scarcely visible from the distant galleries and boxes of "legitimate" theater, vaudeville, or burlesque.[25]

Loïe Fuller's dancing has been described by many twentieth-century scholars as a precursor to film, a way of placing lights on a moving screen, rather than of moving images on a stationary screen.[26] What interests me most in the context of the development of her serpentine dance, however, is that Schwartz draws attention to the audience's learning to see expressive emotion in the midst of continuous motion. Sitting in my library cubicle at the beginning of the twenty-first century, I can fully appreciate the powerful combination of aesthetic swirls and the core dynamic

Figure 8. "Loïe Fuller dansant." Photograph by Eugène Druet. Musée Rodin, Paris

that is their expressive source. In 1892, however, not all audience members had learned to see beyond the usual pose or traditional narratives, especially on the music-hall stage. One aspect of the development of Fuller's work, then, is the way her dancing sponsored a parallel development of a new way of perceiving dance. For the first time, audiences were asked to attend not to the poses at the end of a musical phrase, but rather to the motion between phrases, not to the decorative arrangement of arms and legs, but to the sequence of movement from center to periphery and back again. Fuller's priorities

were complicated by the variety-show format in which she produced her work. In order to understand just how much of a radical departure from the norm her work was, we must revisit the environment in which she first found success.

Figure 9. "Loïe Fuller dansant." Photograph by Eugène Druet. Musée Rodin, Paris

Loïe Fuller made her debut in Paris at the Folies Bergère in October 1892. It wasn't until November, however, that she officially danced under her own name and with the technical support that allowed her to realize many of her original lighting designs. By the end of the year, she had created a spectacular sensation, at-

mically shaking themselves silly, is interested only in one, the one dressed as a spahi officer, with her large, billowing blue pantaloons, her dainty red boots, her gold-braided spencer, and her little scarlet waistcoat, skin-tight, moulding her breasts and showing off their erect tips. She dances like a goat, but she is adorable and common, with her braided kepi, her wasp waist, her large backside, her retroussé nose, and her look of a pleasantly roguish tom-boy.[28]

Finally, he concludes with a description of the theater, which, he insists, has a "real air of the boulevards about it":

It is ugly and it is superb, it is in both exquisitely good and outrageously bad taste. It's also unfinished, like anything that aims to be truly beautiful. The *faux jardin*, with its raised walkways, its arcades of rough wooden lattice-work with solid lozenges and cut-out trefoils stained red ochre and gold, its canopy of pompommed and tasselled material, striped garnet-red and greyish-brown, its fake Louvois fountains with three women back-to-back sandwiched between two enormous saucers of imitation bronze set amid green tufts, its pathways carpeted with tables, rattan divans and chairs, with bars tended by amply made-up women, resembles at one and the same time the restaurant on the Rue Montesquieu and a Turkish or Algerian bazaar.[29]

Remarkably enough, the Folies Bergère looks pretty much the same now as it did then. Although the decor has been revitalized since the nineteenth century, the thematic details remain. The large foyer still has a tacky *faux jardin* motif, complete with plastic ivy climbing up the white latticework. The bar is still huge and active, and the interior of the theater is still clothed in "faded red and tarnished golds." When I attended a show one summer evening in 2003, I was struck by the faded grandeur of the whole building and the sense of history that permeated the environ-ment. As a symbol of Parisian life in the belle epoque and that particular *plaisir à la française* (as the Folies Bergère's publicity terms it), the Folies Bergère attempts to keep up this pretense of joie de vivre even in the midst of declining attendance and revenue. The SARS scare decimated the Asian tourist trade that had helped keep the nightclub hopping, and by the summer of 2004, the club had discontinued its regular nightly spectacles.

Nonetheless, when I attended the "Nuits de folies" show in 2003, Loïe Fuller's legacy was very much present. To begin with, when I asked an usher (who told me that she had spent twenty-seven years working at the theater—fifteen onstage and twelve offstage) if she knew who Loïe Fuller was, she replied, "Of course," and promptly told me there was a Loïe Fuller act in the show. Astonished at my good fortune (*quelle chance!*), I grabbed my friend and a glass of champagne and rushed to my seat. The balcony of the theater is made up of private boxes arranged in a horseshoe shape, allowing the audience to see both the stage and one another. There is a thin runway all along the balcony that performers could (if they were careful) use to get closer to the spectators. (In the show I watched, however, only the acrobats used this edge.) The atmosphere in the theater was very casual, with people drinking and talking during the long pauses in between the various acts. In Fuller's time, it was common for the house lights to be on during the entertainments, so that people in the audience could go to the bar, talk with one another, or attend to the events onstage. Fuller was one of the first performers to insist on a total blackout before her appearance, heightening the sense of expectation in an audience not habituated to the dark.

The "Nuits de folies" show was divided into thirteen scenes, each with a different geographical, ethnic, or erotic flavor. There was the French can-can number, the Spanish flamenco-esque scene, the New York Bob Fosse jazz routine, the Irish stepping dance with Scottish flair (called "Les kilts"), the tango section, and a fairly weird extraterrestrial number with almost total nudity (except for the requisite headdresses and black knee-high stiletto boots). Interspersed among these full company numbers were assorted singers and acrobats. And then there was the Loïe Fuller dance. Choreographed by Claire Duport, this solo in white was categorically different from anything else on the show. To begin with, it wasn't entertainment based on the "flaunt it and smile" organizing principle that underlay most of the other numbers. Although the movement and lighting effects were pretty disappointing (the dancer, for instance, never used the torque or momentum that I believe was a key feature of Fuller's appeal, and the lighting was limited to the usual front and side plot), I appreciated the opportunity to see an abstract vision of movement in the midst of such a panoply of flesh. The incongruity of contexts was striking. Yet even more intriguing was the fact that the audience seemed to take this shift of viewing priorities totally in stride, accepting and applauding the Fuller piece as much as any of the others.

In February 1893, Roger Marx penned a portrait of Loïe Fuller in the *Revue encyclopédique*. On the cover is a photo of Fuller under the title "La danse serpentine." The article begins by lamenting the abominable state of dance, referencing half-naked ballerinas and the "distortions" of the belly dancers currently in vogue. Marx points to Fuller as the savior of true dancing, one who has returned (figuratively speaking) to ancient Greece for inspiration to give her audiences a renewed sense of the spiritual potential of dance. In the fabulously detailed language that would serve as a template for his many later evocations of Fuller's work, Marx describes the effects of her performance.

> Out of the night, the apparition escapes; she takes form, becomes alive.
> Under the caress of the electric beams, she breaks away from the back-
> ground of mourning, abandons the dazzling whiteness of a diamond to don
> all the colors in a chest of precious stones. Thus had the Champs de Mars
> been variously tinted in 1889, but this time, instead of a crystal flame, static

and monotonous, there is a human being, with feminine gestures filled with grace and charm, who lights up, changing colors infinitely. This exquisite phantom runs, flees, returns, and wanders through the multicolored ripples of the electric rivers. She sweeps across the stage with the lightness of a butterfly, skips, and then alights like a bird. . . . She comes forward, gliding with trembling wings, like a bat. Now Loïe Fuller swoops around, turning, her skirt swelling and enclosing her like a flower's calyx.[30]

Images of phantoms, wings, birds, gemstones, water, and flowers—these are the fundamental metaphors that are echoed throughout many of the early descriptions of Fuller's performances in Paris.

But these poetic evocations, wonderful as they are, are only part of Fuller's critical reception. After Marx's essay comes a short biographical section on Loïe Fuller in which a certain "H. C." discusses Fuller's legal "authorship" of her dances. Claiming that France is much more advanced in the matter of copyright than either the United States or England, the author asserts that Fuller can (and has) taken out patents on her costumes and lighting inventions ("une disposition mécanique qui est éminemment brevetable"). Clearly referencing her legal disputes in America, the author declares that even her dancing could be protected if she can prove that each moment was calculated to produce a certain impression on the audience. The problem for the author is that Fuller only applied for copyrights on her dances in France after she had become well-known in England and the United States. As a celebrity, her work had already entered the public domain and could therefore be available to "reinterpretations." As Fuller notes with some irony in her autobiography, "Imagine my astonishment when, in getting out of the carriage in front of the Folies, I found myself face to face with a 'serpentine dancer' reproduced in violent tones on some huge placards. This dancer was not Loïe Fuller."[31]

There is no question that Loïe Fuller had even more imitators than Madonna on an early-1980s karaoke night. But by the end of her first run at the Folies Bergère, Fuller's name had been so successfully marketed as the creator of the serpentine dance that she did not have to worry as much about "the 1,327 soubrettes who have paid Loïe Fuller the compliment of each becoming the 'Only Original Serpentine Dancer in the World'" ("Rumor Says Loie Fuller Is to Wed," *New York Times*, September 5, 1894). By the mid-1890s, the public knew that "La Loïe" was an original artist with an authentic signature. Although she would always take the precaution of patenting her latest technological innovation, Fuller became less concerned about her imitators, focusing instead on developing a succession of variations on the serpentine dance. As her reputation spread, so did her imitators. Ironically, this plethora of unauthorized copies actually served as great publicity. One press article after another compares Fuller and her many imitators, repeatedly asserting the superior quality of Fuller's rehearsed performances: "To rival the pictorial beauty of contemporary burletta and operetta, the variety theatres have their lantern dances, in which Loïe Fuller is still supreme, in spite of her many imitators" ("Trifles Light as Air," *New York Times* supplement, September 13, 1896). When she returned to the United States in 1896 for a series of performances, the *New York Times* ran an article on Fuller entitled "La Loïe Talks of Her Art" in which she gave some advice to aspiring dancers:

> There are 500 people—little misses—who can twirl a few yards of muslin and bob in and out of the focus of a limelight, but twirling a few yards of muslin and playing at touch with the limelight—any girl who is given to kicking her toes at all can do that—do not make a skirt dancer. To be an artist at your business calls for a life's experience. Your profession is so full of subtleties that you have never done learning. I leave nothing to chance. I drill my light men, drill them to throw the light so, or so, and they have to do their business with the exactitude of clockwork. . . . Theme, style, time, all differ in one dance from another. A dance is not built up in a day. (*New York Times*, March 1, 1896)

In her efforts to assert the validity of her artistic signature, Fuller articulated an analytical self-consciousness that fit uneasily with contemporary notions of feminine artistry and "natural" expressivity. By emphasizing the precision with which she orchestrated the visual effects in her performances, Fuller distanced herself from the working-class variety entertainments and entered a middle-class aesthetic discourse. She became an artist, not a dancer. And yet she continued to dance nightly, even when she could have easily substituted someone else in her stead and still retained her choreographic authority. Unwittingly, her focus on work—the elaborate preparations and rehearsals required for her performances—was represented as conceptual, not physical, labor. Losing the materiality of her body, she became the embodiment of an idea, an *idée* as was most famously suggested by Stéphane Mallarmé. Although this process of intellectual abstraction has given us some of the most interesting writing on Fuller, it has also left us a legacy of ignoring Fuller's corporeality and the emotional "impressions" she wished to convey. In the section that follows, I engage with Mallarmé's conceptualizations of Fuller's dancing in order to reanimate the physicality that served as its material foundation. I explore his notion of dancing as writing as well as its inverse, tracing the interconnections between a written and a movement signature. But first, I want to look at two images—one of the skirt dance and one of the serpentine dance—in order to understand what gets lost and what can be gained when the female body gets taken over by a serpentine swirl.

In the December 1, 1894, issue of *Chap-Book*, a semi-monthly publication that reviewed literary and artistic cultural currents, there is an article on "Mr. Bradley's Drawings" by Herbert Stuart Stone. Over the course of a short essay, Stone relates the trajectory of Will H. Bradley's career from advertising copy artist to "one of the cleverest decorative artists" in America. A book illustrator and poster designer, Bradley had begun to attract considerable attention by the mid-1890s. Stone asserts:

"Mr. Bradley is deserving of great praise. A man of slight training, he has come to a prominent place from his splendid sense of the value of black and white. His use of black has always been his strong point; he has massed it deliberately and wisely; his work has been knowing, and it is always self-conscious. It is artistically artificial. It is never accidental."[32] What intrigues me in Stone's description is the phrase "artistically artificial," for it suggests a distinct shift of taste in the decorative arts away from one which positioned nature and artifice as culturally incompatible.

Accompanying this short profile is a series of prints by Bradley. I want to compare the "Skirt Dance" drawing with the one entitled "The Serpentine Dance" (see Figure 11). Both illustrations are in black and white and reflect the growing popularity of the Arts and Crafts movement and art nouveau on the work of this American artist. "The Skirt Dance" is a stylized drawing of a woman lifting her dark skirt to reveal the white mass of petticoat underneath. The erotic potential lies in the sweep of white, which is punctuated by two black legs sprouting out of this virginal landscape. The dancer's face and left wrist are the only other elements of white in the picture, save for a small section of red in the upper left corner. "The Serpentine Dance" was inspired by Fuller's 1893 American performances. In this illustration, the dancer's body is covered over by a swirl of three large black-and-white arabesques. In my performative lecture entitled "Acts of Passion," I critique this

Figure 11. "The Skirt Dance" and "The Serpentine Dance." Print by Will H. Bradley. The Chap-Book, 1894

image for dismissing the physical labor involved in dancing with a few quick swirls of a pen: "By placing two feet, crossed at the ankle, in the lower right-hand corner, Bradley seems to imply the figure under the fabric was demurely sitting in a chair, sipping tea." In this context, however, I wish to look again, considering this image as a manifestation of Fuller's serpentine signature writ large. Tracing the lines, first with my eyes, and then with my finger, I begin in the upper right corner, swoop down and up along the first curve, then take the lower arabesque to swing across the bottom, and up into the central diagonal, which leads me back to my starting point. Swirling across the page, I feel the rise and fall of Fuller's fabrics and the breath rhythm that sustained that looping from earth to sky. I also become aware of the fact that the artist must have worked quickly, imitating Fuller's motion as he swept back and forth across the paper in front of him, for once inside the loop, centrifugal force carries one on. When I consider the image from this bodily perspective, Bradley's work no longer obliterates Fuller's dancing, but rather translates its motion onto the page.

In his book on Loïe Fuller, Giovanni Lista is also intrigued by how the line in Bradley's work saturates the surface of the drawing with its implied motion:

> The veil becomes a space for the lines until it is no more than a surface onto which, like in Art Nouveau, the pure lines appear. The dancer's body is completely absent, all the while being absolutely present as a force creating waves of these lines. It is at precisely this moment that her vital soaring is closest to her being: a pure energy revealing and inscribing the movement of life, the manifestations of the spirit, and the very impossibility of representing it through imitations of nature.[33]

Although his spiritual overtones may be a bit over the top, Lista's articulation of the paradox of Fuller's absence as a body and presence as a force of motion is absolutely on target. I would go even further, however, and argue that Bradley's rendering of the serpentine dance does a great deal more than merely translate Fuller's movement onto the page. I believe that it actually incorporates a new mode of reading design, one that carries a kinesthetic perception at its core.

> To understand that the dancer *is not a woman dancing*, for the juxtaposed causes that she *is not a woman*, but a metaphor summarizing one of the elementary aspects of our form, sword, cup, flower, etc., and *that she does not dance*, suggesting, by ellipsis or élan, with a corporeal writing that would necessitate paragraphs of prose in dialogue as well as description to express, in the rewriting: poem disengaged from all writing apparatus.[34]

It would be easy to dismiss this (in)famous passage by Stéphane Mallarmé as erasing, just as did the black-and-white swirls of "The Serpentine Dance" by Bradley, the material body of the female dancer. A metaphor, the woman dancer depicted by Mallarmé merges with abstract forms to suggest what writing cannot. Like a mysterious text message, she is the disembodied writing, distanced from the hand that writes. But, as in the sketch of Fuller by Bradley, it may be worthwhile thinking about the motion that is left behind. For the reflection on the other side of the intransitive verb in "is not a woman dancing . . ." is disrupted by an intriguing prepositional phrase, "with a corporeal writing" ("une écriture corporelle"). Thus, even as she is disembodied, the dancer leaves a signature, like a ghost writing from beyond the page. I am interested in the role of this "corporeal writing," both in terms of Fuller's legacy of traces, and in terms of the writing that is signed by the dancing. On the way to addressing these questions, let us consider another kind of trace left by Loïe Fuller.

On June 11, 1916, Loïe Fuller inscribed the first page of her new autograph book with her own "corporeal writing." Entitled "The Ghosts of My Friends," this leather-bound volume instructs its readers to "sing your name along the fold of the paper with a full pen of ink, and then double the page over without using blotting paper" (see Figures 12 and 13). The result, when viewed vertically instead of horizontally, is a Rorschach-like image that is quite literally an embodied signature. For, although they are not mimetically representative, these insignias do look, in some weird way, like little skeletons. The symmetry of these figures and their loops and strokes resemble limbs and ribs, and it is fairly easy to distinguish shoulder girdles and pelvises. Fuller's signature on the first page is prefaced by a printed poem by Gerald Villiers Stuart called "Ghosts." A novel twist on the traditional autograph book, this epigraph to the tome suggests that the signatures captured in this way can, in line with popular spiritualist thought, represent the "shadow" of a friend in such a way as to evoke their presence even after death. The friends who signed Fuller's book include August Rodin, Rose Beuret, Flora Haile, May Cobbs, and (believe it or not) Rudolph Valentino. Now, although these writings do not represent in any direct way the bodies of the signers, they do figure the wonderful iconic circularity of dance. For these embodied signatures are both the signifiers and the signified. Fascinating hieroglyphs, their obliqueness is impossible to translate but incredibly seductive—they cry out for interpretation. In this sense, then, they reflect the enigma that faced Mallarmé when he watched Fuller's performances at the Folies Bergère in 1893.

Known as the "father of the Symbolists," Mallarmé penned a series of brief commentaries on theater, mime, and dance, published under the title *Crayonné au théâtre*, in which he articulated what Frank Kermode deems the sources of contemporary poetic comment on Fuller. First in a section titled "Ballets" and then in a short essay on Fuller, Mallarmé describes the symbolic potential of dancing. He is not intrigued by the kind of music-hall skirt dancing that flaunts female flesh and the commodification of their sexuality. Instead, he is interested in ways in which some ballerinas, and certainly Loïe Fuller, are able to transcend those representational frames to become metaphysical embodiments of an "idea." Like a sorceress, Fuller, according to Mallarmé, is able to conjure the mysterious realm of spiritual yearning ("la mystérieuse interprétation sacrée").[35]

In her excellent analysis of Mallarmé's poetics, Felicia McCarren prefaces her

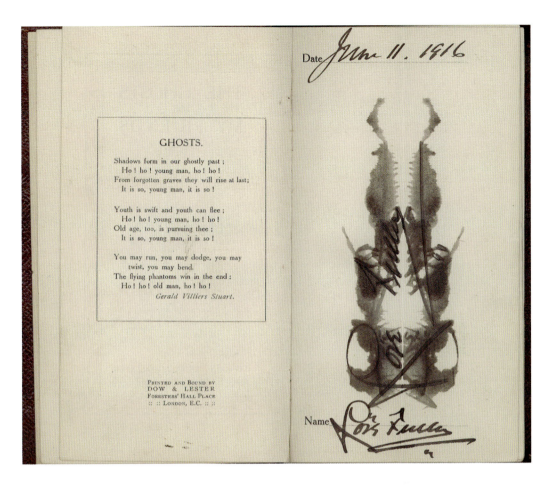

GHOSTS.

Shadows form in our ghostly past ;
  Ho ! ho ! young man, ho ! ho !
From forgotten graves they will rise at last;
  It is so, young man, it is so !

Youth is swift and youth can flee ;
  Ho ! ho ! young man, ho ! ho !
Old age, too, is pursuing thee ;
  It is so, young man, it is so !

You may run, you may dodge, you may
  twist, you may bend,
The flying phantoms win in the end :
  Ho ! ho ! old man, ho ! ho !
            Gerald Villiers Stuart.

PRINTED AND BOUND BY
DOW & LESTER
FORESTERS' HALL PLACE
:: :: LONDON, E.C. :: ::

Name:

Figure 12. Loïe Fuller's autograph book, "The Ghosts of my Friends." Loïe Fuller Collection, Jerome Robbins Dance Division, The New York Public Library for the Performing Arts, Astor, Lenox and Tilden Foundations

discussion of his writings on Fuller by first elaborating on his point of view regarding theatrical performances. Before he even looks at Fuller's dancing, Mallarmé confronts the whole enterprise of spectatorship: "He wants to see something that is not visible: a divine presence manifested in the audience but not represented onstage." Launching her billowing fabrics up to the sky, Fuller can evoke this enigmatic experience without trying to "represent" its emotional affects. Ironically, her ability to conjure up "nothingness" is what catches Mallarmé's eye. McCarren suggests that "the dance comes closer to the Mallarméan poetics of an ideal theater by making-present, rather than visually representing, 'l'idée.' It provides the spectator with the opportunity to imagine, rather than simply to see."[36] For Mallarmé, language (at its best) and dance (at its best) share this capacity to make present without representing:

> The Mallarméan poetics set out in "Crise de vers" defines the relationship between words and things as one in which poetry makes present, through evocation, what is absent. The subject of poetry, then, will not be things

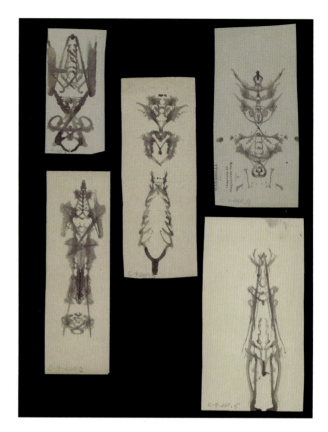

Figure 13. Five "ghost" signatures. Loïe Fuller Collection, Jerome Robbins Dance Division, The New York Public Library for the Performing Arts, Astor, Lenox and Tilden Foundations

themselves. In Mallarméan poetics, language does not so much represent what is absent by naming it, but rather evokes the presence of what Mallarmé calls "mystère" or "enigma," the mysterious functioning of language, the enigma of poetry.[37]

I am intrigued by the play between presence and absence here, the question of evocation freed from the constraints of representation, for I believe it may help us to understand the new kinesthetic language that was the basis of Fuller's serpentine dance. Of course, critics who are less committed to articulating the multiple ways that dancing bodies carry cultural meaning often read Mallarmé's discussions of dance (the "incorporation visuelle de l'idée") as a kind of Platonic transcendence of bodily circumstance into a metaphysical realm. But it seems to me that part of Mallarmé's project was to reanimate language, to have words grapple with the sensate dynamics of gravity, space, and rhythm, even in the midst of reaching, like Fuller's silks, toward the infinite. Julie Ann Townsend points to this paradox in a chapter of her dissertation entitled "Disembodying the Dancer/Incorporating the Poem":

Mallarmé delineates, at once, the research of a metaphysical process toward purity in thought and a physical resistance to such unincorporated operations. He connects the dancer to the poet and the dance to poetry as a strategy to explore an embodied appearance of intellectual processes. This artistic bridge reveals a desire to incorporate the body into thought and to eradicate the limits of the body either through dissipation/disappearance or stabilization/monumentalization. In Mallarmé's model, art would ideally include the material body and the metaphysical *Idée*. In order to accomplish this ideal, he develops representations of a body that inhabits space and time infinitely.[38]

In a letter to his friend Eugène Lefébure in 1867, Mallarmé explicates his own writing process as one that works best when it originates with the whole body. For then, "you get a full harmonious thought, like violin strings vibrating in unison with the hollow wooden box." Describing his efforts to reincorporate his writing one day, he continues: "I tried to stop thinking that way, and with a tremendous effort I braced the nerves in my chest so as to produce a vibration—still holding on to the thought I was then working on, which became the subject of the vibration, that is, an impression; and so that is the way I am beginning a poem I have been dreaming about for a long time."[39]

Attending to the vibrations in his chest, Mallarmé goes to the theater and sees Fuller's dancing, which he calls "intoxicating art and, simultaneously, an industrial accomplishment" ("une ivresse d'art et, simultané, un accomplissement industriel"). In the next paragraph of "Les fonds dans le ballet," he describes what he saw:

In the terrible bath of fabrics fans out, radiant, cold, the performer who illustrates many spinning themes from which extends a distant fading warp, giant petal and butterfly, unfurling, all in a clear and elemental way. Her fusion with the nuances of speed shedding their lime-light phantasmagoria of dusk and grotto, such rapidity of passions, delight, mourning, anger; to move them prismatic, with violence or diluted, it takes the vertigo of a soul as if airborne on artifice.[40]

Conjuring up the traces of her disappearance through the visceral presence of his language, Mallarmé responds to Fuller's dancing through his own body. Writing about this process, he asks, "Que peut signifier ceci?" (What does this mean?), and then answers, "ou mieux, d'inspiration, le lire" (or better, by inspiration, read it).[41] The French word *inspiration* here can move in two directions at once. It can mean both to be inspired and inhalation, or breathing in. Breathing in (and thus attending to the "vibration" in his chest), Mallarmé is inspired to "read" Fuller's dancing without needing to know "what can this mean?"

Overjoyed to leave the realm of mimetic representation in the theater, Mallarmé "reads" Fuller's dancing as if it were a hieroglyph, a visual (and potentially sacred) writing that carries a hidden meaning. Unlike an archeologist, however, Mallarmé is not interested in "cracking the code" or learning to translate that obscure language. Rather than trying to expose or uncover the enigma of the hieroglyph, he wants to be inspired by it to "read" (or see, or even write) differently: "The magic that Loïe Fuller creates, with instinct, with exaggeration, the contraction of skirt or wing, instituting place. The enchantress creates her environment, draws it out of herself and gathers it in again in silence of quivering crepe de chine."[42]

As Felicia McCarren explains, Mallarmé is playing here with the slipperiness between *soi* (self) and *soie* (silk) to indicate how Fuller alternately draws her own environment out of herself and then reinhabits it, blending action and release, inside and outside, self and other, nature and artifice:

> As Mallarmé sits at Loïe Fuller's spectacle, he attempts an explanation of the contradictions of an art generated by the body and ultimately detached from the body, an art of rapidly changing images spun out of a body that is itself described as changing despite its stability. In the dancing body, there can be no clear demarcation of inside and outside; the dancer seems to contain the space in which she is contained.[43]

Beginning with her breath (the primary incorporation of outside and inside), Fuller uses the prostheses of wands and fabrics to write large a central enigma of the dancing body—the ability to merge an articulation of outer and inner space.

Mallarmé's willingness to read Fuller's performances for motion and not for literal meaning comes, I believe, from the viewing priorities set up by her own "new" kinesthetic. His vivid descriptions of her dancing surf along the waves of her expansion, merging with them to experience their motion. In Fuller's performances, these spaces loop from central contraction (the torque) to peripheral expansion (the wings) and back again, creating a series of figure eights that continuously spiral in and out of one another. Fuller's mutability becomes her signature, the morphology of her serpentine dance.

In a chapter on "Morphological Fantasies" in her book *Body Images*, Gail Weiss defines morphology: "The very word 'morphology' has a fluidity that defies discrete boundaries, border, and barriers." She then asks, "What kind of discourse is morphology about?"[44] Etymologically speaking, it would be about shapes, of course. But given the contemporary predilection for making verbs out of nouns (might we say for verbing?), the study of shapes may well become the study of morphing—of changing shapes. Indeed, one of the most complicated but nonetheless important aspects of Fuller's early dance was the subtlety with which she evoked shapes that (like the ghost signatures) called forth interpretations, shapes that were elusively suggestive and enigmatic, but also brought the audience's attention to her very act of shaping.

Watching Fuller's serpentine dance, we can see the suspension of her fabric toward the sky, its movements cresting like a wave. We can follow its looping spiral back toward the ground, intrigued by the process of seeing her silks rise and fall, again and again, each time a little differently. As she grew more skilled, Fuller could manage the syncopation of one side rising as the other was falling, creating an ongoing canon of tumbling images. There was a very seductive rhythm to their appearance and dissolution, evoking the erotic play between presence and absence. These moments of suspension and release were also embedded in a larger narrative structure of gradual build, energetic climax, and subsequent resolution.

In her essay "Alchemic Visions and Technological Advances: Sexual Morphology in Loïe Fuller's Dance," Julie Ann Townsend explores this continual transformation as signifying a lesbian identity. Trying to counter a conservative interpretation of Fuller's voluminous costume as an attempt to cover over her body, thus contributing to a popular reading of Fuller's performances as asexual, Townsend suggests that we read those fabrics as the "folds and contours of labia": "Her masking contrasted the flesh revealed by the *danseuses nues*, but on a more complex iconographic level Fuller may have exposed the genitalia that the *danseuses nues* were forbidden by law to show on stage. I would therefore read Fuller's earlier dances as experiments in the configurations and reconfigurations of sexual morphology—a kind of searching for, or researching of, an artistic identity that had implications for sexual identity."[45]

The question of lesbian spectatorship in Fuller's performances is an interesting one, and one which I will take up at some length in a later chapter on her productions of *Salomé*. In the context of this chapter, I find myself less interested in a literal reading of Fuller's signature shapes as a representation of either female genitalia or a lesbian identity. I simply find this approach too static and deterministic. Instead, I am drawn to read Fuller's motion in all its sexy, slippery—potentially queer— glory. Townsend herself gestures in the direction of a similar reading when she invokes Yvon Novy's description of Fuller's "un-fixable errancy." Later Townsend suggests that "at a time when women's bodies were constrained by corsets, Fuller's representation provided a vision of her body as the site of uncategorizable transformation. . . . Fuller's costumes may have covered her body, but they are also the image of a female sex that is stimulated by Fuller's movements and that in turn caresses and envelops her body."[46]

Seen in this light, the erotics of Fuller's serpentine spirals, their sensuous fluidity and multiplicity, recall Luce Irigaray's notion of *jouissance*, specifically her discussions of female sexuality as "essentially" fluid and mobile. Although (once again) I find myself resisting any deterministic definition of female or lesbian sexuality (either as pathologically static or ephemerally mobile), I do appreciate that Irigaray's conception replaces the Freudian vision of female sexuality as a lack with one of exuberant excess. For I am convinced that it is precisely in the midst of the abundance of shapes, the phantasmagoric excess of imaging in Fuller's work, that we can grasp the radical potential of her dancing body to disrupt both traditional representations of dancing women and the heterosexist norms embedded in watching those performances.

Figure 14. "To my dear little friend, souvenir of Loïe Fuller." Addressed to Gab Bloch. Jerome Robbins Dance Division, The New York Public Library for the Performing Arts, Astor, Lenox and Tilden Foundations

In her essay "The Female Dancer and the Male Gaze," Susan Manning identifies a parallel strategy in the performance work of Duncan and other early modern dancers.

> In my view, it was the kinesthesia of early modern dance that allowed for its choreographic dismantling of the voyeuristic gaze and its address to the female spectator. [Their dancing] projected a kinesthetic power that challenged male viewers to see the female dancer as an expressive subject rather than as an erotic object. . . . In fact, since many female spectators had experienced the same movement techniques that the dancers transformed in performance, their kinesthetic response was particularly intense and led more than a few to identify the dancer's flow of bodily motion as reflective of their own.[47]

Manning's emphasis on kinesthetic responsiveness echoes much of my argument in this chapter about the physical power of Fuller's central torque and the expressive dynamic of her expanding silks. But I believe that Fuller also staged a reciprocal exchange between Manning's "expressive subject" and "erotic object." Repeatedly alternating between creating a space with her airborne fabrics and entering that place, Fuller crafts a dialogue between the inside movement and its outside image, demonstrating the interconnectedness of subject and object.

What is important to me in Fuller's serpentine dance is not, in the end, the staging of her identity as a lesbian, but rather the enactment of its taking shape; not the sexuality performed, but the performativity of desire; not the representation, but the *act* of making present. Peggy Phelan also underscores the importance of the performative in her discussion of Gabrielle Sorère's (a.k.a. Gab Bloch's) vivid depiction of the first time she witnessed Fuller's performance at the Folies Bergère. Included in Fuller's autobiography in a chapter dedicated to Gab, her longtime lover, companion, and business manager (a chapter, by the way, that holds striking resonances with Gertrude Stein's *The Autobiography of Alice B. Toklas*), these words reflect the extraordinary dimension of their relationship in which performance and daily life were intimately intertwined (see Figure 14). In the last section of the chapter, Fuller writes: "And now, fifteen years after, Gab still tells me, when we speak of the impression I made on her at the time she wrote these pages full of ingenuous emotion, 'I never see you exactly as you are,' she says, 'but as you seemed to me on that day.'"[48] In her essay "'I Never See You as You Are': Invitations and Displacements in Dance Writing," Phelan comments: "The performance of the sexual combines both the fantasy of an original consolidation and the force of that consolidation's disappearance [what I would call the erotic interplay between presence and absence]. 'I never see you as you are' is not, for either Fuller or Sorère, the occasion for lamentation. It is rather the reason to keep looking—historically, erotically, imaginatively, spiritually."[49]

Closely watching Fuller's dancing body, Sorère is moved to articulate both Fuller's process—"to seize the unknown her hand becomes coaxing"—and its ephemeral result—"we await with anxious hearts the beauty that passes."[50] Lovingly, she acknowledges both the traces that must pass and the impressions—both visual and kinesthetic—that they leave on a viewer. Because her early dances presented an ongoing transformation of shapes that never solidify into a literal representation, Fuller asked her spectators to look differently, to follow the contours of her bodily writing without stabilizing its meaning. To do so, we must, like Mallarmé, "read" her signature as script, tracing its serpentine spiral by acknowledging the possibility of our own vibration in response.

CHAPTER 2

Becoming Light

Engaging the Dynamics of Color and Space

I f the figure of the serpentine swirl made by her billowing silk costume physically (and sometimes figuratively) effaced the dancer spinning at its vortex,
Fuller's use of light, space, and color reasserted her aesthetic agency to reclaim the
terms of her own representation. Her increasingly sophisticated combinations of
three-dimensional lighting (including the invention of light focused from underneath the stage floor) allowed for a strategic illumination of her dancing, creating,
in turn, a dialogic relationship in which light and color became sources of an active exchange with her movement. Rather than being a static source that framed
her various poses, light seemed to engage her dancing, to bring forth a variety of
expressive responses to the elaborate shifts in color and intensity. Through her active use of light, Fuller developed a dynamic of mutual engagement with the scenic
frame, which, as we shall see, complicated the traditional positioning of women
dancers on the fin-de-siècle stage.

With light, space, and color, as well as fabric, as her dancing partners, Loïe
Fuller was able to fashion a visual spectacle that played across a continuum of
meaning ranging from abstract design to otherworldly environments based on the
sensuous display of color and billowing fabric. Arriving in Paris at the cusp of a
century and in the midst of many cultural changes, Fuller appealed to a broad group
of theatergoers. With amazing foresight, she combined the romantics' envisioning
of light as a magic fluid, illuminating sublime moments of transformation with the
Symbolists' desire for suggestion and metaphor as well as prefiguring a modernist
sensibility to the mobile relationship between figure and ground.

These varying aspects of her appeal can be seen in an 1893 poster by PAL advertising her appearances at the Folies Bergère (see Figure 15). Created within a year
of Fuller's arrival in Paris, this image contains many of the familiar elements of
Fuller's early music-hall publicity, but it also points towards the later, more abstract
evocations of her dancing. We can still see the classic showgirl pose, the form of her
practically naked body (albeit with shoes, of course) vaguely visible beneath a swirl
of colors. Although only her face is turned to the audience, she is smiling, presumably offering the pleasure of her magical transformations to her spectator. And yet,

there is an equally compelling energy in the waves of color emanating from her lights and circling around her axis. Visually, it is unclear whether the woman in the center created these colors or was created by them—a genie emerging from the electrician's lamp. The vibrant reds, blues, and yellows merge together into mauves and greens. These dynamic colors don't passively frame her body for the viewer's gaze. Rather, they obscure it at times, seeming to take on a life of their own. The serpentine design they create evokes, in my mind, a winding road (something along the lines of a Technicolor version of Oz's "yellow brick road"). This poster almost provokes the viewer into searching for various images among the abstract splotches of color. I find it hard to resist seeing, anachronistically, a twentieth-century urban skyline in the upper-left-hand corner of the spiral.

Although Fuller was famous for acknowledging how a marvelous affect may have originally appeared accidentally, she was also astute at keeping in her repertoire whatever fortuitous events the audience responded to. For instance, in a 1896 interview in London with one S. L. B., she admits frankly that

> an absolutely unrehearsed effect may make a performer's reputation more assuredly than all the labor of years—at least, I have found it so. The Rainbow Dance was born in the hour when an inexperienced and careless limelight man's assistant sprinkled me with uncalled for parti-coloured rays. I was, for the moment, astonished—almost alarmed; but the audience saw a rainbow, and I studied to keep the image before them.[1]

As is clear from countless similar interviews, Fuller was quite articulate about how she worked the elasticity of the scenic frame as well as deeply conscious of the emotional timbre of her use of colored lights.

Yet Fuller's popular and artistic successes were more than a sum of her theatrical parts, more than a good combination of artistic curiosity and strategic showmanship. The interplay of movement, fabric, light, space, and color in her performances was always changing, always in flux. Even though she tended to repeat the same dances over and over again, sometimes with slight variations, they were never exactly the same from one performance to another. (Roger Marx repeatedly called her an "improviste.") Much like a structured improvisation, her dancing allowed the audience (especially a knowledgeable audience who had seen her work before) to follow the new and surprising combinations of movement, fabric, and light, to witness the moment of genesis, and to experience in real time the creation and re-creation of her kaleidoscopic images. Although Fuller was known to rehearse her lighting cues fastidiously, the unpredictable interaction between momentum and gravity opened a responsive space where the audience could help construct, or at least select, how they wanted to focus on the variety of images at play. Indeed, this flexibility of meaning seemed over time to engender more and more effusive descriptions of Fuller's dancing, as each journalist or writer attempted to capture the wonder of Fuller's traces of light.

Figure 15. "La Loïe Fuller." Folies Bergère poster by PAL, 1893. Musée de la Publicité, Paris

Here, center stage is the dancer, arms stretched out with her wands, swinging her ample sleeves into circles and vast, parallel figure Ss. Here she is now, lifting the fabric above her shoulders in erect pillars, coiling curls, twisted spirals, turning it into wild waters, rising, swelling, and then sinking waves swirling furiously under the gusts of an unseen cyclone. While the rhythm accelerates, the cadence rushes and the charming creature disappears among the frames and halos of the surrounding spirals, faster the tones alternate and cross, tones of vermeil, and foliage, of azure and blood red; faster they disintegrate, mingle and marry; topaz to lapis, emerald to amethyst, ruby to sapphire, moonstone to aquamarine; the fabric dizzily bubbling, borrows all the iridescences and, as a rainbow, takes all the nuances of the decomposing prism. The vision is never as vivid and passionate as in its vanishing moment when it sinks into naught and turns into darkness.[2]

This extraordinary text by Roger Marx is typical of many descriptions of Fuller's dancing. Most begin by evoking her increasingly expansive use of space as she manipulates her costume in ever larger spheres, first swirling the fabric by her sides and then launching it into spirals above her head. As the music crescendos, the lights begin to accelerate as well, providing an ecstatic shifting and blending of colors that so many artists and writers have tried (rather breathlessly, one senses) to evoke. Images of dawn and sunset, of rainbows, of glittering gems, and the colors of leaves in the fall all cascade into a flow of adjectives that pool kaleidoscopically and then disappear as Fuller's lights fade into a kind of primordial darkness at the end.

When I am sitting in musty archives, reading these kinds of descriptions of Fuller's work, I feel both the thrill of the transformations she achieved in performance and the desire to understand the technical and physical workings that created such magic. This curiosity is not the same impulse as the familiar (and distinctly more jaded) response that suggests that Fuller was simply a master of sleight of hand, employing the latest electrical lighting effects to create beautiful illusions, all the while tricking audiences into believing she was a fairy onstage. As this chapter will document, Fuller actually trained the audience to see many of her most potent lighting effects (including the use of floor lighting) by making visible the light sources.

Refusing the binary of nature and artifice, Fuller was able to create magic in the midst of a conscious and deliberate use of technology. She engaged the expressive possibilities of stage lighting by dancing with, rather than simply in the midst of, color and light. To put it simply, it was neither the dancing itself, nor solely the lighting that projected Fuller into the fin-de-siècle limelight, but rather a potent interaction of the two that created such extraordinary alchemy onstage. By dividing my inquiry into the thematic strands of light, space, and color in this chapter, I hope to unravel, in order to better understand, the key features of one of Fuller's most famous works, "Fire Dance." Then, in the"Becoming Light" section, I attempt to demonstrate how Fuller's energetic dancing engaged those strands to create the whole phenomenon called "La Loïe."

LIGHT

Light makes vision possible. The word light is connected etymologically to words such as enlightenment and insight, and light helps us to see. It is easy, given our penchant for conflating the visible with the true, to assume that light reveals that which was previously unknown or kept in the dark. Indeed, as the historical term Age of Enlightenment valiantly proclaims, light can easily take on the mantle of Western civilization. By dispersing particles as soon as it hits an object, light radiates beyond its source to illuminate the surrounding field. Like colonial expansion, then, light is often pictured as a civilizing force (as in bringing light to the dark continents).

If we refuse this implicit hegemonic paradigm, however, we can recognize that light moves between the visible and the invisible. This is especially important in the theater, where the lighting can either obscure or reveal, veil or unveil. Sometimes theatrical lighting can focus the audience's attention on the figures onstage without implicating itself or revealing its source. (In fact, some lighting designers would argue that the best lighting designs are undetectable because they completely blend into the whole scenic frame and don't call attention to themselves.) At other times, theatrical lighting can create thick, opaque-seeming beams that take on a separate sense of theatrical presence onstage. In the nineteenth-century boulevard theaters in which Fuller worked, and certainly in the Folies Bergère, there would have been a great deal of dust and smoke in the air while she was dancing. In addition to the fact that people were smoking and drinking in the theater itself, the backstage areas were notoriously dusty, and Fuller's many yards of fabric sweeping around must have thrown a lot of that dust into the air. The appalling material conditions of her work environment meant the air was dense with particles and that Fuller's lights would be visible beaming down from their sources overhead and to the sides.

In her performances, Loïe Fuller used light not only to both reveal and conceal her body's motions, but also as a dynamic partner onstage. Although her vision of a spectacle based on color and light was exceptional in many ways, it was not without precedent in the visual culture of late-nineteenth-century France. By tracing the kinds of theatrical effects that preceded Fuller's work, we can begin to recognize exactly how she broke through scenic conventions to extend her performances beyond the traditional frames of nineteenth-century dancing, be it classical ballet at the Opéra or music-hall variations at the cabarets.

In his insightful book *Lighting in the Theatre*, Gosta Bergman traces the concurrent histories of theatrical lighting and the rise of visual spectacles in both home amusements and popular entertainment. In Europe as well as the United States,

rizon gradually changes, becoming more and more overcast, until a darkness, not the effect of night, but evidently of approaching storm—a murky, tempestuous blackness—discolours every object."[6]

This description is remarkably similar to ones given by David Belasco, the famous American actor turned impresario, in his memoirs, *Theatre through the Stage Door*. Belasco underscores the importance of using lighting to create an atmosphere so as to help the audience "feel" rather than merely observe the drama onstage: "Lights are to drama what music is to the lyrics of a song. No other factor that enters into the production of a play is so effective in conveying its moods and feeling. They are as essential to every work of dramatic art as blood is to life."[7] When he became successful, Belasco built a small lighting studio to experiment with different combinations of color and light. Here he attempted to match the quality of natural lighting, such as sunsets, with very specific geographic locations. A lighting designer with a budding ethnographic sensibility, he specifies:

> Nature, in each far-separated locality of the earth, has given a different appearance to the sun and moon and stars and sky, and to the vegetation and fruit and snow and sea. Nature has also given to the peoples of these differing localities their own peculiar esthetic sense of color. If any one doubts that the Japanese have a different sense of the values and relationships of colors from our own, let him study their kimonos or their potteries or their landscape paintings.[8]

Indeed, in speaking of a play with a Japanese setting, *The Darling of the Gods* (which, incidentally, was inspired by Fuller's 1900 Exposition Universelle production of a work by the Japanese dancer Sada Yacco), Belasco insisted that "every particle of color used on the stage, every ray of light cast upon its scenes, was carefully calculated to symbolize its moods, interpret its meaning, and direct and strengthen its emotional appeal."

Although Belasco may be overstating his own importance (as memoirs of this time are wont to do), what is important for our purposes is the exacting nature of his experiments and the real commitment to lighting as a means of communicating the affective quality of drama. Although electric lighting was introduced in theaters in the mid-1800s, it took a while for the technology to be refined enough to produce the kinds of atmospheric effects that both Belasco and Fuller were searching for. It is clear from newspaper accounts of early electric lighting that the new electric arc lamps were seen as much harsher than the old gas lighting. In his column "La vie de Paris" in *Le Théâtre*, the journalist Arsène Alexandre articulated the difference between the standard approach to stage lighting and Fuller's own poetic crafting of lights:

> Before Loïe Fuller, there was lighting, but no one understood how to use it. A harsh and uniform projection, that was all. She brought us this marvelous discovery: the art of modulation, the ability to shift across the spectrum of

color tones, just as we do in sound. The richness of modulations is a distinctive element in modern music and painting, but the theater never dreamed of these possibilities until Loïe Fuller's innovations.[9]

In this excerpt Alexandre uses the term modulate four times in as many sentences to describe Fuller's deft use of light and color. Comparing her work to the richness of musical sounds, he captures how Fuller was able to craft a new technology to suit her own expressive needs. One way Fuller found to reduce the glare of electric lights was to project them through a screen, a cloth, or even glass. Her inspiration for this may have come from watching lighted fountains.

In their book on Loïe Fuller, Richard and Marcia Current attribute Fuller's use of underlighting to an event that took place on the eve of her Folies Bergère debut. In an undocumented citation, they quote Fuller as saying: "The night I arrived in Paris, as we entered the Grand Hotel, I saw, for the first time, an illuminated fountain. There was a female figure in it, and it was lighted from below. The effect struck me at once. I said to my mother: 'I can use that in my dance'" (see Figure 16).[10] Inspirational moments notwithstanding, lighted fountains were pretty standard fare by the end of the nineteenth century, not only as special effects in theater, ballet, and opera, but also in a variety of public festivals and fairs. Although the lighting technology was fairly simple, the effect of colored light as seen through moving water is mesmerizing, even at the beginning of the twenty-first century. Fairs, shopping malls, outdoor urban spaces, even small midwestern towns often feature fountains with colored lights. Indeed, long before I began writing this book, I often found myself gravitating to the public fountains in a town nearby simply to stare at the mix of green, red, and yellow lights projected onto the jets of water shooting into the night sky. L. J. Duboscq, the head lighting engineer for the Paris Opéra, describes his own design for these *fountaines lumineuses* as placing before the lights a revolving disc with multicolored glass lenses.[11] This device is similar to the one Fuller used to create her increasingly sophisticated effects in works such as her "Fire Dance."

In a full-page profile on Loïe Fuller in *The Sketch* dated December 30, 1896, the anonymous author describes in remarkable detail not only the colors of the lights, but where they were positioned as well:

When the music commenced the stage was entirely dark. Suddenly, a light dazzling as that attendant upon the Holy Grail shot down from behind the top of the proscenium and revealed La Loïe clad entirely in white. Then the dances began. . . . Light came from every side. La Loïe danced upon glass, from which the vivid splendor of the head lights was reflected, while from the wings, stage, and orchestra wonderful, luminous streams seemed to flow towards her.

This inventory of lighting effects, which goes on to describe the amazing colors created, is accompanied by an illustration by Louis Gunnis that shows, as the cap-

To our Charming

Rincez-vous L'œil

Hostess

L. JAURIN

tion states, "How the Stage Is Lighted" (see Figure 17). In this black-and-white sketch, Fuller is seen with her signature serpentine swirl framing her body. She seems, however, to be floating in midair. A closer look reveals a rather dapper-looking electrician positioned directly underneath her, holding a large lighting instrument with a flat circle on top. This circle would have contained gels of various colors made by Fuller, and the electrician would have switched the colors as the choreography progressed. Apparently, Fuller dictated the progression of the lighting by various codes, including tapping her foot to signal to the electricians below the stage floor. In this sketch, she is standing on a plate of glass as the light shines right up through her draped costume. There is another stagehand seated in the fly space directly above her, and cones of light are projected in an arc around the back of the stage. Presumably (although they are not depicted here) these lights are also individually manned. While the numbers vary from source to source, Fuller used from fourteen to some thirty-odd electricians (one source claims fifty, but that may be an exaggeration) to run some of her most spectacular and famous effects.

With the help of explicit sources such as this illustration, as well as the fact that Fuller actually patented her costume and lighting inventions in the United States, England, and France, it is possible to get a pretty good sense of what kinds of theatrical technology she was using. For instance, in his encyclopedic documentation of theatrical machinery and effects in nineteenth-century theaters, *La machinerie théâtrale* (1893), Georges Moynet devotes the end of chapter 6, entitled "Optical Illusions," to Loïe Fuller's serpentine dance, cataloging her effects with backstage precision:

> At the Folies Bergère production, which served as a model for all the imitations, Loïe Fuller whirled about in sextuple beams emanating from as many light sources, two of them placed upstage, two others in the wings and a final two placed at the right and left sides of the first gallery; the colors of these lights did not remain unchanged. In front of the lens of each of the lights a glass disk was placed, mounted on a rotating axis, off center in relation to the axis of the lens. The surface of the disk was divided into sections painted different colors which blended into one another. The disk was turned more or less rapidly, tinting the light an endless variety of colors and producing the effect of a kaleidoscope. These colored rays fell on the [dancer] whose flowing skirts caught the passing light.[12]

Figure 16. "To our charming hostess." Watercolor illustration by L. Jaumin; part of a collection of twenty-three watercolors by students at the École des Beaux-Arts presented to Loïe Fuller to commemorate her 550th performance in Paris on March 24, 1895. Jerome Robbins Dance Division, The New York Public Library for the Performing Arts, Astor, Lenox and Tilden Foundations

Although I believe that her lighting sources were visible not only to experts, but to the curious spectator as well, it is interesting to note which descriptions of her performances are limited to discussions of her dancing images and which also note the technical apparatus of her spectacles. Some writers want to preserve the theatrical illusion,

Figure 17. "How the Stage Is Lighted." By Louis Gunnis. Sketch, December 30, 1896. *V & A Images / Theatre Museum, London*

describing the lighting as if it appeared magically, while others underscore the extraordinary use of manpower and technology required to pull off her spectacular effects.

SPACE

One of the hallmarks of modern dance is an acute awareness of the dynamic elasticity of space. Rather than accepting the stage as a static frame (complete with painted backdrop) in which a dancer poses or in which a group of dancers create a pleasing tableaux, modern dance renders space active. Space can be haunting or inviting. Dancers can puncture it, embrace it, or recede from it. With no more dramatic narrative than the energy of their movement, they can dive through space or be sheltered by it. Indeed, a key difference between music-hall dancing in Paris at the turn of the twentieth century and the kind of expressive dancing that Fuller worked with was this awareness of extending the body beyond one's own kinesphere to engage the space all around. Using light and fabric to mark the lines of her energy, Fuller reached beyond herself (both literally and figuratively) to create a sensate interaction with the whole stage.

"La Loïe Fuller reigns over the abysm. She is the mistress of space, she rises up as a sovereign over infinity."[13] This is the kind of highly figurative use of language employed by a certain genre of Fuller's admirers such as Nozière, the writer of these lines. Somewhere in the midst of describing Fuller's evocation of universal beauty and the way she calls souls forth to a kind of pantheistic celebration of Art, Nozière comments on her vivid use of space. He sees her stretching across an abyss, reaching to conquer the black hole of her stage as well as the existential void of infinity. As we know, Fuller draped the stage in black cloth, creating that frightening void. Beginning in total darkness, she moves ever so slightly as the first flicker of lighting appears. Then, as the lighting increases in intensity, her motion grows larger and larger until it seems to stir the whole world into moving with her. As countless descriptions of Fuller's dancing attest, it was truly a riveting experience to see the stage space becoming larger and more dynamic as the dances progressed. In speaking with an interviewer, Fuller emphasizes the powerful psychological dimension of space: "'One has to have space,' she says. 'Dreaming is space, I need no décor, no set, no props, just space!'"[14]

This sense of engaging space originates in the way Fuller initiates movement through her chest and upper body. We have already seen Druet's black-and-white photos of Fuller dancing in natural light in Rodin's garden. Running forward, arms wide open, head slightly lifted, Fuller exudes an expansive openness in her sternum that flows through her arms. More Druet images, shot in a similar setting, show Fuller wearing her famous serpentine costume, complete with wands to extend her movement another ten feet into the air above her head (see Figure 18). Even though she is standing on a small platform and therefore can't actually locomote across

able tension enacted when difference stretches across space. That is to say, whether it is two people or two rays of light or any combination thereof, the spatial tension between them on the stage inevitably sets up a narrative of relationship. Fuller's genius was in constantly rechoreographing the terms of this exchange. That is why she could at once "leave the shadows and absorb the light" and then a second later: "Now, she dances in the color and one could say that it is the light that absorbs her."[17] At times absorbing the light into herself ("s'en impregner"), at other times reaching out toward the light ("s'élever vers lui"), Fuller dances across an expressive spectrum of both active and passive moments. Opening up toward the light and then receding away from it, she was able to recharge the spatial and temporal energies of the stage.

COLOR

"Colors are the actions and sufferings of light in its contest with darkness."[18] Although they worked at different ends of the nineteenth century, Goethe's comment here could easily be referring to the basic dynamic of many of Loïe Fuller's dances. Beginning with a dim lighting (often described as "eerie"), her movement typically became more and more expansive as the surrounding lights increased in intensity and color variation, creating a climactic (sometimes apocalyptic) vision that exploded back into darkness. Fuller's sophisticated use of theatrical lighting was tied to her awareness of the affective emotional qualities of color and light. As many critics have noted, her innovations coincided with similar experiments in painting and, later, lithography. In order to understand more completely just what was at stake in the increasingly liberal use of color throughout the nineteenth century, it is helpful to review some of the aesthetic discourses of the time, for embedded in the critical and popular responses to Fuller's work lies a telling shift in nineteenth-century aesthetic perception.

In an essay comparing the nineteenth-century theorists Goethe, Schopenhauer, and Chevreul, Bernard Howells discusses their responses to a prevailing mistrust of color. This academic position is a result of an aesthetic hierarchy in which line and visual form are seen as empirically measurable and therefore more "objective" and truthful. Color, on the other hand, is seen as a secondary quality because it is dependent on human perception (our retina's response to light) as well as its relative position with respect to the intensity of light and the presence of other colors. At the beginning of the twenty-first century, color has been completely emancipated from form, so it is hard for contemporary readers to understand such a value system. Nonetheless, Howell reminds us, the cultural implications of color discourse in the nineteenth century were critical:

> In it are imbricated other hierarchies which define a certain moment of humanism: reality/appearance, depiction/impression, knowledge/sensation,

rational/irrational, public/private, human/natural, male/female (it is a minor topos of nineteenth-century manuals that line is male, juridical, sufficient for the representation of form, especially of the highest form, the human form, and destined to exercise a strict control over the promiscuities of colour—female—associated with the evocation of *flesh*.)[19]

Loïe Fuller's performances enter this discourse at an interesting historical moment. It is clear from many of the contemporary writings on Fuller's work that her dancing representation is elided with one side of these binaries—that of appearance, impression, sensation, the irrational, and the natural (and therefore feminine) world. On the other hand, the fact that her color and lighting are (literally) connected to the manipulation of electricity and optical effects brings to her oeuvre a certain scientific frame that weighs in on the male, human, rational side of the scale. In fact, Fuller's work unsettles these gendered binaries in fascinating and contradictory ways. That is why Alexandre could write: "She has an artistic eagerness and a sort of scientific instinct which have her searching for, in the area of positive mechanics and optics, new interpretations of her essentially mobile soul."[20] Placing her artistic energy next to her scientific instinct and her physical movement next to her optical effects, Alexandre comes up with a riveting contradiction in terms: "a mobile soul," that is, one that embodies both immanence and transcendence—body and light.

Of course, Fuller wasn't the only artist working with innovations in color. In his essay on color theory, Howells charts Baudelaire's "partial, passionate, political" defense of Delacroix and color in the Salon of 1846:

> Baudelaire sought to neutralize then invert this hierarchy. . . . Line separates artificially objects and parts of objects from each other; it creates stable conceptual identities and emphasizes the psychological distance between perceiver and perceived. Color, on the other hand, blurs the distinction between objects and between subject and object; it corresponds to knowledge in the sense of coalescence rather than abstraction.[21]

Howell's comments on the tension between line, which maintains discrete and separate identities, and colors, which are mutable and fade in and out of one another, help us to more fully comprehend the radical reorganization not only of the stage picture, but also of the whole visual apparatus of the theater that Fuller accomplished with her mature use of lighting effects.

As we saw in the previous chapter, much of theatrical dancing of the nineteenth century, whether it was on the ballet stage or in the music halls, relied on a scopic economy of the gaze in which viewer and dancer are positioned respectively as subject and object. This is hardly new conceptual territory. Dance history and theory have reckoned extensively with the concept of the male gaze, especially when considering the currency of exchanges engendered by the newly privatized Opéra. Yet it may be instructive, given our discussion of the tensions between color and line in nineteenth-century aesthetic theory, to review how the concept of line operated in a variety of nineteenth-century dancing conventions.

Certainly in the nineteenth-century ballet, the question of line was crucial. Even when the formalist tableaus of the Petipa ballets (where the entire cast was structured onstage in a series of symmetrical lines forming symbolic tableaux, as in the beginning of *The Sleeping Beauty*) gave way to more expressive dancing, line was actively debated. But instead of the larger lines choreographed across the stage space, the new line was confined to the ballerina's own body. Thus we have critics such as our famous Théophile Gautier commenting not just on the line of a ballerina's arabesque, for example, but also on the "lines" of her ankle, leg, chin, and even bosom. Similarly, in social and music-hall dancing the endings of musical phrases were often punctuated by individual or group poses that visually consolidated line. Good dancers from various venues knew, of course, how to keep those lines energized and mobile. Nonetheless, as the century wore on, many of the final poses in the *café-concert* halls became increasingly risqué as the skirt "line" was lifted to reveal more and more of the dancer's flesh.

Although she understood well the conventions of skirt dancing, Fuller increasingly eschewed visual lines, favoring instead the play of color and light across the space. In doing so she created a new visual economy that demanded spectators take a more active role in perceiving and registering the various images she evoked. As many writers have noted, Fuller shared an interest in color and light with the impressionists. In a 1929 memorial article written by Valerian Svetloff entitled "Lights That Dance," the author comments:

> The invention of illuminated dancing by Loïe Fuller coincided with the epoch of impressionism in painting. Painters began to see colors and to feel their values in a new and different way. They began to understand that colors depended on light, on distance, on the proximity of other colors, growing darker or lighter, changing, or even wholly losing, their actual nature accordingly. They learnt that shadow is never black, but blue or purple or transparent according to the light and the neighboring colors, just as a pause in music is not mere emptiness, deadly silence, but silent tone.[22]

As we shall see later in this chapter, comparisons of Fuller's use of color with various complex visual and musical modulations being experimented with in other art forms affirm just how expansive her artistic influence was.

In 1893 Henri Toulouse-Lautrec produced a series of fifty extraordinary lithographs of Loïe Fuller. Housed in a large, leather-bound volume in the print collection at the Bibliothèque Nationale, these images sketch a vague outline of Fuller's billowing silks. Each one that I saw, however, was colored differently. Although the shape of the figurative outline remains the same throughout the series, Toulouse-Lautrec hand-painted various combinations of colors for each print and then dusted them with silver, bronze, or gold to create a shimmering effect. Seen together as a series, these images capture the sense of mobility in Fuller's lighting effects. The

*Figure 19. Loïe Fuller. By Henri
de Toulouse-Lautrec, 1893. Bibliothèque nationale de France, Paris*

one I reproduce here reflects a moment of changing colors: the predominantly blue wash shifts into red and yellow as the dancer turns toward another light (see Figure 19).

FIRE DANCE

Fuller's early solos, such as "Serpentine" or "White Dance," presented her audience with an astonishing array of changing lights on moving fabric, calling forth images of flowers, clouds, birds, and other natural phenomena. Although she used a darkened stage before and after each piece, most of the descriptions of the beginnings and endings of her dances suggest the waxing and waning of daylight. Similar to the dawn-to-dusk cycles that were a staple of nineteenth-century dioramas, Fuller's dances seemed naturally to emerge from and recede into the dark. With her newest sensation, "Fire Dance," however, Fuller choreographed a much more dramatic work in which she did not simply emerge from the dark, she battled it.

Presented for the first time as a separate dance in 1896, "Fire Dance" became one of Fuller's most famous and enduring works. A reinterpretation of the "Sun Dance" from her 1895 production of *Salomé* at the Comédie-Parisienne, "Fire Dance" was staged and restaged throughout Fuller's long and varied theatrical career. Most of the time it was presented as a solo, but occasionally, as in its 1922 restaging, it provided the template for a larger spectacle. In it Fuller used underlighting very consciously to hone the interplay between light and shadow. Sometimes she would step over the light to reveal her whole face bathed in red; at others she would play at the edge of the light, allowing only a sliver of her body or costume to catch the light. Pitting light against an all-consuming darkness, "Fire Dance" was at once mythic, spooky, and spectacular.

Indeed, "Fire Dance" could be considered one of the first examples of what Gosta Bergman, in his chapter on the twentieth-century theater, identifies as a "dramaturgy of darkness." Bergman claims that "a great part of modern drama is about light's struggle with darkness, which is directly projected on the stage."[23] Certainly most descriptions of "Fire Dance" suggest a similar struggle, where light becomes fire and is pictured as terrifying, consuming, and destructive. Images of lava and volcanoes pour forth from contemporary descriptions evoking visions of Vesuvius, Herculaneum, the fires of hell, and Pandora's box. Famously, Jean Lorrain declared:

> Molded in the middle of ardent embers, Loïe Fuller does not burn; she filters and oozes light, she herself is the flame. Erect in glowing coals, she smiles, and her smile seems a mocking grin under the red veil in which she is wrapped, the veil she moves and waves like a smokescreen down her lava-like nudity. It's Herculaneum buried under ashes, it is also the Styx and the infernal shores, and it is also Vesuvius with its half-opened mouth spitting

the earth-fire; this immobile nudity which is still smiling in the embers of a fire from heaven, with hell as a veil.[24]

This combination of rising up out of and simultaneously coming down from, this mixing of heaven and hell, in Fuller's "Fire Dance" is beautifully illustrated by a watercolor painted by the early-twentieth-century Russian artist Crozit (see Figure 20). In the view of many critics, "Fire Dance" engaged the expressive possibilities of

Figure 20. "Fire Dance" (Study of Loïe Fuller). Watercolor by Crozit. Fine Arts Museum of San Francisco, gift of Mme. Gilberte Cournand

Fuller's theatrical presence, using her movement and the lighting effects to not only please their eye, but also to grab their guts. Thus, the dance was both abstract and emotional.

An 1898 poster by Georges Meunier advertising Fuller's appearances at the Folies Bergère gives us a wonderful illustration of this aspect of "Fire Dance" (see Figure 21). Unlike the majority of posters of Fuller's work, where the background is a passive dark against which the vivid colors stand out, in this poster the inky black of the background is ominous and threatening. The darkness seems alive, growing around her body like a deadly vine. The effect of the underlighting is ghostly, and her face seems to be masked by shadows. The hot white flames obscure most of her torso, and the red strokes around the edges are morbidly gleeful in their final consummation. In an article in *Le Théâtre* on the 1900 Exposition, Alexandre reflects on the impact of the piece: "It's after that Fire Dance, the dance we have all seen and which we cannot get tired of, where Loïe appears so dramatic and gives us to understand qualities still unknown of mime, and of her ability to be a great artist of fear. She juggles with flames, happy and terrified. The fire reaches its height and then becomes a pile of ashes, which soon disappear—a tiny pile of ashes out of which will rise again the phoenix!"[25]

In 2003 Jessica Lindberg, an Ohio State University graduate student, reconstructed Fuller's "Fire Dance" as part of her master's thesis. In conjunction with John Mueller of the Dance Film Archive at Ohio State University, she created an educational DVD that includes a performance of her reconstruction as well as footage documenting various aspects of the process of restaging this dance.[26] One of the most interesting sections of this multilayered project is a conversation between Lindberg and Megan Slayter, who designed the lights for the piece. Slayter spoke of how she began researching possible lighting combinations for the dance, looking at examples of actual flames, from candlelight to bunsen burners to photographs of forest fires and sunsets. What she noticed was the distinctive combination of colors in the living flames of fire. Although we often think of fire as red and represent it thus, actually there is often a blue underlight and clear white at the hottest part. In a manner that most likely echoed Fuller's combination of scientific observation and theatrical acumen, Slayter and Lindberg then constructed various dramatic shifts in color to parallel the shifts in movement and musical intensity. Although an overall red wash was used at certain key moments, Slayter spoke of how she had to be careful to vary the intensity and colors so as not to tire out the audience's eyes.

This reconstruction of "Fire Dance" begins with Lindberg circling the stage in a ghostly, greenish hue, a sheer cloth covering her face. Releasing her arms to the sides, she mounts a raised box whose glass lid panel allows for the kind of underlighting that Fuller would have achieved with the use of trapdoors. (Although Fuller did patent a pedestal device that raised the dancer above the stage floor such that she would appear to be floating in midair, "Fire Dance" was usually performed over glass inserted into a trapdoor at stage level.) As Lindberg begins to spin

Figure 21. "Loïe Fuller." Folies Bergère poster by Georges Meunier, 1898. Musée de la Publicité, Paris

with her arms at her sides, the silk fabric rippling as she turns, a saturated blue is projected from underneath as a red light from above lights the left diagonal. This early moment is one of the most truly spectacular looks of the reconstruction. In terms that ironically echo Fuller's own modest dismissal of her innovations as products of fortuitous mistakes, Slayter recalled that this striking look was a result of a "happy accident."

Happy accident or not, this tricolored look is remarkably similar to some of the most beautiful and famous images of Loïe Fuller, including the Toulouse-Lautrec lithograph discussed earlier. What is amazing about this particular moment is the way the moving fabric catches different combinations of these three lights, giving the illusion that the lights are changing more rapidly than they really are. In their dialogue concerning the process of staging this dance, both Lindberg and Slayter commented on how the moving fabric creates a kaleidoscopic sequence out of a fairly standard dance light plot. Besides using the two underlights, Slayter intentionally set up sidelights so as to catch the edges of Lindberg's costume with a deep red light that is in direct contrast with the central white light. This combination produced the effect described repeatedly by critics of the day as "flames licking the edges of her dress."

Because she could not locate the original Gabriel Pierné score which was the music for Fuller's "Sun Dance" in her 1895 version of *Salomé*, Lindberg ultimately chose Richard Wagner's "Ride of the Valkyries." This famous piece is essentially an extravagant march with an even beat and predictable changes in structure. Following Kenneth Archer and Millicent Hodson's method of reconstructing historical dances, Lindberg used the musical score to set up a measure-by-measure template onto which she could graft the other primary sources she found. Unfortunately, this process gave the choreography a deadening regularity, which lent a predictable sequence to the movements. Cueing all her changes to the even beats of the music, Lindberg usually repeated her movements such that four measures of spinning to the right would be followed by four measures of spinning to the left. Although the lights were intriguing and beautiful to watch, the dancing seemed rather monotonous, and, with one brief exception, the movement quality was very similar throughout.

My research into Loïe Fuller's performances, particularly those after 1895, suggests that Fuller's relationship to her music was much more spontaneous and flexible than that dictated by Lindberg's method of reconstructing "Fire Dance." Launching her silks into the air and then guiding their descent into various shapes, Fuller must have used a breath rhythm to continue movement impulses across the metric regularity of much composed music. Indeed, she generally worked with live orchestras and often knew the conductor very well (certainly this was true in the case of Gabriel Pierné, the composer of Fuller's first *Salomé* and one of her favorite conductors). In her autobiography, Fuller explicitly notes that the best musicians take their cue from the dancer, not vice versa. A few paragraphs later she adds: "Music, however, ought to indicate a form of harmony or an idea with instinctive passion, and this instinct ought to incite the dancer to follow the harmony without special preparation. This is the true dance."[27]

Watching Lindberg's reconstruction of "Fire Dance," I got the sense that I was watching a series of well-known artistic renderings of Loïe Fuller all strung together to make a dance. What I missed in this reconstruction was the compelling engagement with the lights and space that made Fuller stand out against all her various imitators. Lindberg rarely released her weight to loft the fabric high into the air, nor did she engage many of the spatial diagonals that I am proposing were central to the vitality of Fuller's work. Rather than flowing beyond the frame of the proscenium stage (expanding into infinity, to paraphrase Mallarmé on Fuller), Lindberg seemed curiously contained by it. In the section that follows, I try to articulate how these different strands of light, space, and color came together to create a dynamic whole that inspired legions of artists, especially Symbolists, to represent Fuller's oeuvre—through writing, drawing and painting—in a downright spiritual light.

BECOMING LIGHT

One of the central chapters in Loïe Fuller's autobiography is entitled "Light and the Dance." In this section, Fuller moves away from a more anecdotal approach to the adventures of her life and instead attempts to explain, she tells us, "just what my ideas are relative to my art, and how I conceive it both independently and in its relationship to other arts." Slightly apologetically, she shifts into a more theoretical tone to consider "the question of illumination, of reflection, of rays of light falling upon objects." Through a series of subsections entitled "Color and Light," "Harmony and Motion," "The Music of the Dance," and "The Expression of Sensations," Fuller presents her ideas about human expression. Indeed, over the course of her brief comments on color and lights, music and motion, she delineates the interconnected and interactive nature of these elements in the world and, by extension, in her work.

> In the quiet atmosphere of a conservatory with green glass, our actions are different from those in a compartment with red or blue glass. But usually we pay no attention to this relationship of actions and their causes. These are, however, things that must be observed when one dances to an accompaniment of light and music properly harmonized.[28]

Tellingly, Fuller describes these correspondences between the world and an artist in terms of "vibrations" or "reverberations." Just as the vibrations of light produce color, so the "reverberation" of sensation produces (e)motion. One senses throughout her discourse a vital and responsive energy in the universe, a continual process of composition and fragmentation. Rather than positioning herself as the Godlike figure who creates art, Fuller places herself as an interpreter in the midst of this ongoing motion. She is an individual artist who, by observation and study,

Figure 22. "La Loïe Fuller." By René Lelong, 1910. Bibliothèque nationale de France, Paris

sented over the course of this chapter. In it the very medium of water-color lends itself to a blurring of the lines between the dancer onstage and the lights surrounding her. There is a vibrancy to the colors, even in the midst of their subtle shading and blending (echoing the kinds of color modulation that Arsène Alexander describes). Blocks of color glow across the stage floor, and we can visualize the lights streaming up from below, as well as from the back and high side diagonals. The stronger colors of the lights are reflected in assorted pastels on her light-colored costume. Then too, we can see the expansion of Fuller's movement through the fabric (those three-dimensional diagonals again) and its effects throughout the space.

What strikes me in this painting is the visual dynamism of the whole frame. Everything seems to be in motion. The painting supports my contention that Fuller engaged in an interactive, responsive exchange with the theatrical elements surrounding her. Although in the image her movement is caught and suspended in time, the colors continue to vibrate around her, set in motion by the centrifugal force of her spinning. Fuller's innovations in theatrical lighting, her subtle yet vibrant palette, and her use of underlighting, as well as the fact that the lights had their own choreography, while all important, don't in and of themselves account for the extraordinary impact of her performances. It was her active engagement with these elements that galvanized the stage space, helping to revolutionize her audience's visual imagination. In this sense, Fuller's work parallels many of the changes in the cultural perception of time and space taking place at the end of the nineteenth century both in the United States and abroad.

In his book *The Culture of Time and Space, 1880–1918*, Stephen Kern documents the interconnected discourses of science and aesthetics and their effects on the cultural understanding of space:

> New ideas about the nature of space in this period challenged the popular notion that it was homogeneous and argued for its heterogeneity. Biologists explored the space perception of different animals, and sociologists, the spatial organizations of different cultures. Artists dismantled the uniform perspectival space that had governed painting since the Renaissance and reconstructed objects as seen from several perspectives. Novelists used multiple perspectives with the versatility of the new cinema. Nietzsche and José Ortega y Gasset developed a philosophy of "perspectivism" which implied that there are as many different spaces as there are points of view. The most serious challenge to conventional space came from physical science itself, with the development in the early nineteenth century of non-Euclidean geometries.[33]

The idea of multiple perspectives that Kern identifies here is crucial to understanding Fuller's work. The very nature of her costume insists that the audience see beyond her face or body to the changing undulations of the fabric. In addition, by making the sources of her lighting visible and by constantly changing those sources, Fuller insisted on the mobility of the stage space. Depending on her lights, the space could seem small or huge, comforting or menacing. In the course of several minutes, she could shift from being a lily or a butterfly to being consumed by flames and then completely disappearing.

Once set in motion, Fuller's performances refused the traditional relationship of background and figure present on most of the variety, music-hall, and even ballet or opera stages. In these examples, the lights, scenic decor—even, at times, the other dancers—were arranged (usually in a fairly static manner) so as to formally present and decoratively frame the solo dancer. As we have seen, Fuller's costume covered her body and face. She thereby created resistance to the emphasis on a specific dancing figure, while choreographing the lights to help make the whole space present. This is the same kind of shift in visual perspective that Kern identifies in painting as the "emergence of positive negative space." "For centuries the background had framed the subject as the pillow frames a head. . . . In the modern period the background took on a positive, active function of equal importance with the subject and demanded the full attention of the artist."[34]

Like the emerging modernist artists, Fuller mobilized the whole space of the visual field, inventing not only various lighting effects, but also scenic elements such as her patented mirror room. In this invention, patented in 1893, Fuller arranged a series of mirrors or reflectors around the back of the stage as well as on top of and below the dancing area that reflected and multiplied the image onstage. I imagine the effect would be similar to a Cézanne painting, for instance, where the image of a building or landscape is fractured into multiple, slightly different slivers of itself. Interestingly, Kern cites Merleau-Ponty's comments on Cézanne's work in language that echoes the "becoming" theme of this chapter. In *Sense and Nonsense*, Merleau-Ponty describes how the artist creates "the impression of an emerging order, of an object in the art of appearing, organizing itself before our eyes."[35]

It is this "object in the art of appearing" that captures, I believe, one of the most compelling aspects of Fuller's oeuvre, which was particularly evident in "Fire Dance":

> The Fire Dance that she had imagined was one of her spectacles which made the strongest impression on the public. After securing a total darkness in the theater, there suddenly appeared in the background of the stage a vague and uncertain gleam, a sort of phosphorescence, by moments streaking with its pallid light the shadows, then little by little, this light gains a growing intensity, draws outlines, a human shape appears and seems to flutter in the air, made of immeasurable wings with iridescent colorations, made of ruby, sapphire, and turquoise.[36]

This description of Fuller's "Fire Dance" was written by Henry Lyonnet in a memorial article about Fuller's life and work published in the *Larousse mensuel illustré* in 1928. Penned in the year of Fuller's death, a good three decades after the premiere of that dance, his writing attests to the enduring fascination of her spectacles. Fuller's genius consisted in understanding the pleasure of seeing an image crystallize and then mysteriously disappear, leaving one last trace, a tantalizing flicker of light that promises a later rebirth. This narrative sequence marks the general trajectory of many of her theatrical creations. Yet at the same time, within that overarching structure, Fuller embedded a continuous flow of developing pictures that emerged and shifted from one to another. This sense of becoming—and becoming again—is generated from Fuller's ability to represent not simply an image, but the *very act of imaging*.

When Fuller combines light, space, and color to channel an idea through her body and into the world, she is mobilizing what the Symbolists called synesthesia—

the rhythmic flowering of multiple aesthetic sensibilities into one vision. In his chapter "The Theatre of the Symbolists," Bergman underscores the importance of light for this generation of "poets, dreamers, and theorists and, one may add, of painters": "It goes without saying that light was to play a central role in the Symbolist dreams of the all-embracing work of art: not the atmospheric, illusionary light, but the light that, with all degrees of intensity and colour, can form inner, mental courses of events, can create rhythm." Tellingly, his next sentence points not to Loïe Fuller (whose cultural significance was ultimately limited by the fin-de-siècle music-hall trappings that framed her work), but to Adolphe Appia. What is clear, of course, is that Fuller's innovations in lighting prefigured the radical visions of an expressive theater with mobile lights by an Appia or a Gordon Craig. While Bergman does (briefly) mention Fuller's lighting for her serpentine dances on several occasions, he does not discuss her work in any depth. Nonetheless, his analysis of Symbolist lighting, particularly the contributions of Appia, helps us to understand the concurrent experiments in theater and dance at the beginning of the twentieth century: "But Appia was the first to go the whole way by banning the painted, illusory light and by giving the real light the role of visual music, not serving illusion but the expressive and poetical vision."[37]

Appia's notion of a "visual rhythm" brings us back to Mallarmé, albeit this time with a slightly different focus. Many critical discussions of Fuller's influence on Mallarmé's poetics revolve around his tantalizing commentary about her performances in *Crayonné au théâtre*. In these short meditations, he describes Fuller as mysterious and dreamlike, an inherently elusive figure who conjures up metaphors that evaporate a second before they crystallize. Rather than representing the image of a flower, she embodies it, but only momentarily; these visions appear only to disappear. In an earlier chapter, I discussed the material implications of this play across absence and presence. For the current discussion, however, I want to move beyond questions of images in order to think further about this concept of visual rhythm. In Fuller's dancing, the fabric launches into the air and then dissolves, only to reestablish a slightly different shape. Propelled by her breath, the phrasing of these transitions makes visual a rhythmic pulsing that creates its own vibration.

In a fascinating discussion of Mallarmé's use of Fuller's performance to problematize the whole cycle of spectatorship, Felicia McCarren writes: "For Mallarmé, Loïe Fuller's dance, like the word 'Rhythm' itself, describes a form neither exclusively visual nor exclusively metrical, neither exclusively plastic nor poetic, but somewhere between the two; a form defined by its movement between realms, and defined as movement." Although the psychoanalytic frame of her exploration leads McCarren in a different direction than my particular interests, her research uncovers an intriguing confluence of etymology:

In "La Notion de 'rhythm' dans son expression linguistique," Emile Benveniste traces the origins of "rhythm" to the Greek ruthmos, and considers its shift in meaning from a term used to describe spatial form to a term used to describe aural form. Benveniste attributes the modern meaning of "rhythm" to Plato, who uses the word in its traditional meaning of spatial form, disposition, or proportion, but also gives it a new meaning by applying it to dance. In Benveniste's reading dance is the art in which the form and the content are not simply inseparable from the human form dancing it; to some extent, the formal aspect of dance is itself the human form. The dancing body thus provides the meeting ground for the overlap of "rhythm" in its concrete and abstract, human and extrahuman senses: the form or shape of the body ("attitudes coporelles") and the formal movement of that body in space and time ("mesure" or "metre" of the movement).[38]

In Fuller's dancing, the visual rhythm becomes the aural rhythm becomes the visual rhythm as her billowing images of nature phase in and out of being. Interestingly, in Fuller's time it was widely believed that light, as well as sound, was produced by the vibrations of waves hitting an object. Although Fuller was the most visible current of energy onstage, her audience believed the whole space was alive. They understood that she was, in fact, bringing to light what was present but could not be seen. A selection of press reviews reprinted in a 1914 program, "Loïe Fuller et son école de danse," includes a telling discussion by Léo Clarétie of Fuller's powerful and synthetic vision of the arts:

> It is a transformation: she wrenches and breaks the barriers of genres. Music is a joy for the ears; it can also be a joy for the eyes. She creates [the] pictorial equivalent of music; she sees it and makes it seen. She evokes the otherworldly; materializes what is intangible. She brings to our eyes what we would not see. She mingles and unifies genres . . . she perceives and pays homage to rhythm and universal harmony.[39]

Gathering up the vibrations of light and sound as she gathers in toward her center, Fuller absorbs their energy and then launches a response as she extends her body back into the world. As Claretie testifies in the above tribute, Fuller, by connecting to rhythm through the visual, opens up an intertextual space in which she materializes what has often been left invisible. Attesting to her own sense of their interconnectedness, we find Fuller writing in her memoirs: "Light, color, motion, and music. Observation, intuition, and finally comprehension."[40] In Fuller's performative cosmology, these elements combine to produce a synesthetic experience. The audience witnesses this creative process, for its enactment constitutes the actual stuff of her performance. The gerund in the title of this chapter marks the opening of a reciprocal loop between the artist and her audience that allows both parties to suspend preconceptions about "what" they are going to see and to concentrate instead on the marvel of that vision unfolding in front of them.

In a little leather notebook filled with the names and addresses of various journalists (from an amazing array of regional and international presses), Loïe Fuller wrote a series of mottos—little truisms to live by. On a page near the middle of this book, she has penned: "It is not *what* you see, but *how* you see that counts" (emphasis added). This twelve-word sentence sums up much of what I believe were the more interesting and innovative aspects of Fuller's oeuvre. By shifting the viewers' attentions away from *what* they were seeing—a woman dancing, a butterfly, a bat, a lily—to *how* they were seeing—the physical embodiment of images crystallizing and dissolving in an ongoing cycle of becoming—Fuller helped her audience to see beyond the aesthetic frame of the music hall in which she performed. In doing so, she became larger than the scenic frame, larger that the effusive descriptions of her dancing that anoint her as a force of nature. She became a force of culture, forging a link between dance and the emerging visual paradigm of film. (Many critics see Fuller's work as a precursor to film, suggesting that by placing images and colors on a moving screen, her work, along with other kinds of innovations in an emerging modern culture, allowed people to take the next step: watching moving images on a still screen.)

As a dance historian reviewing the abundant visual images, as well as the journalistic and poetic descriptions of her dancing, I took Fuller's motto to heart and tried to reconstruct not only the *what*, but also—and what is more important—the *how* of her oeuvre. This insistence on process rather than product led me to look at the archival materials with a different focus. Rather than defining Fuller's success by cataloging the number of representations of her by famous (male) artists, I sought to comprehend (physically as well as intellectually) how Fuller actively engaged the elements of light, space, and color to create an ongoing cycle of becoming, and becoming again. Combining abstract images with a kinesthetic passion, Fuller's strategic embodiment of the very act of imaging shed light on her role as a creator, pushing her audience to come to grips with the spectacle of a competent, technologically savvy woman. In the process, she engaged different viewing priorities, setting the stage for the development of theatrical dance in the twentieth century.

CHAPTER 3

Born in America, Made in Paris

Loïe Fuller and the Exposition Universelle of 1900

At the height of her fame, Loïe Fuller loved to announce to interviewers: "I was born in America, but I was made in Paris." This flippant, yet insightful, remark points to the particular intersection of cultural, geographic and national identities which locates one of the most complex and conflicted aspects of her artistic trajectory. As Rhonda Garelick quips, Fuller's success was the product of "the marriage of European aestheticism and Yankee ingenuity."[1] *What* Fuller inspired—the lines of swirling motion in paintings, sculptures, drawings, and poetry, in short, the "look" of La Loïe—came to be seen as quintessentially Parisian. But *how* she inspired—the actual making of her performances—was quintessentially American. Nowhere is this tension more apparent than in her participation in the 1900 Exposition Universelle in Paris. Before I launch into an exploration of the complicated networks of national identity, aesthetic ideologies, technological innovations, and global marketing that formed the basis for this wild world's fair, however, I want to introduce a thematic concept, one that can play a key role in helping us to understand the historical nuances of Fuller's popular and critical reception at the turn of the twentieth century.

At the beginning of his fascinating study of modern Paris, Patrice Higonnet draws an intriguing distinction between myths and phantasmagorias. Myths, he explains, are the narratives that evolve over time to explain the historical prominence of certain politicians, artistic movements, even nations (as in the rise and fall of the Roman Empire). In using myths about Paris as a point of departure for his history of the city, Higonnet admits that he will pay less attention to the facts per se, focusing instead on the perceptions and representations of Paris as the capital of the modern world. Working through the writings of Lévi-Strauss and Barthes, Higonnet distinguishes between what he calls "cosmogonic" myths and phantasmagorias: "Whereas myths enable us to understand, phantasmagorias help us merely to deceive."[2] For Higonnet, myths, although they are often embellished, are in some deep sense true and largely universal. He cites as an example the rendering of nineteenth-century Paris as the capital of science, politics, and modernity. Phantasmagorias, on the other hand, are "illusions"—often self-delusions. Here

Higonnet offers as an example the belle epoque, that fin-de-siècle moment when Paris became "the phantasmagoric, falsely mythical capital of pleasure, sex, and European colonialism."[3]

In his introduction to the book, Higonnet contextualizes his use of the term phantasmagoria. To begin with, he writes, phantasmagorias were "an authentically Parisian phenomenon." As we saw in the last chapter, these magic-lantern entertainments were enormously popular in the nineteenth century and were often so realistic that women screamed when images of bats flew toward them. The second reason Higonnet employs the term is to echo Marx's own use of it in denoting the ease with which political (and, I would add, cultural) ideologies can cover over the economic realities of people's lives—what today we would call the spin factor. (He notes, as an example, the eighteenth-century ideal of a benevolent landowner who is "generous" to his peasants.)[4] For Higgonet, phantasmagorias can either function historically as a specific event (such as Robertson's spectacles) or operate as a signifying system, creating a half-truth that passes as the real thing.

Higonnet doesn't extend his analysis in the direction of popular entertainments any further. Nonetheless, I believe that there is a very interesting analogy here. We can trace phantasmagorias as they morphed from a specific *form* of entertainment in the mid-nineteenth century to a method of *forming* entertainments at the cusp of a new century. That is to say that we can trace their emergence from the theater to the world, from a place to an ideology, from the what to the how.

When Étienne Robertson opened up his phantasmagoric theater to the audience, the threshold of the experience was clear. One bought a ticket and entered the theater through a door. Although the images were believable and realistic, the audience was clearly separated from the events. Eventually the lights brightened, the illusion faded, and people got up, walked out, and resumed their lives. I believe it is this sense of the word that Mallarmé had in mind when he described Fuller's performance as a "lime-light phantasmagoria of dusk and grotto." Phantasmagoria is employed here to reference the mysterious, otherworldly effects of her lighting and motion. But, as Garelick reminds us in her chapter titled "Electric Salome: The Mechanical Dances of Loïe Fuller," "The Mallarmé who loved Loïe Fuller is also the gossipy, dandyist Mallarmé of *La dernière mode*, the Mallarmé who loved department stores, for at her peak Fuller was not just an esoteric marvel, she was also very much the latest fashion."[5]

Indeed, one of the characteristics of the so-called belle epoque was the increasingly conscious and deliberate performances of the fashionable self—the performance of seeing and being seen—in the avenues of the Bois de Boulogne as well as the Champs Élysées.[6] One aspect of this phantasmagoric that prevailed at the end of the century was a slippage of performance outside the previously prescribed theatrical venues. No longer were performers found only on theatrical stages or in the circus. At the dawn of celebrity culture and the ascendence of the dandy, both men and women became increasingly aware of their public personas, in terms not only of sartorial display, but also of physical demeanor. By bringing the theatricality of electrical lighting out into the streets and constructing an endless variety of fantasy sets available to the average pedestrian, the Paris exposition of 1900 built an enormous stage upon which anyone could play. The whole experience itself bordered on the phantasmagoric.

By the end of the century, Paris entertainments had begun to blur a once clear theatrical frame, with spectators getting up and participating in various aspects of the festivities. This was, in fact, the heyday of that particularly Parisian invention, the *café-concert*, in which patrons and performers became indistinguishable as the raucous evenings gathered momentum. Higonnet writes: "Then, after 1880, came a new form of pseudo-popular entertainment of the most phantasmagoric sort imaginable, which was often associated with the name of Aristide Bruant, a cabaret singer and shrewd entrepreneur: this was the café-concert, of which there were more than sixty in Paris."[7]

Interestingly enough, Higonnet marks 1889 as a crucial turning point in the crystallization of the belle epoque because in that year Aristide Bruant, a singer and songwriter, succeeded in commercializing bohemian life, turning it into popular entertainment. This was also the year in which the Moulin Rouge opened its doors and first presented what would become a quintessential motif of Parisian phantasmagoria, the ruffled petticoats of the chorus line in the can-can dance. Encouraged by the huge popularity of the *danse du ventre* (belly dance) in the 1889 World's Fair, homegrown versions of this Orientalist spectacle quickly found their way into the various music halls and cabarets in town. Also during that year Buffalo Bill set up his Wild West show just outside of Paris. These were just a few examples of what might now be called "tourist performances," in which "authentic" local cultures are portrayed for a paying audience ("real" bohemian artists in the cabarets of Montmartre, "real" belly dancers, or "real" cowboys and Indians from the American West). Although Higonnet recognizes that cultural changes such as he is describing are never neatly accomplished over the course of a year or even several years, he sees this burgeoning of popular entertainment on a massive scale as reflective of the sea change in Parisian culture that the belle epoque exemplified.

This was, of course, the world that Loïe Fuller entered in 1892—the world of an increasingly commercialized popular entertainment and a rising celebrity culture. Although they worked in different arrondissements of Paris, engaged in different entertainment forms, and performed in radically different venues, both Bruant and Fuller (as well as Jane Avril, La Goulue, and other fin-de-siècle performers) were famously portrayed in publicity posters by Toulouse-Lautrec, Chéret, PAL, and others in the last decade of the nineteenth century. These images, having lost their historical and artistic specificity by virtue of being reproduced ad nauseum (posters, T-shirts, coasters, paper napkins, umbrellas, etc.), represent a phantasmagoric past of *gai Paris* and are still today a staple product of sidewalk tourist stands in Montmartre as well as in the center of Paris. Although many of my students may never have heard of Loïe Fuller when they first come into my twentieth-century dance history class, most will immediately recognize the Chéret poster created to advertise her early performances in Paris (see Figure 23). Although they cannot connect a definite date or name to the image, they understand implicitly that it deals with a Parisian cabaret scene from a legendary moment in French popular entertainment of the kind most recently reinvented by the twenty-first-century film *Moulin Rouge*. It is important to note that even though these posters originally functioned as publicity for actual live performance engagements, they very quickly became collector's items, thus entering the realm of popular culture as floating signifiers removed from their referent.

At the end of the nineteenth century, commercialized images of Loïe Fuller abounded in Paris. There were Loïe Fuller skirts, handkerchiefs, lamps, small sculptures, and figurines. During the 1900 Paris exposition, Fuller was considered the height of fashion and, in addition to having a theater of her own, was celebrated in a plaster statue situated on the top of the Palais de Danse (which featured a dancer doing a Loïe Fulleresque butterfly dance), as well as being reflected in various other displays. This double (and doubling) of meaning embedded in Fuller's expression "made in Paris"—"made" as in becoming successful as well as "made" as in being manufactured—forces us to recognize both Fuller's complicity within this phantasmagoric marketing of her own image and the limits of her control over the circulation and reception of these representations.

The 1889 Paris Exhibition is best remembered for producing the Eiffel Tower. Considered at the time to be a monstrously impressive feat of human engineering, the Eiffel Tower was the tallest iron structure ever built, a symbol of modernity in its clean, clear lines and exposed infrastructure. The 1900 Exposition Universelle, on the other hand, used technology to recreate on an enormous scale the decorative motifs of an earlier time. Many temporary buildings were plastered (literally) with endless rococo designs. But even the more permanent buildings, such the Petit and Grand Palais erected for the occasion (and still standing), displayed elaborate neo-baroque facades. This exhibition also staged a simulacrum of the world in an astonishing array of "local" transplanted villages that permitted visitors to travel across historical time periods (*vieux* Paris, the ancient East) and various geographic locations. One could visit pseudo-villages from around the globe, including China, Russia, Cambodia, and Tunisia. One could also cruise the Cairo market—complete with belly dancers, of course—or climb a snow-laden mountain in the Alps. The various historical descriptions of these pastiches of night and day, urban and rural, east and west, bedroom and parlor, make me think of a Las Vegasesque similacrum with a decidedly French twist.

For Higonnet, the 1889 exhibition was a mythical event, symbolizing the creativity and foresight of France's engineers and builders. In contrast, the 1900 exposition was a phantasmagoria:

Ideologically, however, what distinguished the Exposition of 1900 from that of 1889 was its relation to technology on the one hand and to contemporary

Figure 23. "La Loïe Fuller." Folies Bergère poster by Jules Chéret, 1893. Jerome Robbins Dance Division, The New York Public Library for the Performing Arts, Astor, Lenox and Tilden Foundations

art on the other—in other words, combining both themes, its relation to modernity. The Exposition of 1889 took place in an era when Art Nouveau formed part of a vast array of "public technologies" and social experiments. By contrast, the Exposition of 1900 presented Art Nouveau as little more than a style appropriate to small, "feminized" domestic objects having no relation to any broader historical trends. The modernizing rationalism of the Eiffel Tower gave way to a more modernist sensibility that was excessively private, not to say privatized, as represented at the exposition most notably by the Maison de l'Art Nouveau designed by Siegfried Bing.[8]

This retrospective world's fair has been seen by critics as a frantic bourgeois reaction to the more radical elements of modernity, particularly as workers, women, and colonial subjects agitated increasingly for sovereignty over their own destinies. What is important in the context of this study of Loïe Fuller, however, is to assess the ways in which this shift from myth to phantasmagoria in Parisian culture affected the presentation, re-presentation, reproduction, and reception of her work. As she evolved from La Loïe, the Serpentine Dancer of the mid-1890s, to La Fée Électricité of the Paris exposition of 1900, Fuller adroitly manipulated the terms of her self-staging in order to mirror (and make money from) these changing aesthetic sensibilities and values. Yet as she became increasingly famous, many of the images made in her likeness became increasingly static. In the process, she became commodified as a style (see Figure 24).

The work of this chapter, then, is to tease out the various cultural forces that came together to shape Loïe Fuller's presence, not only as a performer and a theatrical producer, but also as an ubiquitous image throughout the exposition. Although they are deeply interconnected within an overall belle epoque ethos, I will begin by commenting on two of the main currents energizing this world's fair—the role of electricity as spectacle and the evolution of art nouveau—in order to situate Fuller's work within each of these phantasmagoric elements. Then I will turn to her actual stage performances in order to explore the ways in which her presentation of herself (born in America, made in Paris) echoed, but also at times resisted, the prevailing aesthetic ideologies of that phantasmagoric era, the infamous fin-de-siècle in Paris. But first, a bit of background about the fair itself.

On July 13, 1892, the French government, still reveling in the success of the 1889 exhibition, published a decree announcing a new universal exposition to be held from April to October 1900.[9] This celebration of the beginning of a new century would take place on a scale previously unimaginable, encompassing over 1,500 acres and extending across the newly built Pont Alexander III to both sides of the Seine River. Using some of the existing structures such as the Trocadéro, the Machine Gallery, and the Eiffel Tower, the government also erected a number of new buildings that extended the fair beyond the usual grounds of the Champs de Mars and the Esplanade des Invalides to incorporate parts of the city as well. For instance, the Grand and Petit Palais, which housed the Beaux-Arts and the Arts Français were

BALLET IN THE FOLIES-BERGÈRE. DANCE OF THE TYPE INTRODUCED BY LOIE FULLER.

After a water-color by André Cahard.

Figure 24. "Ballet in the Folies-Bergère, Dance of the type introduced by Loïe Fuller." "After a watercolor by André Cahard." Jerome Robbins Dance Division, The New York Public Library for the Performing Arts, Astor, Lenox and Tilden Foundations built on a small road leading up to the Champs Élysées, thus incorporating that avenue into the stream of traffic to and from the fair.[10]

In preparation for this grand event, the French government built a monumental and ornamental bridge, the Pont Alexander III. Although many believed that its Louis XVI style was overdone, the bridge's vast expanse allowed fairgoers to flow easily from one side of the Seine to the other. Highlighting the implicit theatricality of this fin-de-siècle *folie*, Jean Lorrain waxes poetic: "And the bridge, the Alexander III bridge, how its curve soars into the void! But it is as beautiful as a theorem in geometry, this ellipse of steel spanning the width of the river."[11] The anonymous author of a guide to the exposition is even more effusive: "From the middle of the bridge, it is a fairyland at a glance; the towers, the cupolas, the belvederes, all of the most beautiful conception and harmony of style; and when, in the evening, the great magician Electricity makes them resplendent under the Parisian sky, it is as if we are seeing a magical evocation of Venice, or the décor for a Thousand and One Lights."[12]

This is one of many, many descriptions of similar enchanted worlds at this fair. These magical lands of castlelike buildings (complete with delightful turrets and spires so that they are pretty, but not too imposing) were lit up at night. The term most often used to describe these wonders—*féerique*—is repeated so often that it sounds like a mantra, ringing throughout my research in just about every article or memoir about the Paris exposition that I read. *Féerique*, according to my Larousse, means fairylike, enchanting. Clearly electricity played an important role in creating this magical atmosphere. But the term also strikes me as a bit over the top, like the cloying frosting on wedding cakes. It evokes, I believe, a cultural shift in the way electricity—still a relatively new phenomenon—was viewed at the end of the nineteenth century. This difference gives us a crucial insight into the crowning of Loïe Fuller as "La Fée Électricité."

> A technology is not merely a system of machines with certain functions; it is part of a social world. Electrification is not an implacable force moving though history, but a social process that varies from one time period to another and from one culture to another. . . . Put another way, each technology is an extension of human lives: someone makes it, someone owns it, some oppose it, many use it, and all interpret it.[13]

Thus begins David E. Nye's book *Electrifying America: Social Meanings of a New Technology*. In this fascinating history of the development and commercialization of electricity in America from 1880 to 1940, Nye explores the cultural context, as well as the economic conditions, in which electricity made its debut. He details electricity's evolution from public spectacle through its consolidation as a private luxury and on to its contemporary form as a public utility. Although his comments are focused on the development of electricity in the United States, he often refers to the broader context of electrical lighting, particularly when discussing early innovations in theatrical lighting. Many of his observations about the social meanings implicit in this amazing new source of light translate directly to the fin-de-siècle context in Paris as well.

As he traces the development of electrical lighting from the theaters to the public environments of America's Main Streets, county fairs, and urban squares, Nye uncovers how the meanings connected to it shifted. At first, electric light, especially as it was used in theaters early on, created an atmosphere of the supernatural. It was such a new experience that when it was combined with color and music, people often forgot where they were, held spellbound by what Nye calls "a swirl of synesthetic experience."[14] This phrase echoes countless descriptions of Fuller's performances as mesmerizingly eerie. Nye also documents the meanings embedded in the spectacular light shows of the large national expositions and world's fairs that were coming into vogue at this time. These elaborate public displays used nighttime as a backdrop, emphasizing the theatrical void before the light in much the same way Fuller did by darkening the stage before her performances. In a young woman's diary of the time, Nye finds a description of such an event. Although her effusive writing describes the Electric Tower in the 1901 Pan-American Exposition in the United States, its turns of phrase and metaphors match almost exactly similar descriptions of the 1900 exposition held in Paris a year earlier:

> A few minutes before the appointed hour, the bulk of electric lighting along the paths and within the buildings diminishes until they become tiny specks of flames which soon die away. Suddenly, the buildings, the long lines of lamp pillars, seem to pulse with a thrill of life before the eye becomes sensible to what is taking place. There is a deep silence and all eyes are intent on the Electric Tower. In the splendid vertical panel there is a faint glow of light, like the first flush which a church spire catches from the dawn. This deepens from pink to red, and then grows into a luminous yellow, and the Exposition of beams and staff has vanished and in its place is a wondrous vision of dazzling wonders and minarets, domes, and pinnacles set in the midst of scintillating gardens—the triumph not of Aladdin's lamp, but of the masters of modern science over the nature-god Electricity.[15]

In these municipal and national contexts, fabulous displays of lighting confirmed the technological power of a community and created a visual analogy for an ideology of progress. As I have previously discussed, light symbolizes the civilizing influence of Western technology, the mark of a modern nation. Later, in a chapter aptly titled "The Great White Way," Nye declares: "Electrification thus made possible a new kind of visual text, one that expressed an argument or view of the world without writing, solely through suppressing some features of a site and emphasizing others."[16] As we shall see, the role of electricity—like the architectural features it illuminated—morphed from a symbol of progress and a sign of modernity into a decidedly more decorative feature at the 1900 exposition.

Electricity was used in a largely functional capacity throughout the 1889 exhibition. There were, nonetheless, two notable theatrical displays of its power. The first

cyclamen tints and fall in showers of green and purple light, orchestrations of liquid fire, a riot of volts and ampères. The Seine is violet, iridescent, blood-red. Electricity is accumulated, condensed, transformed, bottled, drawn into filaments, rolled upon spools, then discharged under water, in fountains, or set free on the house tops or let loose among the trees; it is the scourge and the religion of 1900.[19]

In this extraordinary diatribe, Morand anthropomorphizes electricity into a decadent diva, seducing the public with her dazzling artifice. Although the pathologized overtones of his reaction are extreme, Morand's comments are nonetheless consistent with other contemporary discussions of the 1900 exposition, which also revel in elaborate descriptions of the fertile excitement in the streets, the frenetic energy stirred up by the hyped-up pace of the fair. As one such observer reports: "The Exhibition smothers its disparate parts in an ensemble which can be accused of everything except lifelessness; life seethes in this immense reservoir of energy."[20] Many other journalists describe the exhibition as a living organism, again often "seething" with life. It is important to note, however, that "seething" suggests not a balanced ecology, but rather one of continuous consumption—all based, of course, on the steady, inexhaustible current of electrical power. On a practical as well as a performative level,—that is to say, both materially and ideologically—electricity charged the 1900 Exposition Universelle with new currents of desire.

In newspaper articles and interviews of the time, Loïe Fuller was inevitably associated with this kind of boundless energy. Most often, however, these mythic depictions of her persona derive not from her performances, but rather from illustrations of her everyday "American" demeanor. Interviewers repeatedly describe how her brilliant blue eyes light up and sparkle as Fuller becomes animated while discoursing on her latest invention. Even though they inevitably comment on her frumpy, old-fashioned clothing, they also emphasize her intelligence, technological sophistication, and overall theatrical savvy. In an 1899 review published in *The Poster*, the author cites Fuller's thoughtfulness as one important aspect that distinguishes her from other dancers:

> She is not merely the heroine of the few glittering moments during which she occupies the stage of the *Folies Bergère* each night, for she holds in addition a conspicuous place in that society which includes those Frenchmen who in science, art, and letters are adding to the intellectual dignity of the human race. It is not given to the ordinary dancing girl to attract and to retain the interest of writers such as Dumas *fils*, men of science such as Camille Flammarion, and artists such as Rodin. . . . It is Loïe Fuller's crowning merit that she does nothing in her dances which is unintelligent, nothing which is intended merely to provoke the wonder of the vulgar. Her performances are the result of much deliberation, and of prolonged and fatiguing experiment.[21]

During the 1900 exposition, Arsène Alexandre authored an exposé of Fuller that contains one of the most frequently cited passages (aside from Mallarmé) in Fuller scholarship:

> People don't know Loïe's energy, her get-up-and-go. She is what is called *a very pushing woman*. According to the experts, the construction would take six months; actually, it took six weeks. During that time Miss Fuller was architect, painter, decorator, mechanic, electrician, manager, and everything else.
>
> There was nothing more amusing and charming than to see her on the construction site, running around to supervise the work or to correct a mistake, her plum-colored dress disheveled, her hair in wild disarray. One minute she was half-dead from fatigue; the next minute she suddenly came to life and greeted her friends in the midst of her construction (or her ruins—it's hard to say which) with all the vivacity and affectionate graciousness that she knows how to put into her slightest gesture and the slightest word of her fractured French. . . .
>
> She wore out two or three secretaries, though she wrote more letters than any of them. All the while she was carrying on this trade—or, rather, these hundred trades—she also found the energy to dance at the Olympia in the evenings and also, I believe, often in the afternoons. It almost seemed as if it were her ghost that danced and her real self that thrashed about at the exposition, under some torrential downpours, among the carpenters, team-sters, and interior decorators."[22]

This odd English phrase, "a very pushing woman," printed in italics in the midst of typically lyrical French sentences, captures Fuller's Americana image abroad. The combination of resourcefulness and determination that Alexandre portrays in these paragraphs shows Fuller to be a strong and feisty pioneer woman, one whose true-blue American blood could never be diluted by her Parisian successes. This not atypical mythologizing of Fuller's American identity points to an essential difference between La Loïe and most of the other female divas who rose to fame during the belle epoque. Whereas stars such as Sarah Bernhardt were lauded for their ability to just *be* (their performances were seen as elaborately framed visions of an essential self), Fuller's fame is produced by her ability to *do*—to entirely transform herself onstage to the point that she becomes unrecognizable. The incongruity between her pedestrian self and her performative presentations is cited by journalists as one of the most intriguing aspects of her persona. Alexandre calls this "doubling":

> It is true that one rarely sees a person as perfectly twofold [*double*] as Miss Loïe, diverse [*double*] in as many ways as she is. On the streets she is little, on the stage she is huge. In the city she has chestnut-colored hair, on stage

blond—it is true that this shouldn't be surprising, but she is really [*vraiment*] chestnut-haired at home and really [*vraiment*] blonde in her theater. . . . This little plump woman who is cheerful and dressed in dumpy clothes, without much of a sense of style, becomes the marvelous creature of our dreams, dancing lost in the ideal, swirling amid her veils which change shape a thousand times a minute.[23]

What interests me in this fascinating excerpt is Alexandre's repeated use of *vraiment*, or truly. For although he sets up a binary at the beginning of the passage (onstage she appears huge, offstage she is small), in both spheres she is "really," truly herself. With this affirmation, Alexandre refuses an implicit devaluing of the stage as a place of artifice and illusion. Fuller's doubling is not presented as duplicitous, but rather as the natural mutability of a multifaceted person. By highlighting the difference between Fuller's staged incarnations of otherworldly visions and her plebeian, Yankee, "just do it" attitude offstage, Alexandre emphasizes the active transformation at the core of her work, thus keeping Fuller from slipping irretrievably into the phantasmagoria of the fair whirling around her. Unfortunately, he can't hold on forever.

Fuller's early success in Paris was due to the fact that she was able to blend images of nature with the performative excitement of a modern technology to become the metonymic equivalent of an organism powered by light. In the context of the 1900 exposition, however, Fuller became a popular simile: "The ministries of the Left Bank are *like gigantic Loïe Fullers*" (emphasis added). Clearly, within the popular imagination Fuller was considered to be the original performance of spectacular lighting against which all similar public displays are measured. What happens, then, when she becomes an actual attraction at the fair itself? Placed in the midst of gigantic imitations of herself, might Fuller seem like just another similacrum of herself? It is this other meaning of doubling, the one embedded in the duality of performer and image, original and copy, stage and museum, the body and the cast, that I want to take up next as we stroll down the Rue de Paris to visit the Théâtre de la Loïe Fuller.

In his book *Loïe Fuller: Danseuse de la belle époque*, Giovanni Lista records the end of 1897 as the time that Fuller decided to construct her own theater at the exposition.[24] It is unclear to me whether this was a definite decision at that time, or whether she was simply entertaining the possibility of her participation. Nonetheless, many of her friends and advisors encouraged her to build her own theater, and by the end of January 1900 Fuller had officially applied for a spot in the section called L'Art dans la Rue (see Figure 25). As the opening date of the exposition approached, Fuller decided to relocate her theater to the Rue de Paris. This move gave her a prime location, right on the pathway leading from the main entrance of the fair. She was the only non-French concession situated among the various typical Parisian entertainments such as the Théâtroscope, the Maison du Rire, the Grand Guignol, and the Tour du Merveilleux, not to mention the Palais de la Danse, which

was crowned by a plaster statue of Fuller and where Valentine Petit was dancing Fulleresque dances with titles such as "Le papillon" and "Visions nocturnes."

To design the project, she chose Henri Sauvage, a young architect who had recently opened a studio of architecture and decoration (he had previously been involved with designing and manufacturing furniture and wallpapers). At first, Sauvage created a long, tentlike pavilion with a gothic air to the metal decorations ornamenting the roof. When Fuller decided to move closer to the entrance, that building was redesigned and then sold to a Punch and Judy concession called the Guignol Parisien. Sauvage was joined by Pierre Roche in the final stages of design of the new project on the Rue de Paris, and together they created a building with an enormous wave of fabric rippling across its facade. In addition, a life-sized sculpture of Fuller with spread wings was mounted over the entrance archway. In their book on Fuller, the Currents describe this building in terms that help us realize its fantastic (and temporary) nature:

The completed Loïe Fuller Theater, a strange little building, had an air of narcissism about it, totally devoted as it was to the dancer and her reflection in art. Its facade was wrapped in folds

Figure 25. Sculptures of Loïe Fuller in front of her first 1900 Paris Exposition Universelle building. Jerome Robbins Dance Division, The New York Public Library for the Performing Arts, Astor, Lenox and Tilden Foundations

Figure 26. Entrance to the Loïe Fuller Theater at the 1900 Paris Exposition Universelle. Jerome Robbins Dance Division, The New York Public Library for the Performing Arts, Astor, Lenox and Tilden Foundations

of plaster that called to mind her draperies in motion, and it was topped by a life-size Loïe statue, which looked like a great bird about to take flight. All this was the work of Pierre Roche, and so were the curved bas-relief figures of two dancing girls that entwined the entrance. At night the white stucco exterior became ablaze with light, shining up from below. Inside, during the day, sunlight streaming through stained-glass windows gave a kaleido-scopic effect. In the evening, a similar effect was created by electric lights. The stage was quite small, with the auditorium having room for only two hundred seats.[25]

It is difficult to capture in words the bizarre effect of Loïe Fuller's theater at the Paris exposition. Many books devoted to art nouveau illustrate this apotheosis of art nouveau architecture with a design drawing by Sauvage. Although this drawing captures nicely the swirling details of Pierre Roche's plaster decorations, it nonethe-less renders the building weightless and two-dimensional. The ripples of fabric that undulate across the front of the building and the winged-looking statue of Fuller above the entrance are oddly static in their effect. Because there is no attempt to cre-ate any depth or perspective in this sketch, all we see is a plaster facade that seems to parallel the extravagance of the Château d'Eau. This is architecture as spectacle, a weirdly phantasmagoric ode to a mythic dancer.

In his article memorializing her presence at the 1900 exposition, Arsène Alex-andre describes Fuller's theater as the perfect frame (*cadre*) for her work, a place that literally and figuratively embodies her. Not only does the architecture echo the wavelike movement of her silk costume, but it seems to actually breathe with and envelop her. While the outside suggests a stage curtain, the inside provides a kaleidoscopic vision of her influence in the arts:

> In the room, not black, but obscure to highlight the caress of the vivid colors, first you find museum, a very small museum where one discovers a preliminary poem of statuettes, sculptures, pastels, paintings, all celebrat-ing the graceful dancer with the vast wings. Every now and then, the very great painters and sculptors inspire performers, but thanks to performers of genius, there are new schools of art.[26]

Grandly attributing to Fuller the inspiration of new trends in the arts, Alexandre glosses over the blatantly commercial aspect of her concession at the fair.

Fortunately, there are several historical photographs of Fuller's theater at the 1900 exposition (see Figure 26). These images slice through the veneer of fine art and present the theater as a working environment. The ground is muddy and heav-ily trodden in front of the entrance, and shadows and sunlight haphazardly cast images across the front of the building. There is something vaguely tawdry in this photo, which has a kind of circus-sideshow atmosphere. Leaning against bare trees on either side of the entryway are large placards advertising the next show, which is billed as produced by Loïe Fuller (whose name warrants the largest letters) and starring Sada Yacco in her play "The Geisha and the Knight" and a Miss Mabel Knowles in "Danses lumineuses."[27] The dimensions of the theater seem somewhat less grand that the architectural drawings suggest, more like a boutique fair booth than a public theater.

Upon entering the Loïe Fuller Theater, one stepped into a foyer set up as a small museum and souvenir shop. Filled with Loïe Fuller memorabilia such as theater photos, paintings, and small sculptures, this room served up concrete examples of Fuller's elusive spectacles. I can only imagine that this experience must be similar to walking into the lobby of the regional ballet's production of *Nutcracker*, where the local ballet mothers' guild is trying to subsidize the elaborate costumes by selling baked goods, little wooden nutcrackers (made in Taiwan), books, T-shirts, ballet bags, and the like.

Or maybe it was more like walking into the Musée des Beaux-Arts in Nancy, France, to see their exhibition on Fuller, "Danseuse de l'art nouveau" (May 17– August 19, 2002). At that event, three rooms were devoted to displays of Loïe Fuller images, including an enormous selection of small statues by Pierre Roche, Théodore Louis Auguste Rivière, and Françoise-Rupert Carabin, not to mention the gilded lamps by Raoul Larche. At the time that I visited this extraordinary exhibit, I had only been working on Fuller for about a year. I welcomed the opportunity to see the originals of many of the works of art representing Fuller. The exhibition at Nancy featured posters, and many of the photographs with which I was already familiar. Much to my delight, this exhibit also included the limited-edition art book on Fuller produced in 1905, with a text by Roger Marx, and gypsographs (pressed cardboard relief images) by Pierre Roche. Displayed on one wall, each page was covered by Plexiglas, and although one couldn't touch the raised images, they still conveyed an appealingly tactile sensibility.

In the middle of the largest room of the exhibition was a display case with various figurines by Carabin. Executed in a series of six different poses in 1896–97, these statuettes recall the sequential photographs of Edward Muybridge: each one captures a different moment in Fuller's oeuvre. Certain positions in this series clearly evoke Fuller's most famous works, including the serpentine and the butterfly dances. These diminutive figures (most are less than nine inches tall) present a nude upper torso, the full skirt starting only at the waist. There is a youthful spirit that animates each of the poses; they could easily be visions of a young woman frolicking in a summer breeze after bathing in a river. Although the motion of the skirt is superbly rendered, the total effect of these little bronzes figures is quite odd. Lacking any reference to color or light in Fuller's performances, they seem to reduce her dancing to conventional notions of "natural" movement, a stylized version of a young girl's pleasure in spinning around.

A more famous series of bronzes depicting Fuller was also on display in the Nancy exhibition. These were the golden bronze lamps by Larche (see Figure 27). Designed by him and produced in 1900 by the Siot-Décaumille foundry, these

The year 1900 marked not only the apotheosis of art nouveau, but also the cultural emergence in France of the new woman—*la femme nouvelle*, represented in the second International Feminist Congress held at the fair. Active, physical, and mobile, this new woman quickly became associated with the same current of movement and energy that animated the 1900 exposition. In her extensive discussion in *Art Nouveau in Fin-de-Siècle France*, Deborah Silverman remarks how the new woman's entrance into public life paralleled the "tension and new electric energy of the city streets and the 'brand new sparks' of the new century and its promise of technological inventions and 'eternal motion.'" Silverman quotes a contemporary art critic, Marius-Ary Leblond, whose essay "Les peintres de la femme nouvelle" contributed to a seminal awareness of how the portraiture of women was evolving. This *femme nouvelle* rejected her position as an orchestrated object d'art: "The new woman is not beautiful. She looks rather like a boy, and illustrates more than anything the expression of a firm character, a serene soul, a robustly harmonious body."[33] Whether this new woman was represented by the solid statue of La Parisienne or the Pierre Roche's winged image of La Loïe, it was clear in 1900 that her portrait contained the internal tension between modernity as a look or style and modernity as a way of being or force.

Despite the superficial freedom of movement in the style of art nouveau design, this movement was consciously staged as part of a governmental response to a growing anxiety about the new woman, about her flight from the domestic sphere and her threat to the sanctity of the bourgeois family. Like the appliance craze of post–World War II in the United States, art nouveau upped the ante for homemakers. Rather than encouraging women to become mobile and extend their influence to the public world, art nouveau generally captured the *image* of motion, but *contained* it within an increasingly domestic realm. Many of the pavilions at the 1900 exposition, for instance, advertised home decorations and fittings. Some, like the famous Maison Bing, created entire arts and crafts rooms to be discovered and (given the rapidity with which the art nouveau style was quickly co-opted and mass-produced) eventually purchased. That this artistic movement was consciously connected to an anxious response to budding feminism has been amply documented. Indeed, even a cursory look at the cartoons and caricatures mocking the emasculating effect of the 1896 feminist congress (the classic prototype is of a manly woman chiding her husband, who is holding a baby, about preparing dinner as she prepares to mount her bike and drive off) reveals a profound cultural unease with women's new found social mobility.

Fortunately, not all art nouveau was created equal. Although it is easy to place the Larche lamps as part of a conservative retreat into an essentialized vision of an organic, feminine, and privatized interior space (the home, where women belong), there were other cultural currents shaping the production of artistic objects as well. In her introduction to her book on politics, psychology, and style in fin-de-siècle France, Silverman discusses an important aspect of art nouveau—the way it captured a new sensibility about the human body:

One source of this artistic renewal was clearly unprecedented: the meaning of the 1890s craft modernism was inextricably linked to a new French medical psychology that identified the interior of the human organism as a sensitive nervous mechanism. . . . The diffusion of a specific body of knowledge, originating with Doctor Jean-Martin Charcot of the Paris Salpêtrière and his rival Doctor Hippolyte Bernheim of Nancy, stimulated a discourse in the artistic world connecting the organic curvature of modern craft arts to nervous palpitation, hypnotic suggestibility, and the inducement of dream states. The writings and activities of Charcot and Bernheim make it clear that pre-Freudian French psychiatry was charged with implications for the artistic community. Both doctors were immersed in aesthetic concepts and practices, and their redefinition of rational consciousness was generated in part by their experiments with the fluid, dynamic power of images to release unconscious forces. . . . The artist who absorbed the neuropsychiatric theories of fluidity, indeterminacy, and internal tension created art forms more complex, dynamic, and unstable than any institutional framework containing them.[34]

One of the artists most influenced by this burgeoning cultural discourse was Émile Gallé. A native of the Lorraine region of France, Gallé was a second-generation glassmaker whose name quickly became synonymous with glass vases and objects characterized by swirling multicolors. Gallé lived in Nancy, a city heavily influenced by art nouveau, both in terms of its architecture and by way of its decorative arts guild, the École de Nancy, which became a leading force in the development of art nouveau. Gallé's vases beautifully echo the nuanced blending of colors and light in Fuller's performances. They also incorporate a similar blending of abstract design with a more literal depiction of flowers, plants, and animals. Using the techniques developed by the end of the nineteenth century, Gallé combined clear and opaque glass in an ever changing array of colors. He also was famous for using iridescence and metallic highlights in his pieces. When I first saw his work at the Musée des Beaux-Arts in Nancy and the Musée d'Orsay in Paris, I was mesmerized by the suggestive interplay of shape, color, and density. Staring at the cabinet of his vases on display, I felt I was in the presence of something remarkably close in spirit to Fuller's aesthetic innovations.

Gallé was a very successful businessman who had inherited his father's glassworks in 1875. By 1900, his unique objets d'art were in demand throughout the Exposition Universelle. A major figure in the decorative arts movement, Gallé gave a speech at the exposition in which he argued for what he termed "emotional contagion," the idea that forms could have a direct, unmediated emotional impact on a viewer. As Silverman explains:

> Gallé, for whom the artistic process closely resembled the clinical state
> of ideodynamism, proposed in 1900 the ideodynamic quality of visual
> symbolism—that images were converted into ideas automatically and

played with this continuum of symbolic meanings in her dance, gradually metamorphosing from a woman into a flower in the final spiraling moments of the dance, in which her face and body were completely obscured by her costume. Reflecting on these themes, Roger Marx describes Fuller as

> a gigantic lily around a calyx, which is the same body of the dancer, the petals spreading open. . . . This image is prolonged by a thousand little openings and contractions of this inexhaustible vision, this delicate and fantastic plant, which juxtaposes in one symbol, being and nature, and which illuminates, with the smile of a woman, the fragile flesh of flowers.[39]

Unlike her "Fire Dance," where the vivid colors and contrasts of warm and cool shades carried much of the emotional weight of the dance, in "Le lys" it is Fuller's engagement of the space as well as the evolution of the shape of her vast costume that carried the most impact for the viewers. In a black-and-white photograph by Cliché Taber dating from this time period, Fuller is caught in the final moment of the dance. The fabric is suspended above her head, maintained there by her constant spinning. The silk descends in spiraling layers, each of which catches the light differently, creating different intensities within the same color spectrum and completely concealing her body in the process. Described as "incandescent" and "opal-like," the colored lighting for this dance drew on many of the same technical innovations that Fuller premiered with "Fire Dance," but this time she used a softer, more muted palette, as well as multicolored gels: "Her immense spiraling veils were illuminated by multicolored projections, which progressively faded until only a faint silver glow was left at the end of the dance."[40] In the Taber photos, which were taken outdoors in natural lighting, Fuller stands on a large block of stone, her silk costume extending well past her feet and almost to the ground.

Ironically, then, while Loïe Fuller portrayed a lily—that loaded image of a domesticated flower that circulated throughout art nouveau—she also physically embodied it, enacting a transformation that projected an open, changing, and ultimately strong female body. Extending ten feet in either direction, Fuller's soaring wings created in the audience a somatic response to her liberating images of flight. If we consider the impact of Gallé's notion of ideodynamism, we can recognize that even if her body was visually obscured in the final moments of the dance, Fuller's powerful physicality carried its own impact.

During an informal conversation with Jody Sperling, a self-styled "contemporary imitator of Loïe Fuller," Sperling described one of the differences between working with the shorter or longer wands. With the shorter rods, she noted, the dancer has more fine motor coordination and maneuverability at the level of her wrist and lower forearm. This allows for the kinds of flutters and ripple effects seen in the representations of skirt dancing and Fuller's early serpentine dances. With the longer wands, there is less possibility of specific definition in the lower arms and wrists and a greater need to be connected from the central core of the chest all the way out through the hands. Developing strength in the sternum and upper back also were essential for Sperling as she danced with the longer wands.[41] The amount of physical stamina required to lift that much extra silk and launch it so that it catches the air and floats toward the sky is immense. It also requires a definite release of one's weight into the floor and the coordinated use of one's breath. These last two points are, of course, key elements in any modern dance technique, and although they are (quite literally) wrapped up in the fin-de-siècle imagery and enhanced by her lighting effects, I believe that they were nonetheless visible in Fuller's dance. With "Le lys," Fuller was able to embody both the physical strength of the modern woman and her conceptual liberation. Her mobility, transmutability, and expansive use of her costume evoked the impression of a woman's body (even while dancing as a lily) that is free to change.

Temporarily escaping from the phantasmagoria of the 1900 exposition and the (self-) commodification of its commercialized frame, Fuller's actual dancing offered another reality onstage. For both Fuller and her audiences, this alternative was grounded in her American identity. Before we move on to an exploration of her role as an impresario, I believe it is worth exploring this myth of Americanness a bit more fully. It is fairly easy, when reading introductory descriptions of Fuller, to chalk up her American branding to her stocky body, her frumpy appearance, or the notorious limits of her French. Her presence in the 1900 Paris exposition was also a moment of expanding American political, economic, and cultural imperialism, and the American expatriate community was growing in both numbers and influence in Paris. Fuller's self-described role in this community was often to bring French artists and American industrial fortunes together. Certainly, the elaborate correspondence and negotiations she undertook to publicize and market Rodin's artwork in America (however conflicted and problematic they were) attests to her goodwill in supporting his growing international reputation.

In the handwritten manuscript of an unfinished and unpublished essay entitled "America and Americans," Fuller analyzes the stereotype of the rude, self-centered American. She begins with a discussion of how U.S. citizens tend to lump all of America under their own nation. With crystalline insight and a self-awareness rarely attributed to her, Fuller writes: "The American began by having all Yankee-dom-and-Louisiana, nothing'll satisfy him now till he's got all America. He thinks he has it now, and when he finds he hasn't, he'll probably proceed to reach out for it; because he believes he *can* have anything on earth he wants—if he's only willing to pay the price." What follows is a series of amusing anecdotes about rich Americans in Paris trying to buy their way through the French bureaucracy. Then, she shifts the emphasis of the writing by moving on to American women:

> This American woman may never have been to school . . . she was a force, an intelligent and intellectual force, a moral good, and what does it matter whether she knows or cared about the forms and ceremonies of Court life, or any other kind of life—or whether she knows who was the greatest liv-

actor copies exactly the gestures, facial expressions, and physical demeanor of the character type, the emotion will follow. By contrast, most Western acting traditions focus on finding the internal emotions first and then coming up with the gestures that express that emotion.

Although Mauclair contrasts Yacco's psychological interpretations of everyday life with Fuller's abstract images (he calls them metaphysical flights of the soul), I believe they share a similar orientation to the theater. Both Fuller and Yacco focus on the larger theatrical frame, blending expressive movement with pictorial design in a way that engages both the audience members' visual awareness and their physical sensibilities (what was earlier described as ideodynamic or metakinesis). In a city in which there were many serpentine dancers and quite a few "Japanese" dancing actresses, Loïe Fuller and Sada Yacco were able to distinguish themselves from their imitators through the intelligence of their performances. Seen as scientists as well as artists, they both performed with an awareness of the whole stage environment. Their active participation in creating the frame (and their unwillingness to simply be the focus) of their (self-) representations was an early feminist gesture. Although some critics, like Mauclair, recognized this, others did not.

"Sada Yacco in Paris! No one ever imagined that those Japanese prints, which were so popular that they even made their way into Clemenceau's portfolio and into Zola's study, that those precious, stilted kakemonos, would one day come to life."[49] Paul Morand's comments in his memoir reflect what many of the critics said about the Japanese troupe's performances—that they were Japanese prints come to life. Japan was at this time considered an ancient and powerful country with an elegant and artistic culture. Although Japanese prints, fabrics, and ceramic objects could have been found in Europe since the seventeenth century, the opening up of the country to trade in 1853 aroused a tremendous interest in Japanese culture in France. Japanese fine arts and crafts created sensations at all the international expositions in the second-half of the nineteenth century. From 1888 to 1891, Siegfried Bing published an influential arts journal, *Le Japon artistique*. This lavish and beautifully produced publication included essays on various aspects of Japanese art and culture by a distinguished group of writers and critics. Published simultaneously in French, English, and German, it held a pervasive influence throughout Europe. In addition, Bing organized several exhibits of Japanese arts, including one in 1890 at the École des Beaux-Arts dedicated to presenting a survey of Japanese woodblock prints.[50]

Of all the Japanese arts, prints had the most pervasive influence on the aesthetic of art nouveau. When he opened his famous art gallery, L'Art Nouveau, in 1895, Bing showed contemporary Japanese art, especially prints, alongside work by European artists. As a contemporary designer commented: "It took the power of the Japanese line, the force of its rhythm and its accents, to arouse us and influence us."[51] Many poster artists at the turn of the century (including Toulouse-Lautrec) absorbed the stylization of nature in Japanese prints, as well as their blending of foreground and background, their exquisitely subtle shades of color, and the overall effect of stillness in so many of the images.

Manuel Orazi, an Italian printer living and working in Paris, was particularly interested in Japanese prints. His poster advertising Loïe Fuller's theater is one of his finest works, and many of its details, including the circular shapes arising like champagne bubbles on the left, reflect Japanese influence (see Figure 29). These, in addition to his stylized signature on the bottom right, echo the circular shapes on the *kesa* (traditionally seen on a Buddhist priest's mantle) as well as conventions of drawing Japanese family crests.[52] Even the shape of the poster is like a Japanese scroll print, long and narrow. The colors are sensuous and soft, and the way the overall line gathers momentum to sweep across the body and into a wave at the top is quite seductive. Yet what I find most intriguing in this work is the tension between the dynamic serpentine line and the visual stillness of the decorative insignias, suspended in time.

I've been struggling to write about this poster for a long time now. A color copy of the image has traveled with me on all my research trips, and I currently have three in my study—including one mere inches from my pen. It is as if I believe its ubiquitous presence would help me understand my conflicted response to this image. On one hand, I think it has one of the richest and most sensuous color schemes of any Loïe Fuller representation. The depth of the orange and its sinuous retreat through yellow into green, purple, and then blue can keep my eye entranced for a long time, reminding me of the importance of the pure spectacle of color in Fuller's work. On the other hand, the whiteness of the female figure's upper body, blending into a wave, in addition to the stylized curls of her hair, reveals such a tacky art nouveau influence that it practically turns my stomach. On a purely visceral level, I want to dive into the picture. On an intellectual level, I run up against the phantasmagoria of the fin de siècle. Instead of trying to resolve this tension by deciding once and for all whether the image is good or bad, progressive or retro, liberating or stagnating, mythic or phantasmagoric, I prefer to live with this aesthetic ambiguity, recognizing that Fuller's presence at the 1900 Paris Exposition Universelle was equally inflected by both the inspiring and the kitsch.

Figure 29. "Théâtre de Loïe Fuller." Poster for the 1900 Paris Exposition Universelle by Manuel Orazi. Fine Arts Museum of San Francisco, Gift of the Bay Area Graphic Arts Council

HAIL!
SALOMÉ·

CHAPTER **4**

Femininity with a Vengeance

Strategies of Veiling and Unveiling
in Loïe Fuller's Performances of *Salomé*

*To put on femininity with a vengeance suggests the power of
taking it off.*

Mary Russo, "Female Grotesques:
Carnival and Theory" (1986)

In a move that seems to be universally interpreted as a big mistake, Loïe Fuller produced her own version of the Salome myth in 1895 and cast herself in the title role. This "création nouvelle" was billed as a "pantomime lyrique en 2 actes" and ran for less than two months at the Comédie-Parisienne. Most critics panned the play. Jean Lorrain, who had previously been a real fan of Fuller's work (describing her as "the beautiful girl who, in her floating draperies, swirls endlessly around in an ecstasy induced by divine revelations"), penned vituperative remarks that were personally insulting and just plain mean.[1] Various other reviewers (with the notable exception of Roger Marx) registered their disappointment in this new creation by La Loïe. Even late-twentieth-century scholars, writing from a perspective of at least historical if not critical distance, tend to dismiss this fin-de-siècle work as a limp, nostalgic gesture toward the expressive (melo)dramas with which Fuller began her career. Despite the troubled results of her first foray, twelve years later Fuller took on this decadent icon once again—this time when she was forty-five. *La tragédie de Salomé* premiered on November 9, 1907, at the Théâtre des Arts. Although the press reviews for this production were not as personally or professionally damning, the production was a commercial failure and closed after a short run.

Most Fuller scholars chalk up these two failed attempts to play Salome to a bizarre lapse in Fuller's usually astute professional judgment. If they talk about these *Salomé* productions at all, it is usually to discuss Fuller's innovative use of under-lighting in the 1895 version, documenting how Fuller developed the spectacular "Fire Dance" from the production's "Sun Dance" and toured it and other shorter dances independently of the original pantomime. I, however, find myself deeply intrigued and intellectually stimulated by Fuller's desire to repeatedly reinvent this biblical temptress, precisely because the whole enterprise doesn't quite make sense. Why, after having studiously avoided the dancer-as-seductress stereotype so rampant at the end of the nineteenth century, did Fuller decide to enact one of the century's most notorious femmes fatales? What was she trying to accomplish? Why was she compelled to take on Salomé not once, but twice? What strategic uses of the veil are implicated in these stagings? And what, indeed, was she interested in uncovering, or rather discovering, in herself and in her work by "becoming" Salomé?

These are some of the questions that animate this chapter. I believe that an in-depth comparison of her 1895 and 1907 stagings of *Salomé* can illuminate an important shift in Fuller's oeuvre. Not only does each production reveal a singular approach to the subject matter, but each one also reflects a different feminist strategy for confronting and intervening in misogynist representations of sexualized women. Put very simply for the purposes of comparison in this introduction, Fuller's first *Salomé* revised the traditional narrative to create a mystical, "chaste" younger Salomé, who dances to try and save John the Baptist. Here she replaced the deadly seductress with a more positive role model. Interestingly, in her second attempt, Fuller returned to a more traditional portrayal of Salomé as a desperate, desiring woman. For this 1907 staging of *La tragédie de Salomé*, Fuller played with the many known cultural representations of this iconic woman, miming a different approach to the legendary figure in each of the two acts of this production and incorporating both the emotional and the campy in an ironic juxtaposition of citation and expression.

By 1895, Fuller's extraordinary success was predicated on her fluid imaging of cloth and color. Veiling her body, her expansive silks created visions that remained in a comfortably abstract, albeit dynamic, realm. As Mallarmé's "no-woman," Fuller effectively separated herself from the frames of female characterization and traditional narrative (where the public, performing woman usually ended up desperate—or dead). When she enacted Salomé, however, Fuller was forced to confront not only her public's assumptions about who she was, but also the myriad literary and visual representations of this legendary figure literally swarming—like so many insects—across late-nineteenth-century stages as well as in private salons. For the first time since establishing her signature as the original "Serpentine Dancer," Fuller had to revise her performative identity. That she chose to play out her femininity with a vengeance tells us quite a bit about the woman behind the veil.

Rhonda Garelick's chapter on Fuller in her book *Rising Star*, entitled "Electric Salomé," focuses on Fuller's presence at the 1900 Paris exposition. It playfully references the cultural trope of Salomé as a dancer who "unveils," but Garelick never discusses Fuller's performances of this female legend in any depth. Instead, she holds to the common perspective that juxtaposes Fuller with other, more provocative women performers, such as the Orientalized belly dancers parading through the Parc du Trocadéro:

Fuller, it should be recalled, never took her clothes off, never gyrated, and never shocked respectable people. . . . True, she was foreign in France, but hailed only from unsensual America, a country that had (and still has) a reputation for sexlessness and a kind of sanitized heartiness very removed from either Oriental or European passion. Hers was the dazzle not of the body but of machinery, technology, and Yankee ingenuity. In the French imagination, Fuller's appeal was always closer to Thomas Edison than to Josephine Baker's.[2]

As I remarked upon at some length in the previous chapter, Fuller was strongly associated with what Garelick calls "Yankee ingenuity," especially in the context of the 1900 exposition. It is also true that she had a reputation for "cleaning up" the Folies Bergère, enabling the management to create matinees innocent enough for women and children to attend. But, as Current and Current point out in their book on Fuller, by her second season at this nightclub, the director had reincorporated a number of "girlie" acts around Fuller's expanded repertoire. These included women such as "La Belle Otero," a well-known courtesan whose private life and public postures onstage referenced one another. Despite the highly sexualized frame of the other acts in the Folies Bergère, from the beginning of her celebrity status in Paris, Fuller was consistently cast as frank and without pretense or feminine wiles. Indeed, reviewers would frequently point out her charming naiveté. For instance, a reporter from London's *Strand* magazine portrays Fuller as a simple, "bonnie, blue-eyed little woman, plain in her dress, and with a sweet frankness of manner and speech."[3]

Of course, Fuller consciously played into this characterization of her offstage persona. In a famous passage from her autobiography, Fuller writes of her effect on little children, who were frequently delighted with her fairylike performances and whose imaginations, she asserts, are "easily kindled by suggestions of the supernatural."[4] So believable was her fairylike incarnation that these children had a difficult time understanding Fuller's transformation back into an ordinary woman. Citing the example of one little girl who "recoiled with horror" (Fuller's words) when she was introduced to the dancer backstage, Fuller reports that she tried to keep up the illusion by telling the girl that she was merely the fairy's emissary:

The mother and child found their way to my dressing room. . .

The child's eyes opened wider and wider. The nearer I came the further she shrank away.

Quite astonished her mother said: "What is the matter dear? This is Miss Fuller, who danced for you so prettily a few minutes ago. You know you begged me so hard to bring you to see her."

As if touched by a magic wand the child's expression changed.

"No, no. That isn't her. I don't want to see her. This one here is a fat lady, and it was a fairy I saw dancing."

If there is one thing in the world of which I am incapable, it is consciously to cause anyone pain, and, with my love of children, I should never have been happy again if I had caused my little visitor to be disillusioned. I endeavoured therefore to be equal to the situation, and I said to the child:

"Yes, my dear, you are right. I am not Loïe Fuller. The fairy has sent me to tell you how much she loved you and how sorry she is not to be able to take you to her kingdom. She cannot come. She really cannot. She told me just to take you in my arms and give you a kiss, a good kiss for her."

At these words the little one threw herself into my arms.

"Oh," she said, "kiss the pretty fairy for me and ask her if I can come again to see her dance."

There were tears in my eyes as I replied:

"Come as often as you like, my dear little girl. I hear the fairy whispering in my ear that she would like to dance for you all the time, all the time."[5]

Similar references to Fuller's sweet, magical incarnations crop up in almost every historical source on La Loïe, and many them, like Margaret Haile Harris's exhibition catalog, refer to her as a "magician of light."[6] Embedded in these various reports is a very interesting contradiction in terms. Fuller is at once portrayed as a "naturally" unpretentious woman offstage and as someone who can radically transform herself into a fairy or a flower onstage by means of the artifice of cloth and light. Ironically, although many cite Fuller's ability to transform herself by taking on a veil, few will acknowledge the possibility of Fuller's using her extensive theatrical capacities to take off that veil. It seems to me that there must have been something about her offstage persona that limited the public's ability to envision Fuller's performances in any other light.

Indeed, the obsessively repeated iterations of Fuller's dancing persona as "chaste," "correct," and "sans coquetterie érotique" belie a certain anxiety concerning other possibilities. Referring to her presence in the 1900 Paris Exposition, Garelick asserts that "Fuller was a veil dancer who never really *unveiled*." Here Garelick, like many cultural historians intrigued by Mallarmé's references to Fuller, generalizes Fuller's dancing as a series of increasingly sophisticated and technologized serpentine dances, conveniently airbrushing out Fuller's 1895 performances in which she did, in fact, unveil herself—as Salomé: "Fuller's performances provided a whitewashed, apparently de-eroticized version of some of the more lubricious veil dances being performed across the exhibition park at the Trocadéro."[7]

Interestingly, there is also very little material on her first performances of Salomé in Fuller's autobiography. In it her life narration moves very quickly from her early successes at the Folies Bergère to a recitation of all the famous people she has met. Much of this is organized as a series of vignettes about her encounters with artists, philosophers, kings, and queens, and seldom tells us much about her performing career. Even so, occasionally a certain story can be illuminating in surprising ways. For instance, in the middle of chapter 15, titled "Several Sovereigns," Fuller recounts an extraordinary incident. Under the subhead "Massaged by Royal Command," this anecdote describes Fuller's first encounter with the archduchesses of Austria. The recollection is worth quoting in full, for it reveals Fuller's awareness of and responses to a markedly voyeuristic gaze.

> I was once at the Swedish gymnasium at Carlsbad, where machines with electrical vibrations shock you from head to foot. I was just about to dress myself when one of the women of the place came to me, and said:
> "Won't you please return to the hall, and pretend to take the electric treatment again in order that the archduchesses, who are there with a whole crowd of court ladies, may see you?"
> I replied: "Tell the archduchesses that they can see me this evening at the theatre."
> The poor woman then declared to me that she had been forbidden to mention their Royal Highnesses, and that they had bidden her get me back into the hall on some pretext or other.
> She was so grieved at not having succeeded that I returned to the machines, and had my back massaged, in order that the noble company might look at me at their ease, as they would survey an interesting animal.
> They looked at me, all of them smiling, and while they viewed me I never turned my eyes away from them.
> The odd thing was that they did not know that I knew them. I was, therefore, as much amused by them, and without their perceiving it, as they were amused by me.[8]

Clearly Loïe Fuller did not mind being naked in front of a group of titled ladies. Splayed out in all her fleshy glory, she watches the duchesses watching her. In fact, she seems to derive a certain amount of satisfaction from the whole scenario. While I will try to refrain from projecting too much into the situation, I think that it is fair to say that, at the very least, this narrative demonstrates Fuller's acute awareness of her audience and her interest in not only positioning herself as the object of (in this case) the female gaze, but also intervening in that power dynamic by looking back. Compared to the super-sexualized girlie displays at the Folies Bergère, Fuller's dancing may have seemed relentlessly "chaste," as many reviewers have attested. But that posture of asexuality obviously wasn't the only one stoking the fires of her artistic imagination.

Before we turn to an analysis of Fuller's 1895 *Salomé*, I would like to introduce a theoretical discussion that provides a useful framework for thinking about these two apparent anomalies in Fuller's oeuvre. In the mid-1980s, as feminist theory was grappling with questions of theatricality and performance, Mary Russo wrote a short essay that was published in Teresa deLauretis's seminal collection *Feminist Studies/Critical Studies*, and from which I take the epigraph to this chapter. This piece remains, for me, one of the most savvy, succinct analyses of the liberatory possibilities of "making a spectacle" of oneself for women inclined toward theatrical gestures. Russo's essay begins with a proscription that resonates with many women who came of age in the twentieth century:

> There is a phrase that still resonates from childhood. Who says it? The mother's voice—not my own mother's perhaps, but the voice of an aunt, an older sister, or the mother of a friend. It is a harsh, matronizing phrase, and it is directed toward the behavior of other women:
>
> "She" [the other woman] is making a spectacle out of herself.
>
> Making a spectacle out of oneself seemed a specifically feminine danger. The danger was of an exposure. . . . For a woman, making a spectacle out of herself had more to do with a kind of inadvertency and loss of boundaries: the possessors of large, aging, and dimpled thighs displayed at the public beach, of overly rouged cheeks, of a voice shrill in laughter, or of a sliding bra strap—a loose, dingy bra strap especially—were at once caught out by fate and blameworthy. It was my impression that these women had done something wrong, had stepped, as it were, into the limelight out of turn—too young or too old, too early or too late—and yet anyone, any woman, could make a spectacle out of herself if she was not careful.[9]

Working through theories of the carnivalesque by way of the work of Mikhail Bakhtin, Russo delineates both the cultural stakes (what she describes as a double jeopardy) and the political possibilities of claiming the limelight: "The figure of the female transgressor as public spectacle is still powerfully resonant, and the possibilities of redeploying this representation as a demystifying or utopian model have not been exhausted."[10] The intersection of carnival theory with feminist theory produces a cultural analysis of the female body as a "grotesque" body. This body is open and permeable, the body of process and change (the "becoming" body), and inherently female, as opposed to the classical (male) body, which is contained, hard, and timeless—just like a smooth, white marble sculpture. Rather than trying to (hopelessly and often dangerously) pursue a "perfect" classical body, women, Russo suggests, might do well to explore a strategic deployment of this grotesque and excessive body as a sort of feminine masquerade. Playing with the symbolic and cultural representations of women while also attending to the experience of living in a woman's body might well produce some interesting and potentially subversive spectacles. Russo quotes Luce Irigaray's famous passage on mimesis:

> To play with mimesis is thus, for a woman, to try and recover the place of her exploitation by discourse, without allowing herself simply to be reduced to it. It means to resubmit herself—inasmuch as she is on the side of "perceptible," of "matter"—to "ideas," in particular to ideas about herself, that are elaborated in/by masculine logic, but so as to make "visible," by an effect of playful repetition, what was supposed to remain invisible: the

cover-up of a possible operation of the feminine in language. It also means to "unveil" the fact that, if women are such good mimics, it is because they are not simply reabsorbed into this function.[11]

What Russo is getting at here developed over the next decade into feminist discussions of gender as performative. Theorists such as deLauretis, Judith Butler, Iris Marion Young, and Elizabeth Grosz, as well as many other scholars from a variety of fields, began to articulate the ways in which gender and sexuality are implicated in and as embodied performance. To speak of gender or sexuality as performance is not to imply, however, that these experiences are merely theatrical tics—something that is as easy as putting on or taking off a hat or a scarf for effect. As anyone who has any experience in the performing arts—acting, dancing, playing music, singing—understands, all these disciplines require elaborate psychic and physical preparation. What this enactment paradigm does suggest, however, is the possibility of playing it other ways.

As I have discussed at some length in other chapters, Fuller's French reputation was very much cemented to a portrayal of Fuller as a frumpy American matron. At the cusp of the twentieth century, her particular mix of talents—the combination of typically masculine interest in electricity, lighting design, and scientific experimentation, and the typically feminized vocation of performing on public stages (especially as a dancer), seemed in some odd way to render her androgynous. It is almost as if these masculine and feminine aspects of her persona cancelled one another out to render her neuter—or lesbian. For underneath many of these discussions concerning her appearance runs an old-fashioned subterranean current of misogyny and homophobia that seems to assume the reason Fuller did not flaunt her stuff on the stage of the Folies Bergère is connected to her physique (because she did not have the girlie body that would presumably attract men), which, in turn, is connected to her preference for female intimacies. The logic here is twisted and reflects the critics' limited mindset more than the historical record.

These strangely myopic critics tend to pass over the photographic and published evidence of her early career to homogenize Fuller's appearance as plain (or, pointedly, "not beautiful") and her body as stocky (or downright "fat"). Actually, for her time, Fuller was considered cute and "fetching" in her twenties, pretty in her thirties, and still attractive and plump, perhaps, but certainly not obese, well into her forties. As I have just noted in the above episode "Massaged by Royal Command," and as we shall see in our discussions of Fuller's enactments of the Salome legend, being a lesbian does not necessitate a renunciation of a highly feminized, performative sexuality. *Au contraire*.

The Dance Research Collection at the New York Public Library for the Performing Arts houses a series of souvenir cards of Fuller's early theatrical career. I would like to compare two in particular. One is a well-known image of Fuller in a breeches role, such as the one she played in the 1886 New York performances of *Little Jack Sheppard* (see Figure 30). The other is a lesser-known photograph of

Figure 30. Loïe Fuller in a breeches role. Loïe Fuller Collection, Jerome Robbins Dance Division, The New York Public Library for the Performing Arts, Astor, Lenox and Tilden Foundations.

Fuller posing coyly behind a large open Japanese fan (see Figure 31). This soubrette shot shows a young Fuller bare-shouldered, wearing only a pearl choker and a jeweled headband. The assumption, of course, is that she is naked behind the fan, her smile serving as the invitation for the (presumably, but not always, male) viewer to investigate further. This image, which is basically a classic nineteenth-century pin-up postcard, contrasts nicely with the one of Fuller dressed as a boy. Here too, she smiles seductively, but in that knowing, slightly tongue-in-cheek manner that makes male drag so powerful.

The masquerade of the various well-known breeches roles in the second half of the nineteenth century created an interesting liminal place for the imaginative performer. True, these "tights" roles were often guises to flaunt and further sexualize the female performers by revealing her "handsome" thighs.[12] But they could also serve to extend the possibilities of roles for an actress. In this photo, Fuller is standing in a firm, wide stance, her weight leaning back into her right leg in a rather self-satisfied way. Who knows, maybe she had just read her reviews in the *New York Times* that complimented her on her believable acting: "Miss Loïe Fuller, as the

Figure 31. Loïe Fuller posing in front of a fan. Loïe Fuller Collection, Jerome Robbins Dance Division, The New York Public Library for the Performing Arts, Astor, Lenox and Tilden Foundations

hero of the piece, does this little bit very neatly, and indeed Miss Fuller's impersonation is very commendable throughout the play. She looks like a boy, as few women do in breeches, and she acts like one, which is still less frequently accomplished."[13]

One of the few pieces of Fuller scholarship to address La Loïe's ability to play convincingly across soubrette and breeches roles is a short paper given at the 1999 Society of Dance History Scholars annual conference and subsequently published in the proceedings. In it, the author, Tirza True Latimer, focuses on Fuller's dual masquerades as evidence of Fuller's lesbian identity.[14] The reductive reading of the equation of performance with life, in which critics interpret performances or texts as direct signs pointing to an author's "true" identity, is less interesting to me in this context. Instead, I would like to focus on the multiple refractions of images formed by the three-way mirror of Fuller's ironic participation in the traditional frames of theatrical representation. I draw attention to Fuller's masquerade as well as her Sapphic proclivities not in order to confirm her status as a lesbian (which was never really in question anyway), but rather to foreground her early theatrical experiences in "playing with mimesis." These, I believe, served as a theatrical foundation for her later attempts to perform across the hyper "feminine" positions of desire in Salome.

"Salomania touched virtually every aspect of popular and "high" culture, from

Symbolist verse to theatrical parodies, from night club reviews to department store fashions for women."[15] It is generally acknowledged that when in presenting her serpentine dance at the Folies Bergère in Paris, Loïe Fuller created a radical new approach to dancing entertainment. Of course, elaborate lighting effects had been staged before. And too, serpentine dancers had appeared in Paris even before Fuller's arrival. But, as I argued in my first two chapters, Fuller's use of torque and momentum, combined with her active engagement with the lighting, put her performances in a category all their own. When Fuller decided to interpret Salome, however, she was working with a cultural stereotype based loosely on a biblical narrative that had been inscribed and reinscribed (written, painted, enacted) repeatedly over the course of the latter half of the nineteenth century. As Elaine Showalter notes in the chapter titled "The Veiled Woman" in her book *Sexual Anarchy*:

> The most popular veiled woman of the fin de siècle is Salome, the dancing daughter of Herodias. In France, Salome became an obsessive icon of female sexuality for Flaubert, for the artist Gustave Moreau, who did over seventy drawings of her, and for the novelist Joris-Karl Huysmans, who wrote about Moreau's 1876 painting of Salome in *À Rebours* (Against Nature [1884]) as the "weird and superhuman" object of his hero's fantasies of feminine evil.[16]

If Moreau's paintings laid an iconographic foundation for future images of Salome, Oscar Wilde's infamous play, published in 1895 with illustrations by Aubrey Beardsley and staged in 1896, represents one of the most famous literary interpretations.

The "original" story of Salome dancing before Herod and his court appears in the New Testament, in Matt. 14. Presented as a retelling of a past event, the narrative gives only the barest details of the event. Indeed, two brief sentences capture the nexus of her role: "But with his birthday celebrations the daughter of Herodias danced before the guests, and Herod was so delighted that he took an oath to give her anything she cared to ask. Prompted by her mother, she said, 'Give me here on a dish the head of John the Baptist.'"[17] The specific details then about Salome's motive or even about her dancing display were left up to the fin-de-siècle artists and writers to supply. And supply them they did.

One of Gustave Moreau's Salome paintings, a watercolor entitled *The Apparition*, was the major sensation of the 1876 Paris Salon. In *À rebours*, Huysmans's protagonist contemplates Moreau's painting to the point of obsessive fixation. Huysman's description of the work is embellished by grotesque as well as erotic details: "She is almost naked; in the heat of the dance her veils have fallen away and her brocade robes slipped to the floor, so that now she is clad only in wrought metals and translucent gems. A gorgerin grips her waist like a corselet, and like an outsized clasp a wondrous jewel sparkles and flashes in the cleft between her breasts; lower down, a girdle encircles her hips, hiding the upper part of her thighs, against which dangles a gigantic pendant glistening with rubies and emeralds; finally, where the body shows bare between gorgerin and girdle, the belly bulges, dimpled by a navel which resembles a graven seal of onyx with its milky hues and its rosy finger-nail tints."[18] Here is a classic Salome scenario, one in which the dancing girl arouses the viewer's sexual desire, the potency of her sensuous display intensifying as she sheds one veil after another.

In contrast to this Salome figure as the object of another's desire, Wilde's Salome is caught up with her own desire for St. John the Baptist. In Wilde's text (from which the libretto of the Richard Strauss opera of the same name is derived), Salome proclaims her own desire: "I am amorous of thy body, Iokanaan!" Through her archaic-sounding language, Salome ritually evokes the beauties of Iokanaan's body ("Thy body is white, like the lilies of a field . . ."), only to desecrate it as her requests for contact are repudiated by Iokanaan's superior attitude: "Back, daughter of Sodom! Touch me not. Profane not the temple of the Lord God." Practically hysterical with her frustrated desires, the adolescent Salome dances for Herod in exchange for John the Baptist's head, severed from his sanctimonious denial, which she finally claims by kissing on the mouth. Ironically (and intentionally, of course), Salome's infamous "dance of the seven veils" is never described by Wilde. It is only indicated in the play text by a sparse stage direction: "Salome dances the dance of the seven veils."[19] In her book on Wilde, Katherine Worth suggests that Wilde may have been impressed by Fuller's "swirling greens and blues" when he envisioned Salome, whom he described as being costumed in "green, like a curious, poisonous lizard."[20]

Many fin-de-siècle artists interpreted the Salome legend, and I will not attempt to present an exhaustive survey of these representations. So, too, the work of Moreau and Wilde can be (and has been brilliantly) discussed in much greater depth than space permits me to do here. I point to these two examples mostly in order to introduce a continuum of the possibilities available to Loïe Fuller when she conceived of her own version. These precedents stretch from Salomé's dance as an evocation of someone else's desire to its being an expression of her own. These two poles represent either end of the psychic continuum of object and subject across which Fuller staged her own vision of sexuality and desire.

According to a *New York Times* article published in January 1896 to publicize Fuller's American tour, it was Armand Sylvestre, a writer and one of the main librettists at the Folies Bergère, who suggested the role of Salome for Fuller. The article quotes Fuller as saying, upon hearing this remark: "And why can't I be Salome, or whatever her name is, dancing before Herod?" The article continues in its dual description/promotion of the work.

> The outcome was the dignified and dramatic pantomime in which Miss Fuller is the main figure and which she has been presenting at the Palace Theatre, London, and the Comédie Parisienne to crowded houses. It consists of four tableaus, descriptive of the Biblical scene between Herod and John the Baptist. The first represents the prophet visiting Herod, commanding him to put away Herodias, his unlawful wife. Herod refuses at

first, but finally accedes partially, and is angry with Herodias. She studies how she may win him back, and decided [*sic*] that the best way will be to have her daughter Salome dance for him. This is done, and upon seeing the dance Herod accedes to the demands of Herodias. . . . The pantomime is concluded with Herod's dispatching a servant to behead John the Baptist, Salome entering to protest just after the command has been executed. ("Miss Fuller's New Dance," *New York Times*, January 24, 1896)

In preparing her first *Salomé*, Fuller collaborated with Georges Rochegrosse, a popular salon painter, who did the costumes and helped with the sets; Gabriel Pierné, who composed the musical score; and C. H. Meltzer on the libretto. In their book, Current and Current describe Fuller's version as depicting a Salome who is "quite spiritual and essentially chaste" and is a follower of John the Baptist.[21] She dances in order to save his life, rather than out of lust for him. For this lyrical pantomime, Fuller departed from her usual scenic sparseness to incorporate an elaborate palace, complete with a perspectival view of Jerusalem on a backdrop. The visual iconography lent an air of Orientalist decadence reminiscent of Moreau or Flaubert. Nonetheless, one of the key dramatic effects was still the spectacular lighting, particularly Fuller's use of underlighting: "In the floor of the stage are cut six holes, arranged like a triangle. In these openings, which are nearly a yard square, are inserted squares of heavy plate glass upon which Miss Fuller dances. It is impossible to describe the effect which is produced as she circles from one stream of light to another, and her whole performance is said to be a marvel of beauty and grace" (*New York Times*, January 24, 1896).

Promoted as the show that would reveal to the world just how great an expressive artist Fuller was, *Salomé* received warm previews. (One wonders if visions of becoming like Sarah Bernhardt, whom Fuller greatly admired and who was, at one point, scheduled to play Wilde's Salome, danced in her head.) Indeed, the *New York Times* quoted at length a feature praising the show in the London *Figaro* on March 17, 1895, two weeks after *Salomé* opened at the Comédie Parisienne:

As I saw her on the stage of this little theatre—just sufficiently lighted to see the expression of her face—Pierné at the piano, Armand Silvestre and Pierre Berton following the working of the drama in her wonderful dance—it seemed scarcely believable that this small figure, in her ordinary dark walking dress, without the aide of lights or stage accessories, with no word spoken, could move us to the extent she did. Her dance to the sun, her religious dance, her dance of desperation, were all remarkable expressions of the mind, and had such an effect upon us that when she fell at the sight of John the Baptist's head, we all rushed towards her and kissed her. . . . The question now is: What will the public think of it? And will the colored lights mar, or will they enhance, the artistic effect? Of course it cannot be expected that Loïe Fuller will dance every night as she danced at that rehearsal. It is with her more a matter of inspiration than step but there are many points in favor of her repeating the greater part in much the same manner. ("Strange Effects of Expatriation," *New York Times*, March 17, 1895)

Apparently, however, the night that Jean Lorrain went to the Comédie Parisienne Fuller's performance was less inspired. Nevertheless, the savageness with which he skewered Fuller suggests that much of the problem had to do with Lorrain's own expectations about what Fuller should be doing onstage. In the March 9 entry of his journal, published in *Poussières de Paris*, Lorrain begins his review with the effusive, descriptive language reminiscent of his earlier evocations of La Loïe: "Mystery! The colors and nuances of light illuminate and dim in turn, developing into spirals and then suddenly billowing like wings, opening and closing, and then in the middle of this flood of motion and fabric emerges the figure of a woman, her shoulders and arms deliciously pale, appearing all of a sudden between the enormous petals of a giant violet, or the wings of an incredible butterfly."[22] But soon Fuller emerged from the mist of her mysterious effect to take on a more dramatic role in this pantomime: "And it was a disappointment." Disillusioned by Fuller's refusal to remain shrouded by the lighting, Lorrain succumbs to his own frustrations: "One perceives too late that the unhappy acrobat is neither mime nor dancer; heavy, ungraceful, sweating and with make-up running at the end of ten minutes of little exercises, she maneuvers her veils and her mass of materials like a laundress misusing her paddle."[23]

Unfortunately, there is little else in the review that actually describes the show. Who else was onstage? What color were the lights? How did the drama unfold? One gets the impression that Lorrain simply stopped watching the show, fixating on his patronizing conviction that Fuller could only appropriately do one thing— sequester herself behind her voluminous silks and mysterious lighting effects. Lorrain concludes his review with a final diatribe: "Luminous without grace, with the gestures of an English boxer and the physique of Mr. Oscar Wilde, this is a Salomé for Yankee drunkards."[24]

For Current and Current, Lorrain's outburst was "understandable": "Short and fat as she was, Loïe hardly had the figure for Salomé, who traditionally was pictured as statuesque. And Loïe could be seen all too well in the Comédie Parisienne, an intimate theater with a small stage, where she was close to her audience in a way that she had never been at the Folies Bergère. . . . Hence she lost that aura of unreality, ineffability, and mystery that had made her seem a creature of poetic charm."[25] One sees too much—too much body, too much flesh, too much expression, too much woman. No longer hidden by the whirling silk of her earlier costumes, Fuller is criticized for her excess, for exceeding the limits of appropriate display, indeed, for making a "spectacle of herself."

Giovanni Lista, in his massive tome on Fuller, also sees this first *Salomé* as a personal and professional failure for Fuller. Combining his critical evaluation of

One of the critics who found Fuller's *Salomé* particularly successful was Roger Marx, an art critic who also worked for the French government, first as Secrétaire des Beaux-Arts and then as Inspector des Musées de Province. In 1889 he organized much of the Paris Exposition, and for the 1900 exposition he was the curator in charge of selecting paintings. His review of *Salomé* appeared in the April 1, 1895, issue of *La revue dramatique*. The text was then reprinted in a collection of his writings published in a limited-edition art book dedicated to Loïe Fuller, with gypsograph prints by Pierre Roche. Marx begins his review by invoking the Salomes of Flaubert, Moreau, and Huysmans. Although many of the characters, such as Herod, Herodias, and John the Baptist are similarly portrayed in Fuller's production, Fuller's interpretation of Salome is different, Marx informs his readers, "because a miracle of faith replaced the legendary Salome, drunk with blood and voluptuousness, with a mystical Salome—one that is *almost chaste*; it is for John the Baptist that she dances" (emphasis added). Marx applauds Fuller's dramatic gestures and her ability to play across a whole host of emotions: "On her face, passes in turn joy, pity, anger, fear, anguish, each emotion played out with a compelling energy."[29]

Marx next turns his considerable descriptive powers to the final scene, Salome's dance for Herod. Her tells us that Fuller is dressed in a sheer orange silk, with a veil of the same material concealing her face and her chest. She plays with her veil, making figures with the light silk, alternately revealing and concealing her face depending on her position on the illuminated glass squares. One moment she slips away, at which point Marx describes her as being "framed in this fine tissue like an idol." The next moment, she reappears in a black lamé dress and plays the *séductrice* (Marx's word), stirring up Herod's passion: "With a devilish coquetry, she waves her scintillating scarves, which reflect the terrifying flare of the underworld."[30]

This is the moment that sponsored Marx's qualifier of Fuller's Salome as "almost" chaste. In fact, she performs this classic seduction dance not just once, but twice. For when she finds out that John the Baptist has been condemned to death, she repeats the dance—with a difference. Her movements are no longer fluid and graceful, but "jerky and menacing" (*saccadée, menacants*). Bit by bit, her energy fades, and she ends the dance with a poignant, final appeal, "weakened by her agony."

By turns sexy and scary, menacing and pleading, Fuller enacts the gambit of classic feminine gestures. Yet I would argue that she foregrounds the performativity of this masquerade as well—not as parody or drag, but rather by making clear to her audience that she is taking on a dramatic role. Fuller's obvious use of underlighting, her willingness to suspend the narrative denouement in favor of dancing spectacle, and her strategic use of repetition all suggest to me that Fuller was intentionally making visible the triangular relationship of character to body. That is to say, she was making visible her movements between being La Loïe (as in her entrance, the only scene Jean Lorrain liked), quoting classic portrayals of Salome as a femme fatale (did someone say black lamé?) as well as purposefully reinterpreting that role as Loïe Fuller.

Figure 34. "Hail Salomé." Watercolor illustration by Lloyd Warren; part of a collection of twenty-three watercolors by students at the École des Beaux-Arts presented to Loïe Fuller to commemorate her 550th performance in Paris on March 24, 1895. Jerome Robbins Dance Division, The New York Public Library for the Performing Arts, Astor, Lenox and Tilden Foundations

Fuller's multidimensional perspectives on Salome are interestingly reflected in a series of images painted for her by students of the École des Beaux-Arts. To celebrate both her 550th performance in Paris and the free performance she gave for them, these art students threw her a major fete, pulling her carriage through the streets and presenting her with a hand-bound silk folder with commemorative watercolors of Fulleresque images inside. These often exquisite images are housed in the New York Public Library for the Performing Arts; significantly, three of the images are of Fuller as Salome.

One of the most interesting of these paintings is by a certain Lloyd Warren, who signs himself as an ardent admirer. It is entitled "HAIL! SALOMÉ" and depicts a strong, confident, half-naked woman holding a severed head (see Figure 34). We can still see the traces of her most recent movement in the swirl of fabric and jewels spiraling around her waist. Her body is strong and beautiful, and there is an expressive aliveness in this picture that commands attention. This Salome is facing her audience straight on, insisting that we recognize her power and sexual agency. Now, whether this particular rendition was a direct representation of Fuller's show or not is debatable, because apparently Fuller fainted at the sight of John the Baptist's head. Nonetheless, I think the image captures a certain spirit of Fuller's work; at the very least, it portrays a sexy woman with big thighs, suggesting that not

Figure 35. "Loïe Fuller." Watercolor illustration by C. I. Bert; part of a collection of twenty-three watercolors by students at the École des Beaux-Arts presented to Loïe Fuller to commemorate her 550th performance in Paris on March 24, 1895. Jerome Robbins Dance Division, The New York Public Library for the Performing Arts, Astor, Lenox and Tilden Foundations

everyone who saw Fuller up close thought of her in Lorrain's terms as a "laundress." The other two images of Salome reproduce the Byzantine quality of the scenic elements. One portrays Fuller as a young princess, echoing Victorian renderings of Sappho as both Greek and Eastern (see Figure 35). The other is a ludic elaboration of the L in Loïe's name as an Orientalist fantasy in an illuminated manuscript (see Figure 36).

This last image reflects not only the wake of fin-de-siècle Salomania, but also the ripple effects of its popular relative, the *danse du ventre*. For, along with the ethnographic exhibits in the colonial sections of the Expositions Universelles, came the increasingly theatricalized displays of female flesh loosely labeled belly dancing. In an insightful essay, Zeynap Celik and Leila Kinney document how belly dancing moved from its appearance in the fairs' "authentic" Muslim villages through being a staple of theatrical events in those exhibitions to becoming the latest novelty act on the stages of famous Parisian nightclubs:

> For example, while the Islamic quarters in the 1867 exposition were presented with minimal human animation of their architecture, in 1878, theaters were introduced; thereafter, they became indispensable to every Muslim display. In these theaters, music accompanied tableaux vivants from local daily life, in which weddings or shopping at a bazaar, for exampled, were enacted. In spite of the variety of activities presented, belly dancers formed the core attraction from the beginning, to judge by the coverage they received in official and unofficial accounts of the exhibits and their increasingly elaborate choreography in successive fairs. In 1889 the number of spectators who came to watch the Egyptian belly dancers averaged two thousand per day.[31]

What intrigues me about Celik's and Kinney's postcolonial analysis is the theoretical connection they pursue between the Orientalist framing of belly dancing and the overall mechanism of display already embedded in fin-de-siècle popular entertainment in general. The reasons that belly dancing flourished in Paris, they argue, is because it "depended for effect upon a deliberate redundancy of representation." That is to say, in this particular confluence of art and life, the dancers became at once symbols of the "authenticity" of Western Orientalist portrayals of an artistic and literary nature, and yet were, in turn, inflected by them: "If anything, they heightened the 'reality effect' of a body of Orientalist imagery already legitimized by travelogues and paintings."[32]

Enter La Belle Fatma, a certain Rachel Ben-Eny, an Algerian Jew who came to Paris from Tunisia with her father, a musician in that colony's 1878 folkloric exhibition in the French capital. Dancing as a child in the invented "native" display, she grew up on the streets of Paris (where her family had immigrated) and soon became a star attraction, appearing in the 1889 Paris Exhibition in both the Grand Théâtre and in the Rue du Caire.[33] By the time Fuller was engaged at the Folies Bergère in the early 1890s, La Belle Fatma was a regular feature at the nightclub, appearing in the ersatz lobby garden. A Folies Bergère program from December 1892 featuring "La Loïe Fuller" lists "La Belle Fatma" in the entr'acte as "visible au jardin sans supplement" (complimentary entertainment in the garden) between the shows.

Another interesting, albeit inverted, example of the nineteenth-century funhouse of Orientalist reflection and their mediated refractions is that of La Goulue, a famous celebrity

Figure 36. "Hommage du l'atelier Bonnat." Watercolor illustration by Jacquot Defrance; part of a collection of twenty-three watercolors by students at the École des Beaux-Arts presented to Loïe Fuller to commemorate her 550th performance in Paris on March 24, 1895. Jerome Robbins Dance Division, The New York Public Library for the Performing Arts, Astor, Lenox and Tilden Foundations

dancer whose name and image (thanks to Toulouse-Lautrec) was synonymous with such famous belle epoque institutions as the Moulin Rouge. In 1895, several months after Fuller's *Salomé* closed, La Goulue opened her own booth at the Foire du Trône in Paris. Situated between the theater district and the other popular fair attractions (including animals, games, food, and magic-lantern travelogues featuring the Middle East), La Goulue's booth featured two large panels painted by Toulouse-Lautrec. Now housed in the Musée d'Orsay, these panels originally banked either side of the entranceway to her show. On the left side is a typical rendering of La Goulue.[34] She is dancing a *chahut* (can-can) with her partner, Valentin. On the right side is another portrait of La Goulue performing entitled "La danse mauresque ou 'Les almées.'" Here, La Goulue is dressed in a pseudo–Middle Eastern garb, with a black male drummer (complete with turban) and a Middle Eastern–looking woman dressed as a belly dancer playing the tambourine. Despite the Islamic patina to the setting, La Goulue is doing her usual kick-step, can-can routine, and the audience is the typical Montmartre crowd.

This startling confluence of can-can and belly dancing is, of course, precisely

Figure 37. Loïe Fuller posing as Salome. Jerome Robbins Dance Division, The New York Public Library for the Performing Arts, Astor, Lenox and Tilden Foundations

the point about ethnography and exhibitionism that Celik and Kinney are making. In this example of a staged "density of cultural interchange," what matters is less the cultural differences between East and West (although they are very real, of course) than the ways in which women entertainers (that is, their female bodies) repeatedly become the site of the intersection of colony and commodity. Caught up in this landscape of voyeurism, these women enter a phantasmagoria of stereotype and display: "La Belle Fatma [and] La Goulue temporarily vacate one form of identity only to be caught failing to achieve another."[35]

This last line seems to sum up the conflicted position Fuller found herself in when she took on the role of Salome in 1895. Fuller was attempting to reshape her identity as an abstract dancer into one of an equally gifted expressive mime, but her audience wanted to see her do that for which she was famous. This is the dilemma of many performing artists. Although Salome was a new role for Fuller, Fuller-as-Salome also had to contend with the plethora of Orientalist visions of dancing women being staged throughout Paris at the time. That she made irreverent reference to these various copies of copies is made clear in another publicity postcard from 1895 (see Figure 37). Here, Fuller is looking as Middle Eastern as we will ever see her. She is dressed in a series of gauzy fabrics draped and tied around her hips and shoulders and is positioned in a classic girlie or serpentine pose, with her feet in profile and her upper body turned to face the viewer. Her hair is covered by a cloth, and she is holding a piece of material across her face, leaving only her famous sparkling blue eyes to tell the viewer that she is laughing heartily at her own masquerade.[36]

Given the complicated geology of Fuller's first *Salomé*—the many cultural layers of innovation, interpretation, reinvention, and reception that have built up, like sediment, over the years—it is difficult not to read Georges de Feure's poster advertising the 1895 production of *Salomé* as a parable for the "double jeopardy" that Russo points to in her essay "Female Grotesques" (see Figure 38). Trying to place her signature on a cultural icon with as much baggage as Salome, Fuller finds herself pointing forward but looking back. The swirl of her fabrics and the active lettering on the poster all conjure a certain turbulence, an uneasy disjunction that points to the gap between performance and representation across which Fuller plays with mimesis.

In November 1907, Loïe Fuller produced her second pantomimed version of *Salomé*. Entitled *La tragédie de Salomé*, it was staged at the newly renovated Théâtre des Arts. Although the technical preparations took much longer than anticipated, the show ran for only a short while. The libretto was by Robert d'Humière and, like the more traditional fin-de-siècle interpretations of Salome, portrayed this legendary woman as seductive and powerful. The music, by the Alsatian composer Florent Schmitt, prefigured the raw turbulence of *Le sacre du printemps* (1913) by Stravinsky, who was a friend of Schmitt's and to whom Schmitt's score is dedicated. As in Fuller's earlier version of Salome, the overall narrative trajectory of the play was segmented into seven distinct tableaux, each of whose raison d'être was less the dramatic action of the play and more the opportunity to stage fantastic, expressive dances.

The cover of the November 9 program is a weird but not atypical blend of Greek and Eastern motifs (see Figure 39). There is a decorative series of ancient Greek–looking women bacchants drawn over Doric columns, framing another series of studio head shots of Fuller costumed in various Egyptian-looking wigs. The seven scenes of the pantomime are detailed in the program notes. John the Baptist sets the play in motion when he enters Hérode's palace and delivers a diatribe condemning Hérode's and Hérodiade's marriage and the icons, luxury, and "scent" (!) of the harem. As Hérode consults with John the Baptist, Hérodiade schemes. The second tableau is based on "La danse des perles," a duet between Salomé and her mother: yards of pearls are wrapped and draped around Salomé, signifying the luxurious and erotic chains of Hérode's palace. In the third tableau, Salomé performs "La danse du paon" before Hérode and Hérodiade in an extravagant peacock costume.

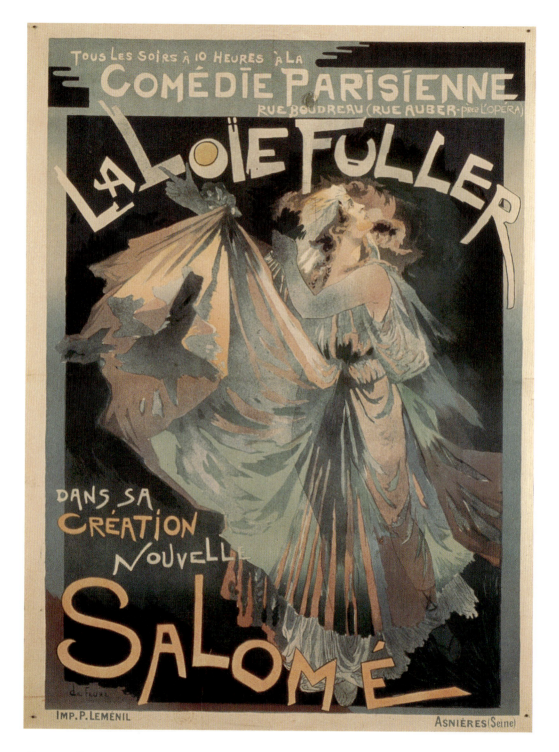

Figure 38. "La Loïe Fuller dans sa création nouvelle Salomé." Poster for Comédie Parisienne by Georges de Feure, 1895. Musée de la Publicité, Paris

Figure 39. Program cover for La tragédie de Salomé, *Théâtre des Arts. Jerome Robbins Dance Division, The New York Public Library for the Performing Arts, Astor, Lenox and Tilden Foundations*

In the climactic moment of the dance, Fuller turns to reveal an iridescent tail of large feathers that she can open into a fan. This outfit was made with 4,500 peacock feathers, a detail available in the press releases, along with other equally impressive statistics such as her use of 650 lamps and 15 projectors to create 10,240 watts of candlepower.[37]

The next four tableaux are much less frivolous. Indeed, they become increasingly ominous and violent. In the fourth tableau, Salomé takes on two serpents that are threatening Hérode and Hérodiade, executing "La danse des serpents" in a manner described as "moitié lutte, moitié incantation" (half fight, half incantation). This ritualized battle ends in a frenzied tarantella. The fifth tableau contains the "Dance of steel." In this section, the music is described as a "fantasmagorie démoniaque," and when Salomé reappears, it is in a blinding and metallic light. The next, climactic scene is punctuated by "La danse d'argent." Salomé, dressed in an elaborate sequined robe of silver and gold, performs a "lascivious" dance for Hérode, who grabs her veils, stripping her naked. John the Baptist quickly covers her up, an insubordination that will cost him his head. Suddenly, blood appears to flow over the stage as Salomé reappears for a final, "La danse de la peur" (The Dance of Fear). In the midst of a furious storm, the head of John the Baptist appears in the sky, driving a tormented Salomé into a "délire infernal."

This final effect, easy enough to achieve with magic-lantern projections, must have referenced, for an early-twentieth-century audience, Gustave Moreau's famous painting *L'apparition* (1876). In this painting, which was all the rage at the Paris Salon that year, a practically nude Salome points an accusing finger at the head of John the Baptist. Although his eyes are fierce and the bloody entrails flowing from his neck are viscerally frightening, Salome doesn't flinch or cower. In fact, the energy running from her chest through her left arm and out her finger is like an electrical charge, and it almost seems as if it is that energy that holds the head captive, rather than vice versa. I evoke this double reading of Moreau's painting in order to foreground the power of Fuller's performance in this final section. Although the dance was called "The Dance of Fear," in this climactic moment Fuller revealed the strength of her mature dramatic persona, interpreting Salome with an impressive dynamism that bordered at times on violent: "And then we have the *Dance of Fear*, in which she reveals her tragic power, transmitting to her audience actual shudders of terror. All this is breathtaking, strangely captivating, and astonishingly new for those, like us, who have followed the joyous and knowing transformations of this genial creature of light."[38]

Considered by some to be "the triumph of her long career,"[39] Fuller's 1907 *Salomé* was seen by both the journal *Fémina* and the newspaper *Le temps* as a feminist statement. In his article for *Le temps* (November 5, 1907), Jules Clarétie wrote: "The other evening, I had, as it were, a vision of a theatre of the future, something of the nature of feministic theatre." An acquaintance of Fuller's, Clarétie had been invited to witness a dress rehearsal of the performance, and it was Fuller's ability to shape at once the production from the outside, as a director and lighting designer, as well as from the inside, as a dramatic character, that sponsored his reflections:

> Women are more and more taking men's places. They are steadily supplanting the so-called stronger sex. The court-house swarms with women lawyers. The literature of imagination and observation will soon belong to women of letters. In spite of man's declaration that there shall be no woman doctor for him the female physician continues to pass her examinations and brilliantly. Just watch and you will see women growing in influence and power; and if, as in Gladstone's phrase, the nineteenth century was the working-man's century, the twentieth will be the women's century.[40]

The marked contrast between Jean Lorrain's remarks about Fuller's 1895 *Salomé* and those of Jules Clarétie describing her 1907 production are striking. It would be easy, of course, to dismiss my rhetorical balancing act as a futile attempt to compare apples and oranges. For one thing, the shows, produced twelve years apart, were completely different. Schmitt's composition for the 1907 production was infinitely more successful than Pierné's music in 1895. Then, too, Fuller took more time to prepare this later show, leaving very little, including her own dramatic gestures, to chance. Whereas those who saw her rehearse in 1895 commented on the improvisational nature of her pantomime, Clarétie described the attention to detail in rehearsals for the 1907 production:

> Then I had the immense pleasure of seeing this Salome in everyday clothes dance her steps without the illusion created by theatrical costume, with a simple strip of stuff, sometimes red and sometimes green, for the purpose of studying the reflections on the moving folds under the electric light. It was Salome dancing, but a Salome in a short skirt, a Salome with a jacket over her shoulders, a Salome in a tailor-made dress, whose hands—mobile, expressive, tender or threatening hands, white hands, hands like the tips of bird's wings—emerged from the clothes, imparted to them all the poetry of the dance, of the seductive dance or the dance of fright, the infernal dance or the dance of delight. The gleam from the foot lights reflected itself on the dancer's glasses and blazed there like a flame, like fugitive flashes, and nothing could be at once more fantastic and more charming than these twists of the body, these caressing motions, these hands, again, these dream hands waving there before Herod, superb in his theatrical mantle, and observing the sight of the dance idealized in the everyday costume.[41]

In addition to all these differences of style and preparation, I would also argue that although the narrative of the 1895 version tried to re-envision a decadent femme fatale, one who is a "chaste" and spiritual figure, it was, ironically, the 1907 return to the stereotype—the seductive and powerful Salomé of Moreau—that was proclaimed "feministic theatre." I find this irony to be both historically and theoretically intriguing. It is particularly extraordinary in light of the fact that the visual traces—the head shots of Fuller in costume—can only be described as patently ridiculous. Crowned in a series of bad wigs, with heavy mascara and pouty lipstick, Fuller looks all the world like a cheap drag queen.

Yet it is precisely the memories of a performance of a drag queen as a legendary female character that provoke me to reconsider these images as traces of embodiment. Ethyl Eichelberger (1945–1990) performed her version of *Clytemnestra* at P.S. 122, a downtown New York City performance venue, in the late 1980s. Put together on a shoestring budget, with some of the intentionally worst costuming ever seen (layers of cheap acrylic curtains from Goodwill together with fake boobs made from stuffed nylon stockings strung across Eichelberger's tall, bony frame), this was ancient Greek (melo)drama splayed out in all its twentieth-century vaudevillian glory. Nonetheless, the power of Eichelberger's dramatic pathos resounded, even in the midst of a campy, S & M–inflected pastiche of late-1980s performance art. A tour de force of solo acting, it was like seeing Aristotle duke it out with Andy Warhol. The show was a thrilling experience for those of us in the audience, at times comic and at times intensely moving. I remember vividly recognizing, in the midst of all the flowing gauze and exaggerated gestures, how Eichelberger used characterization (the stereotype) to more fully realize her "self." In that theatrical space that extends from acting to being and back again lies a transformative power that explains, I believe, an important difference between Fuller's first and second enactments of Salome. Like Eichelberger almost a century later, Fuller played her 1907 Salome with a vengeance, in the process stirring up all kinds of viewing pleasures.

In an essay, Emily Apter recuperates the stereotype from its negative associations with hackneyed convention, reminding her readers that the term derives from the process of printing, "referring to the metal plate made from a mold of composed type." Keeping in touch with the materiality of this notion of "imprinting," Apter proposes a different kind of interpretation, one in which the performance of stereotype—the *act* of imprinting—allows for a critical subjectivity. Referring to Thais, a fourth-century Egyptian courtesan brought back to life by the novelist Anatole France in 1890, Apter writes: "Clothed in heavy gems, and presented to the viewer as an image graven in stone, she embodies the stereotype made pure performative: at once fetishized and mobilized in conceptual and visual space."[42]

This pull between being stuck and being mobile, between being called something and naming oneself, between subject and object, that Apter points to is a place of creative tension in much fin-de-siècle performance. It is connected to Russo's notion of redeploying mimesis in order to make a spectacle (of oneself). For Russo, this repetition with a difference (making visible what is meant to be left invisible) is a golden feminist opportunity. For Apter, it suggests both a feminist and a queer strategy: "Acting and outing, as ontological strategies, commonly rely on essentialist typologies of enacted being that are thrown into definitional crisis by the wild mimeticism of affect." Apter is interested in the ways in which fin-de-siècle enactments of Orientalist stereotypes, onstage as well as in private salons and backyards, opened up a continuum of performativity that allowed women to fashion a Sapphic identity:

> Orientalism, as a nexus of extravagant psychic investments and layered semblance of the type, evolved into feminist and lesbian camp for a number of other more obvious reasons. Not only were women empowered or accorded sexual license through association with the dominatrix characterologies attached to exemplary princesses, queens, seductresses, or women leaders of the East, but, more interestingly, their agency was enhanced by "being" these avatars both on stage and off. Ida Rubenstein, Sarah Bernhardt, Mata Hari, Collette, Lucie Delarue Mardrus, Renée Vivien and others expanded the performative parameters of the historic stereotype by moving their larger-than-life thespian personas into the choreography of erotic everyday life.[43]

Known publicly as a lesbian (although she didn't use that terminology), Loïe Fuller never "performed" her Orientalist diva acts offstage. In this sense, she fits uneasily into the trendy Sapphic circle of Natalie Barney and her friends, who form the nexus of Apter's examples. Although it seems to me unlikely that Fuller's desire to perform Salome (twice) was connected to a desire to "out" her sexuality, it was certainly an opportunity for her to perform a powerfully sexual character. For despite Lista's prediction that Fuller would never reveal herself again, she did, putting on her femininity with a vengeance, even taking off, for a moment, her veils. Indeed, Fuller's 1907 performances of Salome gave her a stereotype into which she seemed able to pour both her body and soul.

During the run of this production, Fuller gave an interview to Camille Mauclair in which she spoke of the connections between what she called the mystery of light and the mystery of the human condition. Her language throughout the article is intensely metaphysical as she distinguishes between work that merely imitates nature (as, she adds, her early incarnations of her serpentine dances did) and art that engages with what she calls the "superior poetry of the real." Mauclair asks Fuller whether light plays a role within her artistic cosmology. Fuller replies:

> Yes. If I use light, it is not just for the pleasure of making a fairyland. Yes, it is pretty to see, but, for me, light has a much deeper meaning. Light: it is the deployment of the soul around a human being, it is a language just as music is a language. There are living lights and dead lights. My art derives from a sense of joy, and here I mean that it has the capacity to instant oblivion, soaring it into another world. Colors in painting are opaque and link it, sometimes to the point of absurdity, to the representation of real objects. But I use live colors, colored scents aroused by a ray of light, and, then, why shouldn't I render into the visible realm that which we dream of?[44]

Although it is hard to parse such romantic notions of light as sublime with the kitschiness of her costumes, I am going to climb out on that proverbial scholarly limb to propose that Fuller's use of lighting at once reinforces and subverts the "wild mimeticism of affect" that Apter identified in fin-de-siècle performance. That is to say, Fuller's lighting—such as the extravagant harsh metallic slices and her refined use of underlighting to create the lavish effect described as blood flooding the stage like a river—served both to materialize the dramatic expressivity of the pantomime and to arrest the spectator's attention with its breathtaking immediacy. I believe that it is this use of light to create moments of visual suspension, rather than the Orientalist signifiers, that best represents Fuller's lesbian double vision.

> There, coming toward me from the other end of a marvelous golden fairy-like room, was what appeared to be a spirit of light gliding along as if swept by the wind with the ends of its flowing garments, transparent in the sun that fell upon her as she approached. Her hair was fair and glistened as if it were of polished gold; her eyes were blue, blue as the sky. She was slight and swayed like a reed in the breeze, her head was set high and thrown well back. All was white, gold, and blue around her. A smile such as I had never, never seen illuminated her countenance and permeated the atmosphere with joy and happiness.[45]

In this passage Fuller recalls the first time she met Marie Alexandra Victoria, then princess of Romania and a granddaughter of Queen Victoria on one side and Alexander III of Russia on the other. It would be easy to read this prose as a classic example of what Terry Castle famously referred to as the "ghosting" effect of the lesbian character in literature. In *The Apparitional Lesbian* (1993) Castle documents the ghostly figures, those pale, wraithlike women who, like their counterparts in nineteenth-century romantic ballets the sylphs, evaporate (or die) right at the moment of physical contact. In spite of the recurrent examples of "denial and disembodiment" that she analyzes, however, Castle's aim is to conjure her "spectral lesbian subject" back into fleshy existence: "For even at her most ethereal and dissembling, . . . she cannot help but also signal—as if by secret benediction—that fall into flesh which is to come."[46] And, indeed, as we read a few lines later in Fuller's evocation of Marie's first appearance, the angel materializes: "She had taken me in her arms and kissed me on either cheek." Thus began a passionate and intimate relationship that was to last for the rest of Fuller's life.

I have been thinking about this vision of Marie amidst a halo of light for several years now. When I first read the passage, I found its fantastic, quasi-spiritual, quasi-erotic overtones puzzling. Now, I believe that it holds the key to understanding Fuller's personal cosmology, in which light and love are mutually evocative. Although Fuller is often cited as one on a long list of turn-of-the-century lesbian public figures, she does not fit into the seductive stereotype of the trendy Sapphic personality cruising the literary salons in Paris at the beginning of a new century. Never self-identified as a lesbian, the traces of her erotic connection to women are always (dis)placed into another "light"—one that alternately reveals and conceals. Yet her pleasure in these connections (including her lifelong partnership with Gab

Bloch) is never in question. Trying to craft the appropriate language with which to talk about Fuller, I am drawn to Castle's last sentence in her chapter on Janet Flanner, the author who, under the pseudonym Genet, wrote a series of "letters from Paris" published regularly in the *New Yorker* from 1925 to 1975: "If, in her magical letters from Paris, Janet Flanner never revealed her sexuality in so many words, what she did share with her readers—her ineradicable, coruscating delight in the world—was in its own way a perfect coming out."[47] Similarly, what Fuller shared with her audiences in her 1907 performances of Salomé was a passionate vision of an (older) woman enthusiastically acting out—making a spectacle of herself—by performing dances of lust and loss in the middle of a (spot)light of her own invention. These acts of passion served to disrupt Fuller's "chaste" image, showing the world that she could, indeed, play her femininity with a vengeance.

CHAPTER 5

Staging the Self

Expressive Bodies and Autobiographical Acts

In January 1907, while Loïe Fuller's *La tragédie de Salomé* was still in its formative stage, Sidonie-Gabrielle Colette donned a transparent veil and a sexy Middle Eastern–looking outfit (complete with breastplates and snake bracelets) to make a serious spectacle of herself by kissing—long and passionately, we are told—another woman. The venue was the infamous Moulin Rouge in Paris. The occasion was the premiere of "Rêve d'Egypte," an Orientalist variation of the Pygmalion theme in which an archaeologist unwraps an ancient mummy to discover a beautiful woman, whom he kisses to bring back to life.

The short pantomime was written by Madame la Marquise de Mornay, otherwise known as Missy, Colette's lover for most of her brief, but, I will argue, seminal career on the music-hall stage. Missy, whose name was spelled backward as "Yssim" on the publicity posters, also played the role of the archaeologist. The packed house included Missy's ex-husband, the Marquis de Belboeuf, as well as Colette's husband, Henri Gauthier-Villars (known professionally as Willy), from whom she was separated but not officially divorced. Having been revived by the kiss, Colette's character proceeded to dance an Orientalist divertissement while the audience practically rioted, booing and throwing whatever was available at the stage. The police censored the show, and although the play's title was changed to "Songe d'Orient" and Colette's mime instructor, Georges Wague, replaced Missy onstage, the show closed two days later. Nonetheless, Colette's fledgling music-hall career was launched by this succès de scandale.

Referred to as the "Scandal of the Moulin Rouge," this legendary incident is usually interpreted as either a supremely public liberatory gesture, Colette's final throwing off of the patriarchal yoke with which Willy kept her creativity subdued, or, conversely, as a rather rash moment within her transitional passage (through lesbianism and across the music-hall stage) that carried her from neophyte scribe to mature writer. Toni Bentley views Colette's audacious performance as a defiant act of self-realization, what she describes as "her transforming device, in searching out her own true identity as a woman." In her book *Sisters of Salome*, Bentley reads early-twentieth-century

Figure 40. Colette as a faun. Bibliothèque nationale de France, Paris

enactments of Salome by Maud Allen, Mata Hari, and Ida Rubenstein, in addition to Colette's performance, in the light of her own autobiographical impulses. Throughout her introduction, she collapses all the historical, cultural, and even personal differences between these women by claiming a universal "Salome effect," which Bentley identifies with a primal, quintessentially female desire to unveil publicly. Indeed, the genesis for her book seems to come from an epiphany during her own first experience of stripping: "Along with my clothes I shed past lives—my European upper-middle-class upbringing, my classical ballerina tutu, my marital allegiance, my good little girl status, the only one I'd ever known. I gained the freedom to be whoever I might have the courage and imagination to be."[1]

Here Bentley indulges in what I consider to be a naive and highly romanticized notion of the liberatory effects of performing (naked) onstage. Whether we dub this as the Salome effect or the Isadora effect, it is a concept embedded in many histories written about the (r)evolution of modern dance. These chart the journey of the "new" woman from Victorian corset to Grecian tunic. Although they may outline briefly a cultural backdrop of dress reform and other early feminist movements and a burgeoning interest in physical culture (à la Delsarte), of utopian idealism and social marginality, these narrations of the development of modern dance usually focus on the life stories and revolutionary gestures of a few exceptional women.

In some ways, this chapter takes up a similar project. I too will describe the lives and achievements of four exceptional women who all performed in Paris at the beginning of the twentieth century: Colette, Isadora Duncan, Eva Palmer, and Loïe Fuller. I too will cite their autobiographies and outline highlights of their theatrical careers. Nevertheless, my project differs from these others in significant ways. I am less interested in finding the "truth" of these women's lives, or even in identifying the liberatory images of "woman" that their performances may have evoked, than in understanding the role that physical experiences of subjectivity played in creating their theatrical and literary legacies. That is to say, I am more interested in their embodied practice than in the mythic images surrounding their lives, even as I recognize the interconnectedness of both.

Although they all lived emancipated lives in Paris at the beginning of the twentieth century, and although they even sometimes shared a stage (or lawn, to be more precise) and a passion for art as an ethical, life-affirming force, these women developed radically different approaches to the stage. Before she became a journalist and full-time writer, Colette worked on the stages of music halls for seven years, traveling all over France with a small pantomime company. Loïe Fuller, who was at the height of her career as the century turned, began to choreograph for her own group of dancers, as well as serving as an impresario for two Japanese theater companies and (very briefly) for Isadora Duncan, among others. Expounding a rhetoric of dance as Art, Duncan, in turn, shunned the music-hall stage and danced exclusively in the concert halls, opera houses, and salons of upper-class European society, launching a career of mythic proportions. Eva Palmer, who once shared a couple of afternoon performances with Colette at Natalie Barney's and who would later marry the brother of the wife of Raymond Duncan (Isadora's brother), recast an early infatuation with Sappho and Hellenism into an ambitious project to revive ancient Greek drama, producing at Delphi two of the biggest theatrical festivals in modern Greece.

There are, of course, overlapping spheres of influence between these women. Some of these have been routinely charted: Fuller and Duncan's brief and mutually unsatisfactory professional relationship, or Colette and Eva Palmer's joint appearances at Nathalie Barney's home. Others, which, to my knowledge, have never been explored, include Colette's invocation of Fuller's dancing and her short portrait of Duncan in *Paysages et portraits*. In this chapter, I hope to map out the unique performance trajectories of these four women as well as their commonalities. For, despite their quite different aesthetics—the disparate looks of their work—these women are connected by two crucial elements: they all experienced their physical bodies as agents of self-expression in performance, and they were all driven to record their ideas in autobiographical writings that doubled as aesthetic and social manifestos.

As genres of representation, performance and autobiography both foreground the problematic relationship of body to signature—of gender to power. Of course, at the beginning of the twentieth century, performing and writing were highly gendered occupations. With few exceptions, women performed onstage, and men wrote about them. This historical fact was reinforced by a cultural alignment of bodily display as feminized (whether the performer was a man or a woman), and the writer's signature as masculine (the pen as the phallus). In the nineteenth-century bourgeois culture that still reigned in Parisian society at the beginning of the twentieth century, these activities were imbued with class values as well. As we have seen in our discussion of Fuller's oeuvre, and as we shall see in reviewing Colette's music-hall days and the reception of Eva Palmer's and Isadora Duncan's work, claims of "aesthetic," "intelligent," and "chaste" dancing and appeals to the idealism of ancient Greek culture constitute various strategies to subvert these overdetermined social discourses. As Julie Ann Townsend asserts in her discussion of the improvisational aesthetics of Colette and Loïe Fuller: "As the dancer takes up the word, she problematizes her status as work of art and artist in one. Through a combination of performance, autobiography, and publicity, women artists reconceptualized the figure of the dancer while rewriting the aesthetics of femininity and women's sexuality."[2] Refusing to be passive instruments of another's vision, these women took responsibility for shaping both the larger theatrical frame and the expressive nuances of their (self-)representations.

When she took to the stage in her thirties after an early apprenticeship as a ghostwriter for her husband, Colette describes the public's view of her as a "woman of letters who has turned out badly." "They also say of me that I'm 'on the stage,' but they never call me an actress. Why? The nuance is subtle, but there is certainly a polite refusal, on the part both of the public and my friends themselves, to accord me any standing in this career which I have nevertheless adopted."[3] In her biography of Colette, Judith Thurman describes Colette's professional debut in 1906 as a "radical coming-out," unwittingly echoing Emily Apter's discussions of acting as outing (this double entendre would be doubly reinscribed, of course, in Colette's 1907 appearances with Missy at the Moulin Rouge): "In 1906, acting professionally was virtually synonymous with prostitution—a transgression of another magnitude, and for a middle-class woman, . . . the class treason was almost worse than the imputed moral turpitude" (see Figure 40).[4]

At the turn of a century that had consolidated (at least in Europe and North America) the separation of private and public realms, to put one's body on display as a spectacle and still claim subjectivity onstage was a difficult and complex balancing act for a female performer. So was claiming the authority of the signature for a woman writer, particularly if the writer had been known as a performer.[5] Resisting the societal strictures of "appropriate" behavior for women, Colette, Loïe Fuller, Isadora Duncan, and Eva Palmer found unique ways to negotiate their specific social and economic circumstances not only to consciously stage their bodies, but also to produce a written discourse that articulated the artistic vision that inspired their work. Whether they began in dance, pantomime, or theater, these women all started with a corporeal practice, producing a physical language that focused on breath rhythms, the dynamic use of the torso, and the articulation of gestures that galvanized space in new and important ways. Then they articulated the cultural potency of that physical work in manifestos that described the meanings of their life missions. Their writings give us their ideas. The photographic images help us to infer their movement vocabulary and the stylistic aspects of the staging of their work. But these visual and written traces are necessarily fragmentary, and rarely do they directly address the implications of this physical engagement with the world—what we might call their corpo-realities. In this chapter, I propose to read through the historical evidence with an attention to the physical practices that created a somatic foundation for these women's courageous and ambitious interventions in the performance culture of their time.

Working in between the stage and the text, my interpretive methodology aligns itself obliquely with one that the feminist literary scholar Nancy Miller proposes in her essay "Writing Fictions: Women's Autobiography in France." In the midst of a discussion that seeks to intervene in glib readings of women's fiction as always already autobiographical, Miller calls for a "double reading," which she describes as "an intratextual practice of interpretation which . . . would privilege neither the autobiography nor the fiction, but take the two writings together in their status as text." This strategy allows Miller to combine the pleasures of French literary theory with the critical attention to historical and material conditions that galvanized North American feminism in the 1980s, giving her access to both (as she terms it) "tropes and sensible shoes." She concludes her essay with her usual panache by adding: "The historical truth of a woman writer's life lies in the reader's grasp of her intratext: the body of her writing and not the writing of her body."[6] Mirroring Miller's strategy of a double reading, I take as my intratext both the body of these women's writings and the writing (that is, the representations) of their bodies.

By the end of her collection of essays aptly entitled *Subject to Change*, Miller comes up against this writing of the body when she discusses *The Vagabond*, an autobiographical novel by Colette that documents, in scrupulous detail, the physical experience of performing in French music halls and society salons in the early twentieth century. Although Miller wants to resist an essentialized discourse that suggest women can *only* write from their bodies, she realizes, in the midst of this fictionalized account of the bodily experience of a touring life, that she must find a way to grapple with the ways these corpo-realities structure an identity of their own making. For *The Vagabond* is a story not only of "a woman of letters who has turned out badly" finding her own way back to writing, but of a woman confronting the double moment of performing in front of an audience—that shifting between objectivity and subjectivity. In language that captures the physical urgency of this double bind, Colette's protagonist, Renée Néré, describes moving between seeing and being seen, experiencing and being experienced, touching and being touched. Recounted in the first person, this short novel is the story of the physical and psychic negotiation between the lived body and its cultural frames. Indeed, it is precisely through its complex interweaving of identity, experience, and representation that *The Vagabond* illuminates how histories of the body can lead to new, resistant enactments of the self.

One of the most famous scenes in *The Vagabond* occurs early on in the novel, when Renée joins her mime partner, Brague, in providing some entertainment for a private reception. They are currently between jobs, and the pay is too good to refuse. Thus Renée is forced to return to the society salons where she once entered on the arm of her husband (now her ex-husband). She is resistant to face again what she describes as "witnesses or accomplices of my past unhappiness," that is, "the women who betrayed me with my husband, and the men who knew I was betrayed."[7] Physically, she is paralyzed; emotionally, she is undone. Standing half naked in the anteroom, she describes her cold hands and the way her Salome wig makes her head ache. Then it is time for her to go on.

With a hand trembling with stage-fright, I wrap round myself the veil which constitutes almost my whole costume, a circular veil of blue and violet measuring fifteen yards round. . . .

The bluish chrysalis which I represent awakens at the sound of a short prelude, and begins to writhe as my limbs slowly loosen. Little by little, the veil unwinds, fills, billows out and falls, revealing me to the eyes of the beholders, who have stopped their frantic chatter to gaze at me.

I see them. In spite of myself I see them. As I dance and crawl and turn, I see them, and I recognize them!

In the first row is a woman, still young, who was for quite a long time the mistress of my ex-husband. She was not expecting to see me this evening, and I was not thinking of her. Her sorrowful blue eyes, her one beauty, express as much fear as amazement. It is not me she fears;

but my sudden presence has confronted her, brutally, with her own memories. . . .

Round the sides and at the back there is a dark row of men, standing.
Packed closely together they crane forward with that curiosity, that cyni-
cal courtesy which men of the world display towards a woman who is considered "déclassée," the woman whose finger-tips one used to kiss in her
drawing-room and who now dances, half-naked, on a platform.[8]

Having detailed over the course of several pages the general attitude of her audience, Renée shifts focus, knowing that the only way to claim her own subjectivity
in this situation is to dance well. She returns to her body to assert her self.

Come now, this won't do. I'm too clear-sighted this evening, and if I don't
pull myself together my dancing will suffer for it. I dance and dance. A
beautiful serpent coils itself along the Persian carpet, an Egyptian amphora
tilts forward, pouring forth a cascade of perfumed hair, a blue and story
cloud rises and floats away, a feline beast springs forward, then recoils, a
sphinx, the colour of pale sand, reclines at full length, propped on its elbows with hollowed back and straining breasts. I have recovered myself
and forget nothing. Do these people really exist, I ask myself? No, they
don't. The only things are dancing, light, freedom, and music. Nothing is
real except making rhythm of one's thought and translating it into beautiful
gestures.[9]

What Colette is describing in this passage is a phenomenological account of how
to replace the anxieties of the stage with a focus on the sensate experience of
performing.

The Vagabond, published in 1910, was written in the midst of an active career
that included such rigors as performing in thirty-two French cities in thirty-two
days.[10] Although her official debut was at the Théâtre des Mathurins on February 6,
1906, where she took the part of a faun in a short pantomime by Francis de Croisset
and Jean Noguès entitled "Le désir, l'amour, et la chimère," Colette had been performing for several years in amateur theatricals held in private salons and gardens
around Paris. For instance, in June 1905, Colette was cast as a shepherd who falls
in love with a nymph played by Eva Palmer, a young American woman testing
the theatrical waters in Europe. The afternoon's entertainment, at Natalie Barney's
house, also included Mata Hari's entrance, naked and riding a white horse, for her
performance of a Salome dance.[11] A year later, Colette again performed with Eva
Palmer, this time in a verse play by Pierre Louys, "Dialogue au soleil couchant." By
the time she mounted the stage at the Moulin Rouge, Colette was a full-fledged professional actress. Her most successful vehicle was the pantomime "La chair," which
she toured from 1907 to 1911, giving over two hundred performances throughout
France.[12]

As Nancy Miller cautions us, it would be a mistake to read *The Vagabond* as transparently autobiographical. Nonetheless, its varied accounts of the physical exhaustion of touring, the endless hours of technical rehearsals, the waiting to go onstage all suggest a real material awareness of the phenomenology of performing. Behind the "barrier of light" that separates the performers from the audience, Colette's Renée Néré revels in the satisfaction of her own competence:

> As soon as the first bars of our overture strike up, I feel soothed and ready for anything, grown all of a sudden gay and irresponsible. . . . From that moment I no longer belong to myself, and all is well. I know that I shall not fall when I dance, that my heel will not catch in the hem of my skirt, and that when Brague handles me roughly I shall collapse without grazing my elbows or flattening my nose. . . . The harsh light sustains me, the music governs my gestures, a mysterious discipline controls and protects me . . . all is well.[13]

These words intersect with the extraordinary range of Colette's theatrical guises to give us a sense of her multifaceted career. The astounding variety of historical images—studio shots, performance photographs, publicity posters, and sketched images—demonstrates Colette's ability to play across the spectrum of popular icons. Some show Colette costumed as an animal, a faun stretched out on all fours, or a cat, crouched low to the ground. In others, she plays the Egyptian femme fatale, either confronting the viewer's gaze directly or seductively playing à la Salome with her transparent veils. Some images are patently ridiculous, such as the one of Colette being carried on the shoulders of a squadron of half-naked male bodybuilders. There is also an intriguing series of shots from the Reutlinger studio of Colette in pseudo-Grecian garb (what is called in the caption a *costume antique*), looking very "aesthetic." There are many photographs of a tired and made-up Colette in her dressing room, of Colette miming onstage in "La chair," especially of the final climactic scene where her onstage lover famously rips her dress to bare her left breast. Then too, there are shots of Colette *en travestie*, dressed either as a gentleman (with cigarette in hand) or as a sailor boy, as well as Colette in a bodysuit or naked, posing like a young girl in a Maxfield Parrish picture. Finally, there is the image of Colette on the cover of *La culture physique*. In this November 15, 1911, issue of the bimonthly journal, which calls itself the "organe de l'Énergie française" (invoking a provocative slippage between body and industry), Colette is profiled as a fervent advocate of physical culture (see Figure 41). Ironically, although Colette exercised in a sleeveless knit bodysuit on assorted gymnastic equipment, the cover shot has her posing like a Grecian statue, standing in profile with one arm stretched up holding the white cloth, which is artistically draped around her torso. This French voguing of Hellenism vacillates between an image of middle-class aesthetic postures à la Delsarte and more lowbrow titillation in the fact that underneath the graceful folds of the fabric, she is naked.

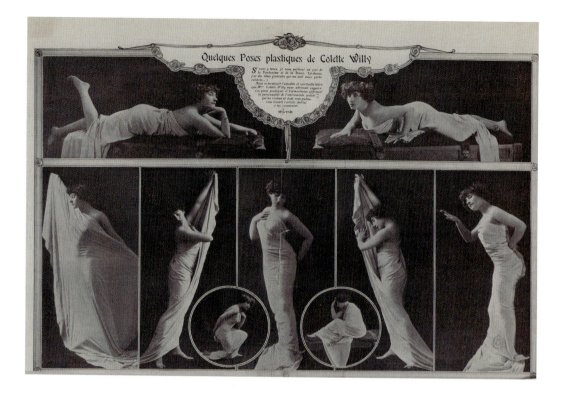

Quelques Poses plastiques de Colette Willy

Figure 41. Colette in La culture physique. *Bibliothèque nationale de France, Paris*

By the time she posed as a cover girl for *La culture physique*, Colette had been seriously working out for about nine years, and her letters to her friends reveal how proud she was of her hard-earned muscles.[14] As a young girl, Colette was outdoorsy and a tomboy. Indeed, until arthritis crippled her in her old age, Colette prided herself on being robust and physically active. When she moved to Paris as a young wife in 1893, however, it took her a while to retrieve her physical self. In 1902 Willy and Colette moved to larger (and lighter) quarters on the rue de Courcelles, and Colette claimed the artist's studio on the top floor, which she outfitted with gymnastic equipment and in which she entertained her friends and distracted herself from her faltering marriage. In *My Apprenticeships*, Colette describes this austere, but inspiring, space of her own:

> Mine had no ornaments beyond the fittings of a gymnasium, the horizontal bar, trapeze, rings, and knotted rope. I used to swing and turn over the bar, suppling my muscles half secretly, without any particular zeal or brilliance. Yet when I reflected on it later, it seemed to me that I was exercising my body in much the same way that prisoners, although they have no clear idea of flight, nevertheless tear up their sheets and plait the strands together, sew gold coins into their coat-linings, hide chocolate under the mattress.[15]

Whether she was conscious of it at the time, Colette was crafting a "modern" woman's body, exploring through her exercise routine the psychosomatic experience of muscular stability and strength. Colette had begun to emerge from the bourgeois cocoon of domesticity, and the photographs of her exercising in her gym reveal a self-possession that contrasts markedly with earlier images. Natalie Barney describes the change in Colette at this time:

> At the beginning of the century, when I saw Colette for the first time, she was no longer the thin, long-braided adolescent cradled in a hammock which a photograph shows us. She was a young woman firmly fixed on solid legs, with the small of her back arching down to a full behind; with manners as frank as her speech, but with cat-like silence in her enigmatic, triangular face; and in her beautiful blue-green eyes a look which did not have to appear seductive in order to seduce.[16]

Thurman affirms Barney's portrayal of Colette at this time, connecting the literal to the metaphoric as she emphasizes the sociological implications of Colette's actions: "In the process of becoming fit, she discovered that exercise strengthens one's morale. . . . She was also, consciously or not, training herself for the profession she would take up when her marriage ended. Colette had understood, precociously, that the true beauty of a woman's muscles is identical with their purpose, and that's self-support."[17] First came the focus on fitness, then the flight. By the time Colette was ready to leave the domestic hearth that had charred her provincial innocence, she had trained with the well-known mime Georges Wague. Eventually, she would join him and his partner on the professional stage. In *The Vagabond*, she describes the satisfactions of this new career: "Solitude, freedom, my pleasant and painful work as mime and dancer, tired and happy muscles, and, by way of a change from all that, the new anxiety about earning my meals, my clothes, and my rent—such, all of a sudden, was my lot."[18]

At the end of April 1907, just months after her debacle at the Moulin Rouge, Colette penned her response to the resultant hullabaloo for *La vie parisienne*. Entitled "Toby-chien parle," this ironic dialogue between her dog and cat contains the defiant language of a manifesto: "I want to do what I want. I want to play pantomime and also comedy. I want to dance nude if the leotard constrains me and humiliates my figure. I want to cherish who loves me and give him whatever is mine in the world: my body resists sharing my gentle heart and my independence!" In the midst of this fierce declamation, Colette describes in the future tense the kind of dancing that she envisions for herself: "I will dance nude or dressed for the sole pleasure of dancing, to time my movements to the rhythm of music. . . . I will dance, I will invent slow beautiful dances where at times the veil will cover me, at times will surround me like a spiral of smoke, at times will stretch behind me like the sail of a boat."[19]

Colette's language here, her "invented" dance with fabric that surrounds her like a spiral of smoke or billows behind her like a sail, so closely resembles published descriptions of Loïe Fuller that it prompts the question of influence. Did Colette ever see Fuller perform? I have not found any mention of Fuller in the abundant scholarship on Colette's life and writings. Yet Colette must have been aware of Fuller's artistic legacy as well as her reputation as an independent and enterprising woman, if only through her husband's circle of friends, for it included some of the most influential fin-de-siècle music and theater critics. We know, for instance, that Colette and Willy frequented the 1900 Paris Exposition Universelle, which opened several months after the publication of *Claudine at School*.[20] It is likely that during this time Colette passed by (if she didn't attend) Fuller's theater on the Rue de Paris. Although I am not really concerned with proving that Fuller had a direct influence on Colette, I find most intriguing a short review by Louis Delluc published in *Comœdia illustré* in January 1913 in which he describes Colette in a series of "poses plastiques": "She plays with a great white veil, in which she surrounds, drapes, and sculpts herself."[21]

Playing with her veil/sail, Colette seems to incorporate Fuller's hieroglyphs-in-motion. In her description of her dancing, Colette abandons the classic narrative and static gestures of pantomime for the improvisational challenge of moving with a large piece of fabric. Reading Delluc, I can imagine Colette tracing Fuller's figures. Yet the reflexive tone of the French verb *se sculpter* shifts the emphasis from the object (what she sculpts) back to the subject (who is doing the sculpting). Thus, using this "great white sail," Colette sculpts herself. In *My Apprenticeships*, Colette recalls her growing awareness at this time of the interconnected poetics of gesture, rhythm, and language: "The melodic and the written phrase both spring from the same elusive and immortal pair—sound and rhythm."[22] As the rhythm becomes the word, my image of Colette doing Fuller dissolves, and I imagine, in turn, the white sail morphing into a blank page, the possibilities of which Colette has learned to explore through reclaiming her body. Moving from the stage back to the page (she would give up performing regularly with the birth of her daughter in 1913), Colette renders, as Nancy Miller notes, "the rhythms of performance *in writing*."[23]

Although Colette gave up performing in music halls, she continued to write plays and, on occasion, act in them. For a theatricalization of *The Vagabond* in 1926 (when she was fifty-three), Colette took on the role of Renée Néré. Certainly, her brief career hustling as an actress gave her a solid foundation in managing her own financial affairs, and she was as proud of this accomplishment as she was of her "lovely muscles." As Renée declares in the beginning of the story: "The music-hall where I became mime, dancer, and even on occasion, actress, turned me also, despite my astonishment at finding myself reckoning, haggling, and bargaining, into a tough but honest little business woman."[24] In this sense, Colette shares with Loïe Fuller a scrappy, practical, get-the-job-done disposition, even though Colette is often cast as typically French (actually Parisian), and Fuller is seen as quintessentially American.

In fact, these two women are remarkably alike in many ways. Neither of them was snobbish about the places where they earned their livings, a trait that clearly separates them from Isadora Duncan and Eva Palmer. Both Fuller and Colette attempted, without much success, to franchise their names at different times in their careers. (Colette started a chain of beauty salons, and Fuller signed contracts at one point for "Les Parfums Loïe Fuller.")[25] Both women also wrote poignantly about backstage life, and they shared the gesture of dedicating moving tributes to the women lovers who sustained them emotionally. Colette wrote about Missy in "Nuit blanche" (published in her 1908 collection *Les vrilles de la vigne*), and Fuller devoted a chapter of her 1913 *Fifteen Years of a Dancer's Life* to Gab. Then too, both these women loved animals, and both were witty, ironic observers of their fellow creatures. The following vignette from Fuller's memoirs could easily have been a part of Colette's writing in *Music-Hall Sidelights* as well:

> In these circumstances Mr. Martin Stein secured for me a dozen performances in one of the beer gardens at Alton, the well-known pleasure resort near Hamburg. I earned there several hundred marks, which allowed us to go to Cologne, where I had to dance in a circus between an educated donkey and an elephant that played the organ. My humiliation was complete. Since then, however, occasions have not been lacking when I have realized that the proximity of trained horses and music-mad elephants is less humiliating than intercourse with some human beings.[26]

Paradoxically, there are aspects of Colette's extensive and varied oeuvre that also parallel Isadora Duncan's writing in *My Life*, even though their personalities were very different. The similarities include documenting the struggles of a woman artist to define herself at the beginning of a new century; particularly a woman artist in love and torn between the security of domesticity and the emotional and financial risks of artistic endeavor. *The Vagabond* is a story of a woman in love who consciously chooses her gritty independence over a bourgeois lifestyle. *My Life* is the story of that same cyclical struggle between love and art, elation and desperation. Like Colette, Duncan claimed the impossibility of writing the "whole truth of her life":

> As I advance in these memoirs, I realize more and more the impossibility of writing one's life—or rather, the lives of all the different people I have been. Incidents which seem to last a lifetime have taken only a few pages: intervals that seemed thousands of years of suffering and pain and through which, in sheer self-defense, in order to go on living, I emerged an entirely different person, do not appear at all long here. I often ask myself desperately, What reader is going to be able to clothe with flesh the skeleton that I have presented? I am trying to write down the truth, but the truth runs away and hides from me. How find the truth? If I were a writer, and had written of my life [in] twenty novels or so, it would be nearer the truth.[27]

Unlike Colette, who did, in fact, write her life through her novels (which is not the same as saying they are *only* autobiographical), Duncan ends the story of her life by questioning the very premise of her attempts to tell its "truth." Yet in the beginning of her autobiography, she seems fully committed to her quest: "My Art is just an effort to express the truth of my Being in gesture and movement."[28] Although she allows for increasing ambivalence about the woman she was, Duncan rarely expresses any doubts about her artist self in the book. Recitations of small, everyday details about voyages, performances, and the constant search for lodgings (travel and home constitute another thematic struggle in *My Life*) are interrupted by visionary declarations, including her most famous pronouncement:

> I spent long days and nights in the studio seeking that dance which might be the divine expression of the human spirit through the medium of the body's movement. For hours I would stand quite still, my two hands folded between my breasts, covering the solar plexus. . . . I was seeking and finally discovered the central spring of all movement, the crater of motor power, the unity from which all diversities of movements are born, the mirror of vision for the creation of the dance.[29]

This mythopoetic tone recurs throughout *My Life*, and its combination of ego and idealism has turned off many a reader.[30] Nonetheless, I want to return to Nancy Miller's concept of intratextual analysis in order to read Duncan's autobiography with what we know of her dancing. My project here is not an attempt to (re)construct a seamless historical account of her work, but rather to juxtapose the written and visual evidence in an effort to capture something of Duncan's physical experience, the texture of her corpo-reality. I place such over-the-top heroic language as "I was possessed by the dream of Promethean creation that, at my call, might spring from the Earth, descend from the Heavens, such dancing figures as the world had never seen" next to the well-known photographs by Edward Steichen of Duncan standing in the Parthenon, or by Arnold Genthe of Duncan dancing the "Marseillaise."[31] Reading these verbal and pictorial texts together allows me to attend to the physical implications of Duncan's written invocations. Reaching up with her arms, face lifted, Duncan calls to the heavens, drawing down from the sky a dynamic tension that cycles through her torso and legs, grounding her energy firmly into the earth.

At the beginning of her book on Duncan's American presence, *Done into Dance*, Ann Daly describes Duncan's amazing ability to make visible what she calls a "narrative of force":

> The general components of force are also those of Duncan's dancing: interaction, motion, directionality, and intensity. Duncan's solos—a single body struggling against, shrinking from, floating on, and thrusting into space— were enactments of agency, the self in the process of engagement with the external world, whether that meant love or fate, oppression or death.[32]

Whether it is the sweet and simple wavelike stepping forward and back of her early dancing, or the more dramatic, weighted, and defiant gestures of her mature work, this interplay of forces moves from the body out into the space around it and then cycles back to affect the body anew. For Duncan, its source is the solar plexus, that "central spring of movement."

What she is talking about, of course, is the breath. Duncan was famous for using her breath to initiate movements, both her dynamic attack and her lyrical suspension. The cyclical nature of the breath, like the waves that Duncan finds so inspiring ("My first idea of movement, of the dance, certainly came from the rhythm of the waves"), regenerates itself, ensuring a continuity of movement that Duncan can then shape dynamically and dramatically. She believed that once started, "each movement retains the strength to engender another."[33] In her essay "The Dancer and Nature," Duncan expounds on what the dancer can learn from the action, suspension, and resolution of the waves. She then extrapolates from these examples to produce a universal law: "All energy expresses itself through this wave movement. For does not sound travel in waves, and light also?"[34] Playing in between these visible and invisible waves, Duncan allowed her breath rhythm to ride over the metrical regularity of musical phrases. This approach to musicality produced a sense that Duncan was creating her own approach by crafting a conscious dialogue between the two forms. Gordon Craig described the first time he saw Duncan dancing:

> Quite still. . . . Then one step back and sideways, and the music began again as she went moving on before or after it. Only just moving—not pirouetting or doing any of those things which we expect to see, and which a Taglioni or a Fanny Elssler would have certainly done. She was speaking in her own language—do you understand? her own language: have you got it?—not echoing any ballet master, and so she came to move as no one had ever seen anyone move before.[35]

Although she speaks of dancing in *My Life*, Duncan rarely calls herself a choreographer. Most of her descriptions, in fact, talk of "finding" movements, almost as if she were simply channeling the motion of the universe through her body. Her inspiration is often metaphysical, found in philosophy, various ideas of "Nature," art, or romanticized visions of the purity of ancient Greek culture so prevalent in her time. Yet it is also physical—for inspiration literally means to breathe in. Mark Franko traces how Duncan negotiates this back and forth between presence and absence in his discussion of the concept of expression in early modern dance: "Duncan's personal poetic statements weave between these two poles. In her writing, she becomes personally identified with a carnal source of inspiration, yet that present source retains its miraculous, elusive, evanescent connections to an elsewhere."[36] When she reaches up toward the heavens, with her feet firmly weighted into the ground, Duncan literally embodies this tension between establishing her material body and evoking the metaphoric world around her.

Popular sentiment, along with many mid-twentieth-century dance histories, has long regarded Isadora Duncan as the "mother" of modern dance, placing her at the top of a lineage of expressive movements that can be traced through multiple generations. Even contemporary modern dance pedagogy, although it doesn't look like Duncan dancing and doesn't talk about "soul" anymore, can trace its sources to a Duncanesque belief in "authentic" movement that comes from somewhere inside the dancer's body. Both Franko and Daly try to unpack these taken-for-granted facets of Duncan's legacy, Daly by analyzing the cultural discourses implied by her use of such contested terms as "woman" and "nature," not to mention "American," and Franko by exploring the political ramifications of Duncan's bodily practice. Although their critical agendas differ, both Daly and Franko attend to how the dialogue between physical sensation and kinetic impulse in her dancing produced an extraordinary performing presence. Franko describes this potent state as "pre-expressive" or as "power in reserve."[37] Daly also tries to capture this ineffable quality:

> Presence—the magnetic sense of fullness that certain dancers possess— it is as difficult to define as it is to overlook. It is something that cannot be taught per se; it is not contingent on technique, but it is tied up with some discernible physical/mental skills. It has to do with focus, with concentration, with one's saturated attention to everything surrounding and everything within. It has to do with a quality of bodily listening as well as bodily singing. It has to do with skin as well as muscle. It has to do with filling every moment as if it were eternity.[38]

This performative presence—what Daly perceptively describes as the attention to "skin as well as muscle"—is not a miracle of spirit (despite Duncan's claims to the contrary), but rather the result of a practiced attention to both the internal sensation of a movement and its outside form. Duncan shifts the priority from executing a static, picture-perfect arabesque to translating for the audience her experience of engaging, suspending, and retreating from a pose that doesn't stop but that extends the line of the body from the hand through the opposite leg. At one point in *My Life*, Duncan describes the difference between the "mechanical movement" of an "articulated puppet" taught by the ballet schools and her own dancing.

> I on the contrary sought the source of the spiritual expression to flow into the channels of the body filling it with vibrating light—the centrifugal force reflecting the spirit's vision. After many months, when I had learned to concentrate all my force to this one Centre I found that thereafter when I listened to music the rays and vibrations of the music streamed to this one fount of light within me—there they reflected themselves in Spiritual Vision not the brain's mirror, but the soul's, and from this vision I could express them in Dance.[39]

If we read past Duncan's exaggerated mythopoetic tone, we find that these "vibrations" of music and light—what Duncan also calls waves—quite closely echo the language that Loïe Fuller uses to describe her own translations of energy into motion. Separated from her spiritual "Vision," Duncan's "centrifugal force" and its "vibrating light" that fills her body are remarkably similar to the visual dynamism of fabric and light which characterized Fuller's serpentine dance. In chapter 2, "Becoming Light," I explored how Fuller's work intersected with contemporary discourses on light, physics, and electricity. I also referenced Deborah Jowitt's discussion of Duncan as a "dynamo," a "charged and vibrant" body. Although they channeled the scientific and aesthetic discoveries of their time in very different directions, Fuller and Duncan shared the radical ability to mobilize the space around them, reflecting the possibility of a dialogue between their movement innovations which has been overlooked by much of modern dance history.

As we have seen, Fuller used the torque in her body to launch her silks into the air. Once they were aloft, she was able to ride that cycle of momentum, shaping the fabric's descent through the undercurve such that it regenerated its own flight. This riding of the wave, so to speak, is exactly how Duncan conceived of her own motion. Both Fuller and Duncan used this cycle of suspension and release to motivate their movement phrasing. In Duncan's dancing, this most often took the form of simple, mostly symmetrical undercurves and overcurves, whereas Fuller's work elaborated this pattern into increasingly complex figure eights. These dancers shared a core physical experience: the exchange between expansion and contraction and the resultant opening up or condensing of the space around them. Of course, how they shaped the experience dramatically and how they placed themselves within their respective theatrical and historical frames were, needless to say, very different.

In their books on Fuller, both Lista and the Currents quote Louis Vauxcelles's famous quip: "Isadora sculpts, Loïe paints. Useless to compare them."[40] Indeed, it seems to have been pretty much the accepted wisdom—both then and now—that Loïe Fuller and Isadora Duncan were polar opposites. If Fuller is aligned with theatrical artifice and modern technology, Duncan is seen as the embodiment of nature and the ancient Greeks. If Fuller is categorized as a modernist, Duncan is seen as a romantic. While one was perceived as androgynous or masculine, the other was seen as highly feminine. Although they both gained a lot of weight as they aged, one was most often portrayed as dumpy and frank, the other as beautiful and coy. One was openly (yet privately) homosexual; the other publicly (and performatively) heterosexual. Fuller's body (mostly) disappeared under a mass of silk, while Duncan's was shockingly revealed by her light tunics. These kinds of distinctions have become so ingrained over time that it seems positively heretical to begin to break them down. And yet, in Paris at the beginning of the twentieth century, both dancers were seen as enterprising, independent, and eminently American women. If we shift the dynamic of their comparison from an either/or to a continuum, we can begin to discuss their differences and similarities without setting up a hierarchy of influence. For, as we know, Duncan and Fuller did share a mutual admiration for one another's work.

Fuller's memoirs, *Fifteen Years of a Dancer's Life*, were written at the height of Duncan's fame, just at a time when Fuller was beginning to work more as a choreographer and director for her own group of young dancers and less as a performing artist herself. Perhaps this is why she doesn't mention Isadora Duncan by name in a chapter describing their first meeting and brief interaction. Or perhaps it was because she was still offended by a report she heard suggesting that Duncan, when asked by a reporter if she had worked with Fuller, not only refused to acknowledge Fuller's early mentorship of her career, but even claimed that she didn't know her at all. In any case, the first paragraphs of Fuller's chapter "An Experience" clearly identify Duncan, if not by name, certainly by reputation:

> She danced with remarkable grace, her body barely covered by the flimsiest of Greek costumes, and she bade fair to become somebody. Since then she has arrived. In her I saw the ancient tragic dances revived. . . . I told the dancer to what height I believed that she could attain, with study and persistent work.[41]

In this last sentence lay the beginnings of Duncan's and Fuller's miscommunications, the result of their different working styles. Fuller saw the possibility of launching Duncan, just as she had successfully launched Sada Yacco, whom Duncan had seen at the 1900 Exposition Universelle and very much admired. But this chapter documents the resulting tension between Fuller's energetic managerial style and Duncan's intense privacy about her creative preparations. Thus, while Fuller was bustling about making all the necessary arrangements for Duncan's debut—hiring an orchestra, sending out invitations, visiting dignitaries to persuade them to attend, ordering a buffet for the reception after—Duncan was lying about with an air of indifference to all the preparations on her behalf.

More that simply a difference of personalities, this tension was a result of what I see as a crucial ideological separation that still often distinguishes modern dance from other forms of stage dancing. The moment of creation in modern dance is an intensely private ritual, a communion with an internal source of inspiration and a belief, as Duncan describes it, that the body is a temple. In the music hall, on the other hand, creation is largely a public affair, a result of trial and error, with stage-hands running about, music blasting from various sound checks, people waiting in the wings for their turn to go onstage—a real cacophony of activity. I certainly felt this when I was working on my *Dancing with Light* piece. I began the dance by crafting movement alone in the studio, just like countless modern dancers before me. But I quickly realized that because light was my movement partner, I had to create the dancing in the theater, with all the lights and glass floors in place. That meant that I also had to contend with construction in the scene shop, blaring radios, and even people walking across the stage. At first it was disorienting for me (just as the idea of rehearsing in a hotel lobby must have been to Duncan), but eventually I got used to it. Aside from her first mythic moment of inspiration dancing with color and light, Fuller's stories tend to be about "study and persistent work," while Duncan repeatedly memorializes her solitary moments of divine inspiration.

Isadora Duncan's chapter on Loïe Fuller in *My Life* begins in a curious fashion:

The Western nightingale had once said to me, "Sarah Bernhardt is such a great artist, what a pity, my dear, that she is not a good woman. Now there is Loïe Fuller. She is not only a great artist but she is such a pure woman. Her name has never been connected with any scandal."[42]

Having quoted her friend, Duncan devotes much of the rest of the chapter to stories of being scandalized by Fuller's troupe of "beautiful but demented ladies." Many historians cite Duncan's portrayal of Fuller's highly affectionate company of young women. I am not interested in belaboring or even deconstructing Duncan's reactionary responses to the Sapphic subculture in which she found herself, although her comments about Gab are, in this sense, quite revealing: "I was at once attracted by this personality but felt that her enthusiasm for Loïe Fuller possessed her entire emotional force, and she had nothing left for me." What her chapter on Loïe Fuller does confirm is how much Duncan admired Fuller's artistry. Watching her performances night after night, Duncan describes Fuller as a "luminous vision" as well as "an extraordinary genius" whose "generosity was unbounded": "That wonderful creature—she became fluid; she became light; she became every colour and flame, and finally she resolved into miraculous spirals of flames wafted toward the Infinite."[43]

In February 1912 Claude-Roger Marx (Roger Marx's son) wrote an article for *Comœdia illustré* entitled "Les danses de Loïe Fuller et d'Isadora Duncan," in which he discusses the similarities and differences of their two schools of movement and thought. Both these innovators, he notes, have revitalized dance by reconnecting it with nature: "After centuries of convention, dance regains strength through its contact with nature."[44] Marx then proceeds to distinguish between Fuller's and Duncan's conceptions of nature, articulating the different pathways that each artist forged in her desire to affirm dance as a legitimate art form. For Marx, Duncan is an archaeologist, one who has captured in her movements the simplicity and harmony of the ancient Greeks. Fuller, on the other hand, uses light and fabric to create an ongoing motion from which images of nature spontaneously burst forth—"flower, insect, storm or flame." As the article plainly reveals, the son, like his father, was a Fuller apologist. Nonetheless, his analysis is perceptive, for it points to Duncan's and Fuller's different relationship, not only to the concept of nature, but to the arrival of the modern world as well.

Even though she certainly took advantage of her historical position as a "modern" woman, Duncan fetishized Greek culture. In her hybrid Hellenism, she wedded her notion of an eternal and inspiring "Nature" to Platonic ideals of "Beauty":

> In no country is the soul made so sensible of Beauty and of Wisdom as in Greece. Gazing at the sky one knows why Athene, the Goddess of Wisdom, was called "the Blue-Eyed One," and why learning and beauty are always joined in her service. And one feels also why Greece has been the land of great philosophers, lovers of wisdom, and why the greatest of these has called the highest beauty, the highest wisdom.[45]

This first paragraph of Duncan's essay "The Dancer and Nature" establishes the marriage of beauty and wisdom through which Nature reveals herself as a woman dancing. Later in the same essay, she declares: "Woman is not a thing apart and separate from all other life organic and inorganic. She is but a link in the chain, and her movement must be one with the great movement which runs through the universe; and therefore the fountain-head for the art of the dance will be the study of the movements of Nature."[46]

As Daly makes clear in her chapter "The Natural Body," Duncan's nostalgic return to Greece was an "anti-modern impulse," one that shunned the technological advances of the early twentieth century: "'Nature' was Duncan's metaphorical shorthand for a loose package of aesthetic and social ideals: nudity, childhood, the idyllic past, flowing lines, health, nobility, ease, freedom, simplicity, order and harmony."[47] Eventually, of course, Duncan evolved choreographically from her early renditions of a sweet and gentle nature in her "La Primavera" days, in which she enacted a number of figures in Botticelli's painting (complete with flowers circling the neck and waist) to representations of "Nature," which included fierce and destructive energies as well as harmonious ones. Certainly, by the time she was dancing her Greek vignettes such as "Orpheus" or "Iphigenia in Tauris," Duncan's expressive palette had expanded to include both Apollonian and Dionysian themes.

Figures 42–44. Isadora Duncan. From a series of watercolors by Abraham Walkowitz. Jerome Robbins Dance Division, The New York Public Library for the Performing Arts, Astor, Lenox and Tilden Foundations

Despite the (dis)ingenuity of her rhetorical strategies linking "Nature" to ancient Greece (and thus, Daly notes, nudity to nobility), Duncan's heroic manifestos, collected in her book *The Art of Dance*, justified both her revealing costume and, to a degree, her radical lifestyle, which included a celebration of free love and motherhood out of wedlock. In the context of this chapter, it is interesting to review a brief portrait of Isadora Duncan written by Colette and published posthumously in *Paysages et portraits*. In a section called "Danseuses," Colette comments ironically on the enthusiastic women applauding at one of Duncan's Paris performances, making fun of the society ladies who cheer Duncan and imitate her "Tanagra" dress (albeit with a chest-to-knee corset underneath): "They acclaim her but they don't envy her. They salute her at a distance, and they contemplate her, but as an escapee—not as a liberator."[48] Colette, having been subjected to a similar hypocrisy, sees beyond this response, guardedly acknowledging both Duncan's "naive" idealism and her dancing genius. She describes how Duncan danced with her whole body, her whole being: "As soon as she dances, she dances with her whole being, from her loose hair to her naked and hard ankles. . . . She dances and never mimes" (see Figures 42–44).[49]

It is this concentrated unity of focus—her presence—that Abraham Walkowitz has captured so compellingly in his many drawings of Duncan's dancing. Reflecting

Colette's remark that "son corps parle plus que son visage" (her body speaks more than her face), Walkowitz leaves Duncan's face blank, allowing the viewer to focus instead on how her head follows the expressive motion of her torso. More important, Walkowitz's sketches and watercolors help us to comprehend how Duncan was able to transform her ideas about nature into a fleshy, weighty corporeality. In his work, Walkowitz blends watercolors (or shading) with ink lines to represent the hallmarks of Duncan's fame: the poetic tension of her stillness, her luxurious open reach to the sky, the lively skipping of her incarnation as a bacchant, and the contracted anguish of loss. More than specific movements or gestures, however, Walkowitz's drawings evoke the vital spontaneity of Duncan's pleasure in dancing:

> My idea of dancing is to leave my body free to the sunshine, to feel my
> sandaled feet on the earth, to be near and love the olive trees of Greece.
> These are my present ideas of dancing. Two thousand years ago a people
> lived here who had perfect sympathy and comprehension of the beautiful
> in Nature, and this knowledge and sympathy were perfectly expressed in
> their own forms and movement. . . . I came to Greece to study these forms
> of ancient art, but above all, I came to live in the land which produced these
> wonders, and when I say "to live" I mean to dance.[50]

Isadora Duncan spent much of 1903 in Greece with the whole Duncan clan. Led by Raymond Duncan's fierce desire to reinvent an archaic Greece (one not sullied by modern equipment or politics), the family crossed the Ionian Sea in a small fishing boat to make their first pilgrimage to this ancient land. The chapter in *My Life* documenting this odyssey is filled with poetic quotations from Byron and Homer, as well as depictions of Isadora and Raymond gamboling about the Greek countryside, drunk with Plato.[51] Its euphoric tone is also inflected with wry comments about bedbugs, hard wooden planks for sleeping, and the assorted perils of the countryside, not to mention the astonishment of the modern Greeks at this band of foreigners who looked like ancient sculptures come alive. The rest of the story is well-known, a testimony to the quixotic myopia of a radical American fundamentalism. Dressed in tunics and shod in sandals, the Duncans bought some land with a view of the Acropolis and proceeded to build their house, Kopanos. Eventually, it dawned on them that there was no water to be had in the area, and although Raymond would have deeper and deeper wells dug (at Isadora's expense), eventually they would give up the fantasy of living in Greece permanently, and Raymond would return to Paris to start a theater school there.

While in Greece, the Duncans met the Sikelianos family: Philadelpheus, an archaeologist; Angelos, who would become a renowned poet and later marry Eva Palmer; and Penelope, a singer, who became Raymond's wife. The alchemy between the Sikelianos family and the Americans was very interesting. Both Penelope and Angelos helped Raymond actualize his dreams of living like the ancients, and the impulsive utopianism of the Americans (not to mention their financial assistance, which, in the case of Eva Palmer, was considerable) also helped the Sikelianos family to dream of reaching back past the modern Greek state to reconstruct the simplicity of peasant life as well as the humanitarian power of ancient popular theater. Reading about their work together, it seems clear that without Eva Palmer's presence in his life, it is unlikely that Angelos Sikelianos would have written his best work. In 1927 and again in 1930 Angelos Sikelianos and Eva Palmer-Sikelianos produced two epic theatrical festivals at the ancient theater in Delphi, which included athletic games and exhibitions of folk art and featured Eva Palmer-Sikelianos's stagings of Aeschylus's *Prometheus Bound*, the first time in modern Greece that anyone had attempted to mount ancient Greek tragedy in an outdoor setting of that scale. (In 1930 she also staged Aeschylus's *Suppliant Women*.)

In some ways, Eva Palmer-Sikelianios's place in this chapter is an odd fit, and it would not surprise me if most readers had never heard of her before. Two years ago, neither had I,[52] even though, at the beginning of the twentieth century, Palmer's family name was so well-known that Sarah Bernhardt canceled an American tour with her because the press's interest in the young Eva threatened to upstage the "Divine Sarah." By the end of the century in America, Eva Palmer-Sikelianos was known mostly in America as an early lover and lifelong friend of Natalie Barney. Nonetheless, Palmer-Sikelianos has long been honored in Greece as the woman who helped realize her husband's dream, someone who learned to speak Greek like a native and who promoted Greek culture throughout her life. She is also remembered as the director and choreographer who successfully recreated the mythic power of the ancient tragic chorus in the outdoor setting at Delphi. In this sense, Palmer-Sikelianos managed to accomplish what Isadora Duncan loftily envisioned when she wrote her short essay "The Greek Theater": "Greek Tragedy sprang from the dancing and singing of the Greek Chorus. Dancing has gone a long way astray. She must return to her original place—hand in hand with the Muses encircling Apollo. She must become again the primitive Chorus, and the drama will be reborn from her inspiration."[53]

Born in 1874 to a well-to-do and well-placed New York City family, Palmer had all the advantages of money, connections, and liberal-thinking parents. Her father introduced her to some of the most radical thinkers of the late nineteenth century, Robert Ingersoll among them. Her mother developed both her fine musical sensibility and her interest in the arts, sponsored in her an awareness of social injustice, and modeled for her a fervent belief in women's suffrage. As she grew up, Palmer went to schools in the United States, France, and Germany, giving her a patchwork education that was long on English literature and short on mathematics. Precocious but undisciplined, Palmer took up the challenge posed by M. Carey Thomas, the legendary president of Bryn Mawr College, who flatly told Palmer it was unlikely she could pass the entrance exams. She studied hard ("eighteen hours a day for six months") and managed to gain admission to this bastion of women's education and classical studies, where she spent the next two years studying Greek for the first time and immersing herself in English literature. She also directed the annual class plays, pleased when Thomas suggested that she direct *Hamlet* the following year. In her memoirs, Palmer writes that Thomas "had also a knack of sensing and encouraging one toward one's own strong but still unexpressed leanings."[54] I suspect that it was her pleasure in the more practical, hands-on nature of theater that compelled Palmer to abandon the scholarly, cloistered setting of Bryn Mawr for the freedom of Europe, where she spent a year in Rome with her brother before settling in Paris in a pavilion near Natalie Barney's place in Neuilly.

From the time she was first sent to school, Eva Palmer evinced a passion for recitation. Her autobiography recounts numerous occasions of standing on a chair performing Shakespeare, Swinburne, or Poe to a spellbound group of her schoolmates. They were witnesses to some of Palmer's first attempts to merge language and rhythm, and although she was told by a teacher to stop—these events were considered "too exciting" for the girls—Palmer's passion for "melody in words" was ignited. In a chapter entitled "The First Delphic Festival," Palmer connects these early experiences to her later work:

> So this impetus toward the singing of words was for long obscured; and Mrs. Dowe's negative imperative was perhaps still working, while entirely new conceptions of Greek Choruses were building in my consciousness. But then I no longer was interested in either reciting or acting myself. I had come to long for many voices, for many women, or preferably many men, expressing in perfect individual freedom, and in perfect composite unity, the complete inner meaning of the word.[55]

In Paris, Palmer studied acting and performed in amateur theatricals such as those with Colette in Natalie Barney's garden. Her striking long red hair and beautiful eyes led both Sarah Bernhardt and Mrs. Patrick Campbell, another well-known actress of the day, to invite her to play in Maeterlinck's *Pelléas et Mélisande* with them. In both cases, her professional aspirations were thwarted; one because of Bernhardt's fear of being upstaged, and the other because Palmer refused to give up her friendship with Natalie Barney, the association with whom Mrs. Campbell claimed was bad for her protégée's reputation. In any case, Palmer recounts: "I had seen by that time a good deal of back-stage politics and meanness, and my ambition to go on the French stage, or any other stage, was not so ardent as it had been."[56]

During the spring of 1905, while Palmer was trying to decide what to do with her life, she met Raymond Duncan and his wife, Penelope Sikelianos, and their baby. Upon hearing Penelope sing Greek ecclesiastical melodies, Palmer had an epiphany: "I felt that I had heard music for the first time; heard a human voice for the first time."[57] Because of worker strikes that threatened to become violent on the first of May, Palmer invited the Raymond Duncan family to move out to Neuilly with her. Soon the house was in the midst of a mini–Greek revival, with Raymond painting friezes on the walls and the women sewing their own apparel. Eventually they built a loom and decided to try to weave a cloth that draped and folded just like the fabric on ancient statues. One afternoon while resting, Penelope explained the shifts in tone that Palmer found so compelling in her singing:

A mode . . . is not a scale; it has nothing to do with the piano. Each mode
has special intervals of its own, which do not exist on the piano. A mode is a
mood; and a Greek song uses the mode which suits its content: one mode if
the words are gay, another if they are melancholy, another if they are mar-
tial, and so forth. We have many musical modes. We therefore have infinite
melodic variety.[58]

Inspired by the sound and rhythm of the language and intrigued by a lifestyle that
sought to capture the essence of ancient life, Palmer went to Greece with Raymond
and Penelope and there met Angelos Sikelianos, with whom she would find the
focus for her life's work in the theater.

In the introduction to her autobiography, *Upward Panic*, published in America
some forty years after her death in Greece, John Anton writes: "Ultimately, *Upward
Panic* is more the biography of an idea than the autobiography of a person, of an idea
that swept the person in a steady course toward self-realization."[59] Written at the
instigation of Angelos, *Upward Panic* tells us very little about Palmer-Sikelianos's
mature personal life in Greece, moving from the anecdotes of living and acting in
Paris quickly into manifesto mode. Inspired by Nietzsche's *Birth of Tragedy*, her
husband's epic poetry, and her studies of Greek culture, Palmer-Sikelianos set out
in the mid-1920s to stage *Prometheus Bound* at Delphi. As her guiding mantras, she
kept two lines in mind, the first from Plato's *Republic* and the second from Aristotle's *Poetics*: "The tragic chorus is the union of poetry, music and gymnastics"
and "The tragic chorus expresses in movement the character, the sufferings, and the
actions of the actors."[60] What helped her transform these lofty ideas into a living,
breathing, moving theatrical unit, however, was her extraordinary facility at movement analysis.

It is unclear to me whether Palmer-Sikelianos ever had any specific movement
training, either in some kind of Delsartesque living pictures during her youth in
New York City (which is a good probability) or as part of her studies in acting
in France. Maybe she was just naturally perceptive at distinguishing the physical
dynamic of stance and gesture, both on and off the stage. In any case, her autobiography contains a number of compelling descriptions of people's physical personalities. For instance, near the end of her chapter "School," while she is expressing a
certain admiration for what she calls M. Carey Thomas's "great vitality," Palmer-
Sikelianos recalls how Thomas, long since retired, returned to campus one day
while Palmer was directing a Greek play for the senior class:

It was just a matter of entering the room walking through the aisle, and sitting down. There were many people present. She alone was alive. I tried
afterwards to analyze the technique of it, and find out just how she did it;
how she walked; how slow, how fast; whether her slight lameness added in
any way to her extraordinary dignity; what were the almost imperceptible
gestures of her hands; how she greeted a few friends. But there was no technique. It was just pure magnificence.[61]

This attention to detail, to the pacing of a walk, to how a person carried his or her weight or emphasized his or her ideas with a gesture, is a mark of Palmer-Sikelianos's directorial eye, one attuned to the nuances of physical comportment.

One of Palmer-Sikelianos's most perceptive movement descriptions comes in her chapter on Isadora Duncan. Even before Palmer met Raymond Duncan, she had seen Isadora dance several times ("We all felt that the shackles of the world were loosened, that liberation was ahead of us"). Indeed, at the beginning of her chapter on Duncan, Palmer-Sikelianos recalls how everyone originally thought of Isadora as the embodiment of Greece: "What she did was always connected with Greek vases and Greek bas-reliefs; and only gradually, after a number of years of unquestioning gratitude for what she brought us, one began to date the vases which were evoked by her dancing."[62] Palmer-Sikelianos's search for the movement forms of an ancient, archaic Greece led her to recognize the inconsistencies in Isadora's gloss on Greece, ones that Duncan herself pointed out in the end of *My Life* when she claimed that "it has often made me smile—but somewhat ironically—when people have called my dancing Greek, for I myself count its origin in the stories which my Irish grandmother often told of crossing the plains with grandfather."[63] Nonetheless, Palmer-Sikelianos's articulation of Duncan's movement style is very perceptive:

> Her arms were beautiful, and the soft undulations were infinitely charming to a world which knew only the tiresome stiffness of the ballet; but there is not a single example of any work of Greek art before the fourth century which resembles Isadora's dancing. It was always flowing. Even in powerful dances like her "Marche Slave" and her Chopin "Polonaise," the lines of her body went into curves. She always faced her audience frankly, head and chest in the same direction. There was never the powerful accent of a strong angle, and never the isolating effect of keeping the head in profile with the chest "en face" which is characteristic of archaic Greek art. Even in moving around the outside circle of the stage, it was always straight ahead, more like a child running, with none of the pause and power which are added by what I have called the Apollonian movement in the dance.[64]

As we know, Isadora used her classical connections to legitimize her own dancing and distinguish her work as "Art." Eva Palmer-Sikelianos, on the other hand, was interested in using a more archaic movement vocabulary, not because she was dedicated to being strictly "authentic" (she wasn't), but because she thought that this Apollonian style best carried the dramatic power of the tragic chorus. Thus, in a photograph of Raymond Duncan's 1912 Paris production of Sophocles' *Elektra*, we see all the members of the cast (including Raymond, Penelope, and Eva) moving in a series of sharp juxtapositions: feet in profile, arms bent at the elbows in sharp angles, with the heads often facing in the opposite direction from the feet. In his portrait of Eva Palmer-Sikelianos in *The Splendor of Greece*, Robert Payne recounts comments of a modern Greek actress that reveal how Palmer-Sikelianos's skill at movement analysis created a foundation for her uncanny ability to animate history.

> She was the only ancient Greek I ever knew. . . . She had a strange power of entering the minds of the ancients and bringing them to life again. She knew everything about them—how they walked and talked in the marketplace, how they latched their shoes, how they arranged the folds of their gowns when they arose from the table, and what songs they sang, and how the danced, and how they went to bed. I don't know how she knew these things, but she did![65]

One of the tools available to Eva Palmer-Sikelianos in her search for the appropriate gestures and movements in reconstructing the role of the chorus in ancient Greek drama was a book called *The Antique Greek Dance*, written by Maurice Emmanuel and originally published in French in 1896. In this massive tome, the author meticulously cross-referenced gestures and positions of the body found in Greek sculpture, bas-reliefs, and vase paintings with passages from poetry and drama. He categorizes these designs into three basic groups: gestures that are ritualized and symbolic, gestures of everyday life, and mostly decorative gestures. Moving from poetic rhythms to music rhythms to dance rhythms, Emmanuel reconnects the visual and the written evidence, creating an encyclopedic documentation of ancient Greek movement styles.

It is unclear whether Eva Palmer-Sikelianos ever consulted this exhaustive reference. In her autobiography she speaks of going to museums to look for visual evidence and consulting archaeological texts but never directly mentions Emmanuel's book. There are, of course, some obvious similarities between Palmer-Sikelianos's directorial choices and Emmanuel's interpretations of ancient ritual and dramatic postures. For instance, in the group of ritual and symbolic gestures is a gesture of worship referenced in a sculpture from the Berlin Museum and described as a boy "holding the arms out with the palms up."[66] This is exactly the position that the Oceanides chorus takes in *Prometheus Bound*. In a photograph by the Greek artist Nelly of the 1930 production, we see a semicircle of women facing Prometheus in this supplicating pose. Later in Emmanuel's book there is a section entitled "Chorus of the Dance" in which he analyzes the movements of groups of women, including the folk dance that Palmer-Sikelianos used in her choreography, as well as the Pyrrhic or warrior dances, which were also included in the Delphi festivals. In this section, Palmer-Sikelianos would have found clear justification for her belief that the chorus moved as a rhythmical unit in circular patterns, using their whole bodies to create a wavelike ripple across the stage space. In any case, Palmer-Sikelianos was pointedly less interested in historical accuracy per se than in reviving the spiritual aspects of Greek drama. In response to a compliment by a Mr. Buschor, the director of the German School of Archaeology, concerning the "archaeological correctness" of her 1927 production, Palmer-Sikelianos declares:

Figure 46. The Ocean-
ides. From Eva Palmer-
Sikelianos's 1927 pro-
duction of Prometheus
Bound. *The Archive of*
Performances of Greek
and Roman Drama,
University of Oxford,
Leyhausen-Spiess
Collection.

"laws" delineate how "the attention of actors, chorus, and audience was centered on a point, the orchestra, and formed circling waves of power which increased in intensity as the drama unfolded."[71] She describes this moment as the "thrill" of great performances, the moment when audience and actors experience a mutual sense of belonging, an awareness of their shared humanity. Van Steen connects this focus in her directing to Sikelianoses' larger project of creating a university: "Her choice of circular and centripetal choreographic movement within this 'sacred' setting of nature and ruins expressed her belief that a simple, primitive form could help to transmit the Delphic Idea. The Sikelianoi's ideal was to create a universal center of centers, a university, at Delphi, which would unite peoples around spirituality and Art."[72]

This ideal university proved to be elusive. After depleting her own fortune and after many attempts to secure state institutional support for the Delphi Festivals, Palmer-Sikelianos returned to the United States to try and interest Americans in her ideas and raise money. While in the States, she worked with Ted Shawn and his men's group at their dance retreat at Jacob's Pillow and also staged *The Bacchae* at Bryn Mawr and Smith Colleges. Eventually she returned to Greece, where she died after suffering a stroke at a performance held in her honor. As I write, there are still a lot of gaps in Eva Palmer-Sikelianos's biography. I wonder, for instance, how much she was aware of the American dancers appearing in Greece in the 1910s and 1920s. In February 1914, Loïe Fuller and her troupe gave an outdoor performance at the Athens Stadium. It is possible that Palmer-Sikelianos saw or heard of Fuller's performances, but so far as I can tell, there is no documentation about any interaction between these two women artists.

The last line of Anatole France's introduction to Loïe Fuller's autobiography (first published in French in 1908) reads: "There you have to the life this Loïe Fuller, ... who reanimates within herself and restores to us the lost wonders of Greek mimicry, the art of those motions, at once voluptuous and mystical, which interpret the phenomena of nature and the life history of living beings."[73] For someone who had been acclaimed at the Paris Exposition Universelle of 1900 as "La Fée Électricité" and had played Salome as recently as 1907, the rhetorical shift evident in France's language is remarkable. Indeed, this idealization of an eternal nature and universal humanity, with echoes of Greek antiquity, attests to Fuller's amazing ability to reinvent herself. I will now return to Fuller's work with her dance group to analyze how she incorporated the contemporary cultural evocations of "nature" and "Greek" in her stagings of what were essentially modernist theatrical landscapes.

It is important to remember that early on in her career Fuller had invoked the "origins" of dancing in ancient cultures to distinguish her movement inspiration from the music-hall dancing that framed her first appearances in Paris. She disassociated her movement style from that of academic dancing, but Fuller had long connected her work to the ancient Greeks, who "danced with their whole bodies—with their head and arms and trunk and feet."[74] In 1908, however, the term "Greek dancing" clearly referenced Duncan's dancing and that of her imitators. Fuller was thus careful to distinguish her school of dance from that of her early protégée:

> By no means is my kind of dancing like Isadora Duncan's, although there are one or two points in common. The two kinds are as different as night and day. Miss Duncan's dancing is essentially a cultivated art—a learned kind of dancing that takes much practice—whereas mine is natural, inspirational, and spontaneous. Miss Duncan imitates the movements of dancers as represented on Greek vases and her pupils copy her. I and my pupils give the original natural expression and movements which inspired the Greeks when they made their vases.[75]

What Fuller meant by "natural" dancing can be seen in the photographs taken by the American Harry C. Ellis of Fuller's young students rehearsing outdoors (see Figure 47). This extraordinary series of action shots shows a group of long-limbed girls in turbans and tunics, skipping, swinging, and generally cavorting in a fairly chaotic manner. They are usually leaping in the air, sometimes with their faces to the sky, sometimes curled over, with their arms continuing the C curve of their body. Although they may be all doing the same thing (skipping, for instance), they are not all doing it in the same manner or at the same time. This makes for a random

visual field, but it also gives their movements a sense of spontaneity and individuality, two qualities that Fuller wanted to cultivate in her group. Unlike similar photographs of Isadora Duncan's pupils (trained by her sister, Elisabeth), which portray young girls moving as a unit, all with the same leg forward and the same lifted chest, Fuller's students exude a sense of the wilder, less tamed side of nature. Rather than cultivating her dancers, Fuller seems to have simply let them loose. The press often remarked—generally favorably—on this *adorable troupe enfantine*: "Far from inflicting the same lessons on everyone, Loïe develops the individuality of each of her students, which gives these young bodies the freedom that life tends to drain from us."[76]

Despite her strategic differences from Duncan, Fuller's "Muses," as they were often called, wore the stylized tunics and bare legs made famous by Duncan. Although her movement vocabulary differed substantially from Duncan's, Fuller was savvy enough to cash in on the trend for "aesthetic" or "natural" dancing that was sweeping her home country at the time. Thus, on her 1909–10 North American tour, one of Fuller's troupe, a young German woman named Gertrud von Axen, performed solos—both on Fuller's programs and separately—that apparently were remarkably similar to Duncan's early work.[77] In the Fuller Collection at the New York Public Library for the Performing Arts is a program for a concert of solos by von Axen to the music of Beethoven and Schubert given. The heading notes that the concert is given "By Special Arrangement with Loïe Fuller." The cover photo shows von Axen with her arms outstretched in front of her, her upper body leaning away, with the end of her wrapped tunic draped gracefully down her back. The

inside carries Fuller's endorsement: "Miss Fuller considers Gertrud Von Axen the most perfect and real Greek dancer before the public today," and the back excerpts press comments from Fuller's recent tour. Von Axen's performance was predictably acclaimed as "graceful," "charming," and "spontaneous"—exactly the descriptions used when Duncan was first dancing. For a while, Fuller employed several other young women soloists as well as a young man named Paul Jones Chute. Three of these muses, Gertrud von Axen, Irene Sander, and Orchidée, left Fuller to dance at the Plaza Theatre in New York City, although Orchidée returned to the company in 1911.[78]

Figure 48. Loïe Fuller and dancers in cloaks. Jerome Robbins Dance Division, The New York Public Library for the Performing Arts, Astor, Lenox and Tilden Foundations

Alternately billed as "Loïe Fuller's Ballet of Light," "Loïe Fuller and her School of Dance," or "Loïe Fuller and her Muses," the company usually presented an evening of dances that ranged from *A Midsummer Night's Dream*, set to Mendelssohn's music, or *Prometheus* (basically Fuller's "Fire Dance" en masse), with a score by Scriabin, to more abstract works set to modern, impressionistic music such as selections from Debussy's *Nocturnes*, Stravinsky's *Feu d'artifice*, or Armande de Polignac's *Orchestrations de couleurs sur deux préludes*, a piece that was composed expressly for Fuller's company. Works such as *A Midsummer Night's Dream* sketched out a vague narrative—"In a forest, a Shepherd sleeps and dreams of fairies, gnomes, and elves . . ."—onto which Fuller would hang a series of atmospheric events that swept like waves across the stage. There is a photograph of the company in a bucolic setting, perfectly arranged like a picture, with Loïe Fuller on the far right, draped in flowing fabric (see Figure 48). Although it is more staid than the frolicking action shots by Ellis, one can imagine the curtain rising on the tableau, with the lighting gradually growing brighter, like a rising sun, as the stage action begins.

The more abstract works were essentially music visualizations, in which Fuller's exquisite lighting effects were further enhanced by the manipulations of fabric (often with little mirrors sewn onto it to reflect the lights) by the girls onstage. No longer a solo figure evoking fleeting images of a lily, clouds, or fire, Fuller was now working with a larger palette, allowing her to create an impressive series of theatrical landscapes. In the same way that Duncan's dancing realized "a narrative of force," Fuller's choreography now depicted the forces of nature. Lista describes Fuller's work at this time in terms that echo Emerson's notions of the transcendence of nature: "She thinks, like Emerson, that human beings, to truly communicate with the universal aspects of nature, need to downplay their unique position in the world."[79] Unfortunately, most of the visual documentation of these works by Fuller is in the form of still studio shots, with the young girls of her company posed in formal tableaux. There are two outdoor photos, however, taken at dusk, that give us an idea of the kinds of atmospheric play of light and shadow that would become a trademark of her later work (see Figure 49).

Fuller thought of her music visualizations as a "new form of art." In a 1914 interview, she describes her efforts to merge "pictorial orchestration" with "magical lighting":

> Specialists of the dance do not understand that I aim only to give an harmonious impression trying to express the spirit of the music. I intend to continue it, in some way, to continue it as the waves unfurling on the shore continue to obey the breath of the wind. I try to follow thus the musical waves in the movements of the body and in colors; I am trying to create a harmony between sound, light, and movement.[80]

Although some music critics disparaged Fuller's dances for betraying the music, others claimed she had unified the different genres, creating a fusion of sound, movement, and light. Clearly refuting a previous commentary, Jules Clarétie calls her work a "transposition": "Music is a joy for our ears, she gives us again a joy for our eyes. She renders the music pictorial. Claude Debussy is translated, he is not betrayed."[81] Distinguishing Fuller's efforts from either ballet or what he dubs decorative spectacle, Lista also suggests that Fuller was on to something new: "In fact, it was really about creating a new form of expression, neither ballet nor decorative spectacle, but rather a sort of tableau vivant which unfolded like a pure music visualization."[82] I find the phrase "a living tableau unfolding through time" intriguing, for it points to the future of cinema but also recalls the earlier nineteenth-century magic-lantern shows that depicted landscapes changing dramatically from dawn to dusk, or with the arrival of a storm. Once again, Fuller was harnessing technology to produce exquisite images of nature.

Occasionally, Fuller participated in these creations (playing in *Prometheus*, for instance), but mostly she served as the company's choreographer and director. One exception was "La danse des mains" (Dance of the Hands) (see Figure 50). This solo, inspired by Rodin's sculptures of hands and his observation that the soul can express itself through any part of the body, was performed in total darkness, with

only her hands illuminated. Several of Fuller's programs for 1914 contain a sketch entitled "La danse des mains," which portrays four sets of hands in different expressive gestures; clawing the air, commanding attention, holding something, or simply reaching toward the sky. Writing in *Le Théâtre*, Jean d'Orliac echoes Rodin's aesthetic sensibility: "The entire human being, with all his multiple emotions, is evoked by these expressive fingers whose rhythms move her supple hands."[83] If Fuller's music visualizations were changing landscapes that indicated her future directions in cinema, "La danse des mains" pointed toward the expressive montage of light, shadow, and close-up that would mark her signature on this new medium of film.

In response to a question from an interviewer for the *Dramatic Mirror*, Fuller

Figure 49. Open-air rehearsal with Loïe Fuller's dancers. Jerome Robbins Dance Division, The New York Public Library for the Performing Arts, Astor, Lenox and Tilden Foundations

once declared: "It is an American monopoly to combine stage dancing with self-respect."[84] This chapter has explored the theatrical work of Colette, Eva Palmer, Isadora Duncan, and Loïe Fuller with an eye to understanding how that self-respect was cultivated in the bodily practices of these women and how they learned to stage that experience of physical subjectivity for the world to see. Through their embodied training, these women learned how to mobilize the space, enact force, and strategically use language to articulate the metaphysical implications of these often audacious acts. Each of these women was a true innovator. Thus, there are no easy conclusions, no overarching summations about their individual pursuits of art, life, and liberty. Nonetheless, the references and cross-references of their theatrical practice help us to comprehend the fascinating multidimensionality of their work. Although they all lived in Paris at the beginning of the twentieth century and probably all walked the streets of the 1900 Exposition Universelle, their mature professional careers would lead in different directions, even to different countries. Yet their autobiographical writings (which, as we have seen, have the urgency of manifestos), when read together, reveal a similar sensibility with respect to movement observation and a common curiosity about recent trends in art and science. Intelligent and well-read, these women were also aware of the powerful spiritual lessons of everyday existence. In this sense, then, they all were true humanists. They were encouraged at the beginning of a new century by the potential for their own personal and professional realization, and they shared a fervent desire to communicate those possibilities to the world.

Figure 50. Loïe Fuller in "La danse des mains." Jerome Robbins Dance Division, The New York Public Library for the Performing Arts, Astor, Lenox and Tilden Foundations

CHAPTER 6

Resurrecting the Future

Body, Image, and Technology

Intoxicating art and, simultaneously, an industrial accomplishment.
Mallarmé on Loïe Fuller, "Les
fonds dans le ballet," 1893

The epigraph, a famous and ubiquitously cited sentence penned by Stéphane Mallarmé, sets the stage for my final chapter, which focuses on the intersection of body, image, and technology in Loïe Fuller's long and varied career. Many Fuller scholars point to this sentence as indicative of the fascinating combination of art and industry, beauty and technology at work in Loïe Fuller's turn-of-the-century spectacles. Like Rhonda Garelick, who uses this quotation as an epigraph to her chapter on Fuller, "Electric Salomé," these writers often proceed, however, to evaluate *only* Fuller's industrial achievements, attributing her theatrical successes solely to her mastery of the technical apparatus involved in her costuming and increasingly sophisticated lighting effects: "Fuller differed dramatically from other stars of her era in that her popularity owed more to *technē* than to conventional talent, personality, appearance, or grace."[1] Variations on this sentence can be found in virtually every survey of the history of modern dance, relegating Fuller to a realm outside of expressive movement. I propose instead to focus on her "industrial accomplishments" in the midst of this "intoxicating art"—to look at the ways in which Fuller used machines to connect with and energize her physical expressivity.

I began this book with a desire to challenge the conventional wisdom that relegated Fuller to the role of "mechanical wizard," a woman with a great deal of backstage savvy but no particular physical grace or dance technique. According to Garelick, "She had turned herself into an illusion-producing machine, devoid of any apparent bodily characteristics."[2] In recovering a bodily presence that had been written out of history as a spectacular absence, I have argued that Fuller's movement was a good deal more than simply a motor aimed at setting her fabric in motion. In my first two chapters, I analyzed how Fuller's dancing was, in fact, kinesthetically expressive, enumerating how she used a central torque in her body to launch her silks, and

Figure 51. Loïe Fuller onstage with underlighting in "L'archange." Photograph by Eugène Druet. Jerome Robbins Dance Division, The New York Public Library for the Performing Arts, Astor, Lenox and Tilden Foundations

a dance writing seminar for journalists, was oddly dominated by a blatant refusal on the part of some panel members to seriously engage with any sustained reflection (or even interest in) mediated images in dance. The general tone was summed up by one person's comment along the lines of: "I don't pay much attention to screendance because I prefer live performance." Even when challenged by audience members (many of whom made dance films or videos), who reminded the panel that much contemporary dance includes both live bodies and visual images, the oppositional categories of natural and artificial remained unquestioned. It was amazing to me, as I sat in the audience, to witness such a deep resistance to media in dance, and I began to realize how fully the rhetoric of the natural human body has seeped into dance studies, even at the beginning of the twenty-first century, a moment of massive mediatization throughout the world.

As a performer, choreographer, and feminist scholar, I truly appreciate the importance of sweating, breathing, dancing bodies, especially the intriguing possibilities of audience response and the performer's own "looking back" provided by live theater. Still, I find the inability to imagine another relationship besides that of opposition between dance and technology deeply distressing. It not only limits our ability to fully understand Loïe Fuller's oeuvre, it also forecloses the critical discussion of an increasing amount of dance performance currently happening in theaters and art galleries, on the streets, on screens, and in cyberspace. Offering an alternative perspective, Auslander articulates the *always already* interconnectedness of the live and the mediated:

> That the mediated is engrained in the live is apparent in the structure of the word *immediate*. The root form is the word *mediate* of which *immediate* is, of course, the negation. Mediation is thus embedded within the immediate; the relation of mediation and the im-mediate is one of mutual dependence, not precession. Far from being encroached upon, contaminated, or threatened by mediation, live performance is always already inscribed with traces of the possibility of technical mediation (i.e. mediatization) that defines it as live. Although the anxiety of critics who champion live performance is understandable given the way the economy of repetition privileges the mediatized and marginalizes the live, theorizations that privilege liveness as a pristine state uncontaminated by mediatization misconstrue the relation between the two terms.[6]

Following Auslander's lead, we can move beyond the polarization of bodies and machines to a model of dance and technology as a continuum. On one end lies the informal studio or salon performance, with live dancing but little or no theatrical lighting and minimal costuming. On the other end is the completely mediated environment of hyperdance or cyberdance. In between lies the range of dances with which most of us are familiar. These are choreographies that combine live bodies with a variety of technologies, such as lighting, sound, costumes, and scenic elements, including scrims and sometimes projected images. Another way that dances and technologies are mutually implicated comes from the relationship between technique and technology. For dance techniques are, in fact, technologies. This is true even of dance techniques that claim to free the "natural" movements of the body.

In his treatise "The Question Concerning Technology," the twentieth-century philosopher Martin Heidegger reconnects the terms technology and technique with their etymological root, *technē*, an ancient Greek concept that refers at once to the skills of the artisan and the visionary power of the artist. Heidegger also links *technē* to *epistēmē*, a way of knowing the world. Thus dance techniques and media technologies are not simply about the capacity of machines (or even the dancer's body-as-machine), they also concern how we come to know the world. For Heidegger, this knowledge is not a passive recognition of what already exists, but rather a method of "bringing forth," a "revealing" of a truth: "Thus what is decisive in *technē* does not lie at all in making and manipulating nor in the using of means, but rather in the aforementioned revealing. It is as revealing, and not as manufacturing, that *technē* is a bringing-forth. . . . Technology comes to presence in the realm where revealing and unconcealment takes place, where *alethēia*, truth, happens."[7] Although his philosophical language is incredibly dense and at time repetitious, what I appreciate in this essay is the idea that technology could render, rather than efface, presence—be it theatrical presence or a more existential being-in-the-world.

Fuller's own writings connect technical knowledge and scientific invention with artistic inspiration as she flows back and forth easily between descriptions of a certain technical apparatus and the theatrical effects it can create onstage. Because of her failure, in 1892, to copyright her choreography as intellectual property, Fuller shifted her strategy and proceeded to legally protect herself by patenting her inventions for lighting and set design. Because she patented these devices in almost every country she frequented, we now have an incredible body of evidence about her use of the devices she engineered to produce many of her most spectacular effects. Nonetheless, it is important not to disembody these inventions as mere theatrical machines, but rather to recognize that their "bringing-forth" or "revealing" in the Heideggerian sense of these terms happens in the midst of Fuller's physical embodiment of them in performance. After describing her lighting discoveries in an interview, she once proclaimed: "I wanted to create a new form of art, an art completely irrelevant to the usual theories, an art giving to the soul and to the senses at the same time complete delight, where reality and dream, light and sound, movement and rhythm form an exciting unity."[8] Born in the nineteenth century, Fuller nonetheless enthusiastically embraced twentieth-century technology to help her achieve this "new form of art."

Three of Fuller's best-known inventions were registered with the U.S. Patent Office between 1893 and 1895. These consist of her "Garment for Dancers," her "Mechanism for the Production of Stage Effects" (essentially her device for underlighting), and a mirrored room she called a "Theatrical Stage Mechanism" (see Figures 52–54).[9] I have direct experience with the first two of these patents, and it dience away from attending to the usual trappings of the music hall (pretty, perky women dancers smiling at the audience and showing lots of leg). Instead, she introduced them to alternative ways of seeing bodies in motion. According to the film scholar Tom Gunning,

> Fuller blended the techniques of electrical ballets or illuminated fountains with a new taste for spectacle composed of gradual transitions and organic motion. In addition to Symbolism, Fuller's dances have long been associated with Symbolism's more popular and commercial cousin, Art Nouveau, for which Fuller's art of motion served as much as an inspiration as an example. . . . As Klaus-Jurgen Sembach has pointed out, the origin of both Art Nouveau and motion pictures in the 1890's underscores their shared concerns with motion and expressiveness.[10]

In chapter 1, I discussed the myriad ways in which Fuller's sequential expanding and contracting in space taught the audience to see movement not as a connected series of poses, but as a rhythmic transition that spun out from center to periphery and back again, teaching her viewers how to read motion beyond the face at the center of the spotlight.

Fuller's widely acclaimed new art of motion inspired early filmmakers. Besides foregrounding movement as transition, Fuller's extravagant lighting effects led early cinematographers to grapple with the issue of color, and many early films were based on variations of Fuller's serpentine dance (executed by a variety of imitators with a range of skills). Some of these films were hand-tinted frame by frame. These early dance films were a staple of what Gunning calls the "cinema of attractions." Like the music-hall format they were often imitating, these films were short and nonnarrative, and their subjects included travelogues, trick films (like the early phantasmagorias), erotic displays of women undressing, and elaborate fairy spectacles. In 2002 the Fuller scholar Giovanni Lista collaborated with the Cinémathèque de la Danse to produce the short montage *Loïe Fuller et ses imitatrices*. In a brief twenty-five minutes, one can see no fewer than fifteen filmed serpentine dances, including six variants by Thomas Edison and at least one by Louis Lumière.

Several of these films were also produced as "folioscopes" or flipbooks. I own two reproductions of these late-nineteenth-century novelty books. The first one is entitled, ironically, "Isadora's Dance" and shows a mediocre Loïe Fuller imitator mostly facing forward and swirling her wands from side to side. Originally printed in 1897, the black-and-white "flipix" is billed on the inside cover as a "Living Photograph." The instructions read: "Draw thumb over top edge and pictures will appear as if ALIVE." Although there are only a few really good sequences of fabric in motion in the whole book, the ability on the part of the book's creator to slow down and analyze consecutive frames is amazing. A much more beautiful example is Louis Lumière's 1897 "Danse Serpentine." These film frames are reproduced in what is called a "pocket film" format, a little flipbook done "in the manner of Loïe Fuller." This hand-painted film/book was executed by a much more sophisticated dancer using more fabric and more space. The film is shot from farther away so that one can really see the designs of the colored fabric. Although some of the sequences of shots have jarring jump cuts, the hand tinting is exquisite and helps to give the viewer a sense of the rich wash of colors on fabric that made Fuller's dancing such a fin-de-siècle sensation.

At the end of her chapter "Choreocinema," Felicia McCarren compares Fuller's live performances with Edison's 1895 film of Anabella in ways that anticipate my own comparison of these flipbooks. McCarren's analysis articulates the important difference between these two spectacles as that of visual attention. Each of these mediated dances sets up different viewing priorities, asking the audience to *look* in radically different ways. Fuller, she claims, does not aim to seduce her public. Hers is a "performance of pure motion and the movement of silk, wings, panels, petals, turbulences—in Mallarmé's words—around and across her body."[11] In contrast, Anabella "performs not turbulences or forces of nature but simply 'Anabella'—herself." McCarren continues:

> The difference between the two imitators—"Loïe Fuller" dancing for Lumière and Anabella dancing for Edison—could be described as a difference of focus. Like many of the stage dancers of the nineteenth century, Anabella dances for someone—in this case her cameraman—as if he were her patron. She dances for her immediate audience. "Loïe" dances for an eye that the camera only points toward but that film will eventually make possible: the global marker for technobodies, the publics created across the century. Fuller herself, conceiving her dance for the camera, is aware that this eye is greater than dancer, audience, or cameraman: it is historic, it is enormous; it extends in space and time.[12]

Much of Fuller's theatrical legacy comes from patent no. 513,102, "Mechanism for the Production of Stage Effects," which is the design for Fuller's famous underlighting. The drawing and description of the original dance calls for a glass pedestal, but later paragraphs also suggest the possibility of a glass floor instead (which was what Fuller ended up using most of the time). After a detailed mapping of figure 1 (including parts A–J), Fuller explains the desired theatrical effect: "By turning on the light from below and by illuminating, if desirable, from the wings of the stage by projected light, the figure will, as before stated, be apparently suspended in the air. Graceful evolution may be performed without marring the illusion" (lines 73–79). In the Rodin Museum archive there is an early studio photograph of Fuller experimenting with a modified version of her pedestal underlighting (see Figure 51).

In the spring of 2003 I collaborated with lighting designer Jen Groseth on a piece we called *Dancing with Light*. For the final section of the work, we built a glass floor through which we could project multicolored lights, just as Loïe Fuller would have done. Although the movement vocabulary for this section was my own, the experience of performing on top of colored light was one of the most extraordinary sensations I have ever had onstage, and it helped me understand much of Fuller's "surfacing from a furious ocean as if waking up from a nightmare" (see Figure 56).[15]

From 1909 onward, Fuller's choreography for her ever-changing group of young muses took her interest in the expressive possibilities of fabric and lighting to new heights. Although some of these company dances had a hint of a narrative, most often they were pure music visualizations that transferred the potency of her solo work to the entire proscenium stage, something like her "Fire Dance" writ large. Descriptions of these group works remind me of the dioramas and optical spectacles of the mid-nineteenth century, with their spellbinding play of atmospheric light across a landscape. This time, however, Fuller was staging the equivalent of an IMAX show. Fuller's work, especially her sublimation of the human form, coincided with the aesthetic agenda not only of the Symbolists, but also of modern stage designers such as Adolphe Appia and Gordon Craig. Sally Sommer calls Fuller's stagings "a theatre of pure motion, plastic and imagistic," and describes how, "with the help of the magic lantern and scrim silks, she turned the stage itself into a continually shifting and changeable form as the dancers 'passed through a mystery of luminous material.'"[16]

In these performances by her extended company, Fuller created what she called "Ballets of Light," in which atmospheric tableaux unfurled before the audience, punctuated by various untitled dances known only by their numbers. Her shift in directorial priorities is evident in the program for her 1909 season at the Metropolitan Opera House in New York City. Here, Fuller's "Ballet of Light" is divided into three sections, and extended descriptions are given for each one. In scene 2, for instance, acts such as the "Rolling Clouds" give way to the "Passing of the Lights" and "Approaching Fires" until the "Volcanoes—Eruption" take over and "The Cleansing Fires" burn before she finishes with "Dance No. 3." In this work, Fuller is clearly moving away from creating choreographies in the manner of dance numbers, choosing instead to focus on the development of moving images over time.

In the Fuller Papers at the New York Public Library's Dance Research Collection is a manuscript version of Fuller's playbill for a week of performances at the Kaiser Krone Theater in Kiel. This document is truly remarkable, not only because it provides an invaluable opportunity to witness Fuller's own interests and priorities (some titles are larger than other, some credits are in bold and underlined several times, etc.), but also because it includes extensive notes concerning her "newest scientific creation," the "Radium Dance." Her program for the last three days includes this dance with its "Special Black Decorations." Written in poetic form, her director's notes explain:

> The Radium is a soft-strange light.
> It is like the moon
> it throws no rays
> it is not brilliant

and it must be seen in absolute darkness.
It is a new unknown light
and should not be looked upon
or judged by a bright light
and it should be seen very near.

What follows is five pages of scripted scientific information about radium, including what it looks like, where it comes from, how much it costs, and what it will do to you if you touch it. Fortunately, Pierre and Marie Curie, who had officially discovered the element not long before, persuaded Fuller that it was too dangerous to actually use radium to draw designs on her costumes, so we can assume the lighting effects she used in this dance approximated its luminous glow.

Although Fuller died before she could investigate the theatrical possibilities of black light and fluorescent paints, her partner, Gab Sorère, teamed up with the Mazda company in 1938 to produce an evening of "Ballets et lumières." Billed as a tribute to Loïe Fuller (who surely would have loved playing with black lights), this program included some of her old favorites, such as "Fire Dance," as well as a new repertoire with black lights. This second half of the program included works titled: "Étoiles," "Le voile magique," and "Fleurs et cristal," among others. With black lights, the effacement of the dancers into the landscape of lighting effects was complete: the audience could only see the movement of the fluorescent lines painted on their costumes. Critics immediately understood how these dances continued Fuller's legacy as the "Priestess of Light," commenting on (and explaining) the surprising effects and the technical perfection as well as the high level of aesthetic intention. The front page of the program carried endorsements from a number of famous people, including a quote from Rodin, who thanked Fuller for "opening the pathway for an art of the future"—a telling epitaph for someone who was known not only for her dances, but also increasingly for her work in the early cinema.

FROM STAGE TO SCREEN

"There once was a woman who caused the light to dance."[17] This comment by an early-twentieth-century critic reveals the degree to which Fuller had moved from a combination of physical expression and visual image (dancing in light) into abstract spectacle (where lights dance). Dances such as Fuller's renowned serpentine dance have been described by twentieth-century scholars as a precursor to film, a way of placing lights on a moving screen (rather than moving images on a still screen). In her group works from the 1910s to the 1920s, she worked with large scrims that could reveal or conceal dancers and stage spaces depending on how the lights were focused. After World War I, Fuller became increasingly interested in the dynamic of these images on the screen, reshaping her early fascination with magic lanterns and expanding her repertoire by featuring moving images created by shadows. In

In chapter 2, I discussed how Fuller's "Fire Dance" exemplified what Gosta Bergman described as a "dramaturgy of darkness." Developing from tiny silver flame to raging fire and back to a dying light, "Fire Dance" staged an archetypal battle of light and dark. In many ways, Fuller's shadow dances can also be read as the struggle between light and dark, good and evil, individual will and the larger forces of a world intent on war. Directing "Les ombres gigantesques," Fuller had become adept at foregrounding, in the midst of her fairy tales with their witches and enchanted lands, the sometimes terrifying cultural references to the political shadows haunting Europe at the time.

In 1920 Loïe Fuller created a full evening-length fairy tale, *Le lys de la vie* (see Figures 59 and 60). The narrative for this stage extravaganza was adapted from a children's story written by Queen Marie of Romania, an intimate friend of Fuller's. As she was staging the work, however, Fuller was becoming more and more intrigued with the possibilities of film. Soon, she sketched out some ideas in the form of a storyboard, eventually, with the assistance of her artistic collaborator and life partner Gab Sorère, directing a cinematic version of the story. Produced in 1921, this film expands upon many of Fuller's earlier theatrical experiments even as it weaves these visual effects into a cinematic narrative. (The staged version was later reprised for the Metropolitan Opera House in October 1926 as a tribute to Queen Marie, who was then visiting America.) In his discussion of *Le lys de la vie*, Giovanni Lista takes pains to distinguish between a filmed version of a staged dance and Fuller's adaptation of this work for film. Indeed, he argues that Fuller was interested in exploiting the possibilities of the cinematic medium, transposing her ideas by drawing on her latent cinematic eye. Perhaps it was because she knew very little about filmic conventions, but quite a lot about visualizing motion on the screen, that Fuller's first foray into the cinema was hailed as a *miracle cinématographique*, making a profound impact on the nascent field.

Figure 59. Image from Loïe Fuller's film Le lys de la vie. *Bibliothèque nationale de France, Paris*

Le lys de la vie is a fairy tale of two princesses competing for the love of a handsome prince in search of a wife. For the film, the staged choreography and effects were transposed to the landscape of southern France, where idyllic gardens, sun-dappled woods, and the ocean provided the perfect backdrop for unrequited love and a mythic journey. Fortunately, beautiful black-and-white programs still exist, complete with a condensed narrative and stills from the film. This documentation helps us to fill in the gaps in the second half of the film, which is currently unviewable. The original pellicle is housed at the Musée d'Orsay, but there is a copy of the first half of the film available to the public at the Cinémathèque de la Danse in Paris.

The story begins and ends with the classic line "Once upon a time. . . ." At the beginning, this opening operates in a typical storybook fashion, indicating a mythic time and place and getting the audience ready for the heroic quest that makes up the entire second half of the narrative. By the time this phrase is reprised at the end, however, it opens the possibility of other stories, or even other readings of this particular tale. This dual perspective or double reading is further enhanced by the pauses in the cinematic *déroulement*, where the storyline is cut in favor of odd events or spectacular effects. One of these weird repeated motifs is a monkey who is always looking in the mouth of a tiger-skin rug. For a contemporary viewer used to films that suture the close-up shots, sounds, and other effects together into a seamless narrative, *Le lys de la vie* seems disjointed at first. Because the astonishing effects often take precedence over the development of the story, Fuller's film can be situated in between the early cinema of attractions analyzed by Tom Gunning and the later crystallization of a smooth narrative form in film.

Nonetheless, there is a storyline. It includes a king, a queen, two princesses (Mora and Corona) and their various friends and animals. One day, a prince from a faraway kingdom appears searching for a bride. Both princesses fall instantly in

Figure 60. Negative image of dancers from Loïe Fuller's film Le lys de la vie. *Bibliothèque nationale de France, Paris*

love with him. These events are then suspended while Corona goes off with her "fidèle bouffon," the court mascot, and reads "a marvelous book filled with beautiful legends." Here, she encounters the tale of the lily of life, a magical flower that can restore happiness—but only to others. Suddenly, the prince falls ill, which prompts Corona, the more adventurous princess, to travel across wild and fantastic lands in search of the lily. She is aided in her quest by the fantastic creatures of the forest, who immediately recognize the purity of her soul. Corona evades the sirens and meets an old crone, who gives her a "light" that will keep her safe and help her on her journey. Finally, she finds the miraculous flower, rushes back, and revives the prince, who, alas, wakes up and falls in love with her sister. In despair, Corona runs off to the woods and dies of a broken heart, but her body is retrieved by a group of women in white and carried off, presumably to join another world. The story ends as it began ("Once upon a time"), suggesting that Corona's story continues, but in a different realm.

In her very interesting discussion of *Le lys de la vie*, Julie Ann Townsend calls it "the most explicit development of the 'queer' in Fuller's work." Besides the various strange and erotic vignettes between different animals, a princess and her servant (a dwarf), and children, who mirror the embrace of Mora and the prince in an early use of the split screen, there is also a freewheeling, slightly improvisatory effect to all the narrative disruptions. Here, Townsend claims, "desire, like the body, is a living, moving screen onto which any image can be projected." Pointing out the possible feminist and lesbian readings of Corona, who turns away from the heterosexual romance and follows her own journey (basically the entire second half of the film), Townsend aligns the heroine with the transformative world of spirits. But, she insists, "I do not think that this is a fatalistic rendition of lesbian love; rather, Fuller's depiction of the concrete ways that imaginary worlds enter into interpersonal relationships implies that the fantasy is ultimately achievable."[21] Although I have, at times, resisted Townsend's readings of Fuller's dances as a lesbian morphology, I find her argument about the transformative and unstable aesthetics in the film very persuasive. There is something intriguingly "errant" operating here, something about the odd combinations of story and cinematic effect in the film, something that refuses to settle down or hold its shape, something, well—queer.

Le lys de la vie employs a variety of spectacular technical effects, many of which had not been used previously in the cinema. In addition to her usual repertoire of lighting options, including underlighting and a very sophisticated use of shadows, Fuller spliced negative images directly into the film, creating intriguing juxtapositions of light and dark as well as breathtaking images of other worlds. The eerie effects of these negatives, where bodies seem to glow with light, create a cinematic moonscape across which the dancers romp like jubilant glowworms. Writing for *L'avenir du cinéma*, Gustave Fréjaville was positively jubilant about Fuller's ability to evoke "the marvelous, the fantasy, the surreal, a story or fairyland." He claimed that Fuller had, in fact, found the proper use of film: "Moving lights can create ghosts, sprites, and fairies which have neither substance nor weight."[22]

Fuller and Sorère also played with slow motion, crafting a strange, suspended atmosphere by instructing the dancers to move slowly as the cinematographer cranked the film as fast as possible. This then novel effect was used exclusively in the second half of the film, giving Corona's journey the quality of a dream. Remarking on the fluid and expansive "plastic movement" of the work, Jean Faltier-Boissière wrote in *Le crapouillot*: "Nothing is more graceful than these supple dancers slowly rising toward the sky, with flowing scarves and executing the most astonishing arabesques, or of the witches, who seemed to swim slowly in the air."[23]

Both dance and film critics were extremely enthusiastic about *Le lys de la vie*, describing it as "enchanting," "dreamlike," a "miracle of grace," and a "masterpiece," among other superlatives. One critic, writing in the program booklet, also raved about the "trancelike" quality of her filming, claiming it as one of the "purest creations of our screens." Recalling the very first reviews of Fuller's dancing, M. Borie writes in *La liberté*: "Miss Loïe Fuller finds an intensity of effect and expression in a pastoral simplicity that highlights her thoughts and gestures, as well as her use of light and visual perspective; it captures the eye and the imagination of the spectator. . . . Miss Loïe Fuller has created a poem written with light and shadow, a poem that comes from an art so noble and so pure that none can rest insensitive to its crystalline beauty."[24] Indeed, many writers commented on the poetic quality of the film, describing Fuller's play with light, rhythm, and movement.

The term poetic, which is used repeatedly to describe Fuller's oeuvre, captures the importance of form over content. The meaning in a poem is usually derived less from the formal linguistic structure of the sentence than from the rhythmical quality of the language—the ways it ebbs and flows, speeds up or slows down. Cinema can also be poetic. This is especially true of experimental cinema, where the director's priority is not necessarily to create a seamless narrative, but rather to choreograph the movement and phrasing within a sequence of shots. Much of the avant-garde film in France in the early twentieth century was interested in getting at this essence of moving pictures—the play of light and motion.

"I would like a cinema freed from literary subjects, one whose subject was lines and volumes. . . . I evoke a dancer! A woman? No, a line skipping with harmonious rhythms." These words by Germaine Dulac, a feminist, socialist, and pioneer in avant-garde cinema, echo Mallarmé's pleasure in finding his aesthetic vision come alive in Fuller's early spectacles. A writer as well as a filmmaker, Dulac's critical essays help us to comprehend the importance of Fuller's work for filmmakers in the 1920s. For Dulac, cinema was essentially "an art of movement, and by movement I mean the unfolding of life itself."[25] She identifies three levels of movement in film: the movement of the images themselves, the actual motion of the film strip in the projector, and an aesthetic vision or spiritual force that constitutes the creative movement between the shots. In this visual rendering of the cinematographer's ideas—in motion—lies the potential for magic and transformation of vision. In his introduction to Dulac's *Écrits sur le cinéma*, Prosper Hillairet, the collection's editor, explains: "The aesthetic of Dulac is tied to the corporeality of cinema, the materiality of movement with its speeding up and slowing down, its drawing together and distancing, its harmonies and its ruptures, its complications and its evolutions."[26]

Dulac considered Fuller's *Le lys de la vie* one of the first successful attempts to choreograph for the new medium of film. Several years later, René Clair (who played the character of the prince in Fuller's film) collaborated with the artist Picabia and Jean Borlin, director of Les Ballets Suédois, on a mediated performance entitled *Relâche* (1924). Informed by the pacing and populist environment of the music hall, *Relâche* was meant to be a send-up of conventional ballet. Clair's contribution was a short film called *Entr'acte* (which literally means intermission, confusing the audience about whether they were to leave their seats or stay). With its focus on the rhythms of movement across frames, Clair's film continued the legacy of Fuller's experiments in cinema.

In her discussion of Clair's work, Townsend makes an interesting parallel between avant-garde film and modern dance, quoting Clair's manifesto: "Cinema should not be restricted to representation." Clair believed that once it was freed from its overdependence on narrative, film could then open itself up to what he, quoting Dulac, calls a "visual symphony." Townsend elaborates:

> Like music or dance, Clair seems to look towards a film that is a series of images in which each one emerges as meaningful through its relation to the other images in the film, as part of an overall structure or "rhythm" of images. Clair's film explores movement and rhythm as the organizing principles of a semiotic system by drawing on a terminology established by modern dance aesthetics and Symbolist writings on dance, which pre-date Clair's film by some forty years. His interest in these aesthetic problems may reflect his role in Fuller's 1921 film *Le Lys de la Vie* [which] was his first acting appearance and his introduction to the world of cinema. . . . In addition, Clair's shots of the dancer in *Entr'acte* utilize the technique used by Fuller as early as the 1890's of lighting dance from underneath the dancer to produce visual illusion of partial bodies and ghostlike images.[27]

The section of the film that Townsend is referring to is, for me, one of the most striking early examples of dance on the screen. By switching the usual orientation of the viewer and slowing down the dancer's descent, Clair deconstructs the classical aesthetic of the ballerina's *pas de chat*. As this sequence repeats over and over, we lose the dancer for the motion, as the rise and fall of her tutu begins to morph into the taking off and landing of a big white bird.

Perhaps one of the fullest realizations of Fuller's cinematic vision is the 1934 film *Les ballets fantastiques de Loïe Fuller*, produced by André Morron with Fuller's dance company under the artistic direction of Gab Sorère. The cinematic direction was provided by George Busby. Starring Amelia Baker, who is incredible in Fuller's solo "Le lys," this film is divided into fourteen separate danced sections. Liberated from any narrative and taking advantage of the great advances in filmic techniques since 1921, *Les ballets fantastiques de Loïe Fuller* has some very inventively shot movement sequences. One of these is Baker's solo. As Baker runs down a wide, terraced pathway of grass, white silks flowing behind her, the camera also zooms in, such that the viewer experiences the immediacy of that kinesthetic rush of approaching someone. Once she reaches the bottom of the hill, Baker begins to turn and swirl, lofting the costume into Fuller's serpentine designs as the camera moves to a high diagonal. This allows the viewer to see the movements of fabric from above, capturing the billowing white clouds of fabric among the trees. In its combination of image and motion, art and nature, silk and bark, the sequence is extraordinarily beautiful.

Other inventive effects in this film include the ghostlike figures made by the novel use of double exposure (where the background of woods can be seen through the dancers) and the play of spraying water or falling flower petals in front of the images to create an interesting juxtaposition of foreground and background. In addition, the film constructs a fascinating dialogue between the movement of the dancers and the movement of the camera. For instance, in the section called "Bataille de fleurs," the dancers first appear moving through the woods, tracing a serpentine pathway toward the camera. Dressed in Grecian tunics with scarves, the dancers begin to skip in a circle, each dancer holding the scarf of the dancer in front. At first the camera is still, and the dancers swoosh by one after another. Then the camera switches orientation and follows one dancer, revolving at the same time with her. This keeps the dancer in the center of the shot so we can actually see her while the background of woods spins by, giving the viewer a slight sense of vertigo. This obvious shifting between stillness and movement, foreground and background reminds me of the work of the contemporary filmmaker Sally Potter, whose cinematic eye has always seemed to be influenced by a real choreographic sensibility. In such films as *Orlando* and *The Tango Lesson*, Potter dissolves the line between lens and image, creating a visual texture in which the camera dances along with the movement being filmed. In *Les ballets fantastiques de Loïe Fuller*, the camera is similarly embodied, and the work is a testament to the possibility of a rich collaboration between dance and film initiated by Fuller before her death.

TECHNOLOGIES OF GHOSTING

The issue of *Nouvelles de danse* dedicated to exploring digital technologies is entitled "Interagir."[28] A composite, made-up word (I couldn't find it in any of my French dictionaries), this term has interesting resonances for me. When I was a college student, engrossed in reading continental philosophy and French literature, I was inspired by the verb *agir*. For me at the time, this word was closely tied to the uniquely French and existential notion of a *littérature engagée*—that is to say, a politically engaged writing. *Agir* means to act, to do something in a way that has a real effect, that produces results. It suggests taking something on with a kind of passionate commitment, reinforced with a physical tenacity. *Agir*, then, is to live fully.

Add *inter*, which means between or connected to, and one comes up with a word that insists on an active engagement with the world.

Nostalgic musing aside, *interagir* is the Francophone equivalent of interact, as in interactive technologies. But I am hoping to hold onto some of the energy implied by the root of *agir* to emphasize the full and fully physical embracing of body and machine, especially as I draw a bridge from Fuller's engagement with light, motion, and screens to more recent experiments integrating dance and technology. Time, expertise, and the mooring of this historical project do not allow me to present any kind of overview, even a highly selective one, of the range of contemporary work in mediated performances or screendance. There is, however, one example of the interweaving of body, image, and technology that has intriguing resonances with Fuller's oeuvre and that I would like to explore here. This is the 1999 collaboration between body and machine, between the dancing of Bill T. Jones and the visual design of Paul Kaiser and Shelley Eshkar entitled *Ghostcatching*.

Before I delve into a discussion of this mixing of flesh, sweat, and digital tracing of Jones's movement vocabulary, I want to recall two strands of ideas from chapter 1, "Serpentine Signatures." The first strand concerns Mallarmé's perception of Fuller's dancing as a series of hieroglyphs, what he calls the "incorporation visuelle de l'idée." Connected to her body but freed from static representations of some*thing*, this corporeal writing (*écriture corporelle*) reveals the mystery of language itself, the rhythmic dynamic of creation and dissolution—of absence and presence. Although Mallarmé translates what he is seeing in terms of ideas and the enigma of language, he does so by attending to his somatic response to her motion (those vibrations in his chest). Perfectly in sync with Fuller's own philosophy about the exchange of movement ideas and visual form between performer and spectator, Mallarmé's poetics are structured as a serpentine figure eight. In this spiraling Möbius strip of a reception theory, Fuller's dancing pulls an (e)motion from her body and renders it in space as a figure, which, as it expands and billows and starts to fall, creates a responsiveness among the viewers, who in turn breathe with the motion as it descends only to be guided through another trajectory and another figure.

The second moment in that early chapter that I want to reconfigure here is my explanation of Fuller's autograph book, entitled "The Ghosts of My Friends." In this example of corporeal writing, the signature (done in ink, without blotting paper) shifts spatial orientation (from side to upright) and becomes a model of a skeleton, oblique traces of an embodied signature. I would like to suggest that this early-twentieth-century exercise in ghostwriting is a precursor of contemporary experiments such as *Ghostcatching*. At the heart of this comparison lies the whole question of a dancing signature, the question about whether there is an identifiable trace for each body that remains after the body is gone, and, if so, how we might capture it.

In his essay from the *Ghostcatching* catalog, Paul Kaiser relates both the prehistory of the project (a commission to translate the late Keith Haring's drawings to the computer) and the genesis of the project's title:

Before we could start, Bill had to have twenty-four markers taped to his body. He looked balefully at these markers, and then at the lights, the cameras, the tripods, the screens—at all the technology of reproduction surrounding him—and said he felt he was breaking a taboo. "Dancers have a strange piety," he said, "a romantic notion that only the ephemeral moment of performance counts." To the purist, recording was a blasphemy—like some people not wanting their picture taken for fear of losing their soul. He said we were "ghostcatching," and the name stuck.[29]

Ghostcatching relies on motion-capture technologies to extract the movement potential of an individual and then convert that via algorithmic mappings into a virtual format where the traces of that body's original movement can morph and dance and choreograph themselves in different variations infinitely. This process is based on what Kaiser calls "continuous keyframed animation" and another process developed by Robert Breer called "rotoscoping," in which only certain lines are traced by the motion capture to create what in the hands of Kaiser and Eshkar would become the "spawns" or little Mini-Me's that developed out of Jones's "original" virtual figure.

When it first appeared in an installation at Cooper Union, many of the critical discussions of *Ghostcatching* focused on the tension between Jones's usual focus on the cultural markers of identity on his body and the visual abstraction of his virtual "ghosts." In her essay on *Ghostcatching*, subtitled "An Intersection of Technology, Labor and Race," Danielle Goldman quotes Jones as he addresses an audience of university students: "Do you see the sexual preference of the person, the race of the person, the gender of the person, and then, can you see what they're doing?"[30] This kind of double vision that Jones identifies is especially crucial in performances such as his 2002 solo *The Breathing Show*, in which he juxtaposes his bodily presence—his breath, voice, movements, and sweat—with the visual traces of his virtual self. Like the dual perspectives of simultaneity that I highlighted earlier in this chapter, the live and the digital in this work operate within ironic juxtapositions of connected separateness—"intoxicating art" *and* "industrial accomplishment."

In his essay "Dance and Technology: A Pas de Deux for Post-Humans," Kent De Spain quotes Jones as he remembers his first experience with motion capture and his initial sense that there was absolutely no way these technologies could keep up with his movement, could capture the essence of his dancing. Jones relates that he soon changed his mind: "When I saw the dots swirling around on the computer screen later, I was mesmerized, and I was quite moved. Because, though there was no 'body' there, that was my movement. It was different than video, it was disembodied, but there was something 'true' in it, and I was respectful, more respectful, then."[31] It is important to point out that these figures on the screen are a result not of pure machinery, but rather of skilled artists inventing and using those technologies. Like Mallarmé watching Fuller, Kaiser and Eshkar watched Jones for a long time before they created the score for their virtual spawns of his dancing. Trained as visual artists, they responded to the changes of flows and intensities of his lines, the fluid dynamics of his movement. In an essay on *Ghostcatching* evocatively titled "Absent/Presence," Ann Dils explains how, in the midst of all the co-motion sponsored by Jones's traces and their spawns, she felt that her own role as spectator was "unusually active."[32] It is this active witnessing that is called forth in the enigmatic translation of body and line between dancer, image, and viewer.

Understanding what is "true" in the figures swirling around in *Ghostcatching* without interpreting them as being "actual" representations of Jones's body forces the question of traces that this book has been grappling with over the last two hundred–odd pages. Mediated dance makes obvious the process that dance historians encounter in the course of their research: the paradoxical absence of body and presence of figure. Looking at the parallels between Fuller's traces of light and *Ghostcatching*, I want to consider a critical question for dance studies: When the performance is over and the dancing body is long gone, what constitutes its movement signature? How do we hold onto its immediacy—how do we learn to read that signature as a cipher for a (once) live body?

For me, the key to this reconstructive study is to replace traces with the act of tracing, thus implicating the viewer's body in the process of seeing. If we return to Mallarmé's notion of a corporeal writing that makes present without representing, we can begin to "read" *Ghostcatching* not with nostalgia for what has been lost, but rather with a sensibility for what might be gained in the translation between body and line. Prefiguring many of the contemporary debates about body and image, Fuller's dancing presented an ongoing transformation of shapes that never solidified into literal representations. She asked her audience to look differently, to follow the contours of her bodily writing without stabilizing its meaning. If we take our cue from Mallarmé's embodied reading of her dancing as script, we can begin to look at contemporary mediated dance like *Ghostcatching* with another kind of lens. We can learn to follow those moving signatures in a way that carries kinesthetic perception at its core, implicating both the past and the future in a new visual economy.

Working on Fuller at the beginning of the twenty-first century has also helped me to see contemporary mediated dance differently. For instance, while I was in the thick of researching and writing the manuscript, I also had the pleasure of seeing Bebe Miller's *Landing Place* at Dance Theater Workshop in New York City, both as a work in progress and two years later as a finished piece. This multimedia dance uses a combination of motion-capture and video projection with live dancing to explore the themes of sensory, spatial, and cultural dislocation. As the work developed, I began to appreciate how the sparse constellations of lights projected quirky figures that mirrored certain movement qualities of the dancers. There was also a background projection of various landscapes from time to time. These two-dimensional elements provided a sort of virtual environment within which the dancers moved with a raw, sensuous physicality. I am not sure that I would have seen the same kinds of interconnections between the digital figures and the live dancing bodies if I hadn't been thinking about similar correspondences in Fuller's spectacular use of movement and technology. Indeed, exploring the theoretical connections between Mallarmé's notion of Fuller's swirling figures as hieroglyphs and motion-capture imaging (such as that used in *Ghostcatching* or *Landing Place*) helped to liberate my thinking about the role of technology in graphing a dancer's movement. This notion of a corporeal writing in dance refuses a common nostalgia about preserving the "real" body and encourages a willingness to follow these odd traces beyond the absent dancer to the figurative presence of movement dynamics illustrated by her or his digital ghost.

of *Dance History Scholars Conference*, comp. Juliette Willis (Stoughton, WI: The Society, 1999), 53.

9. Clipping, Loïe Fuller Papers (1872–1913), folder 267A.4, Dance Research Collection, New York Public Library for the Performing Arts.

10. Fuller, *Fifteen Years*, 33.

11. Mark Franko, *Dancing Modernism/Performing Politics* (Bloomington: Indiana University Press, 1995), 1.

12. Ibid., 8–9.

13. Flitch, *Modern Dancing*, 83.

14. Fuller Papers, folder 267A.4.

15. Flitch, *Modern Dancing*, 86.

16. Ibid., 84.

17. Ibid., 84–85.

18. Quoted in Flitch, *Modern Dancing*, 88.

19. Quoted in Sperling, "Loïe Fuller's Serpentine Dance," 53.

20. Fuller, *Fifteen Years*, 40.

21. Sperling, "Loïe Fuller's Serpentine Dance," 55.

22. Gilles Deleuze, "Mediators," in *Zone 6 (Incorporations)*, ed. Jonathan Crary and Sanford Kwinter (New York: Urzone, 1992), 281.

23. Hillel Schwartz, "Torque: The New Kinaesthetic of the Twentieth Century," in *Zone 6 (Incorporations)*, ed. Jonathan Crary and Sanford Kwinter (New York: Urzone, 1992), 91.

24. Ibid., 75.

25. Ibid., 101.

26. For discussions of Fuller's connections to early experiments in film (including her own) see Rhonda Garelick, *Rising Star: Dandyism, Gender, and Performance in the Fin de Siècle* (Princeton, NJ: Princeton University Press, 1998); Julie Ann Townsend, "The Choreography of Modernism in France: The Female Dancer in Artistic Production and Aesthetic Consumption, 1830–1925" (Ph.D. diss., University of California, Los Angeles, 2001); Tom Gunning, "Loïe Fuller and the Art of Motion," in *Camera Obscura, Camera Lucida: Essays*

in Honor of Annette Michelson, ed. Richard Allen and Malcolm Turney (Amsterdam: Amsterdam University Press, 2003). 75–89; and the work of Felicia McCarren.

27. J.-K. Huysmans, *Parisian Sketches*, trans. Brendan King (Sawtry, England: Dedalus, 2004), 31–32.

28. Ibid., 39.

29. Ibid., 44.

30. Roger Marx, "Loïe Fuller," *Revue encyclopédique* 52 (February 1, 1893): 107–8.

31. Fuller, *Fifteen Years*, 53.

32. Herbert Stuart Stone, "Mr. Bradley's Drawings," *Chap-Book* 2, no. 2 (December 1, 1894): 57.

33. Lista, *Danseuse*, 288.

34. Stéphane Mallarmé, *Oeuvres complètes*, (Paris: Bibliothèque de la Pléiade, 1945), 304.

35. Ibid., 305.

36. Felicia McCarren, "Stéphane Mallarmé, Loïe Fuller, and the Theater of Femininity," in *Bodies of the Text*, ed. Ellen Goellner and Jacqueline Shea Murphy (New Brunswick, NJ: Rutgers University Press, 1995), 220, 221.

37. Ibid.

38. Townsend, "Choreography of Modernism," 78–79.

39. Stéphane Mallarmé, *Selected Poetry and Prose*, ed. Mary Ann Caws (New York: New Directions, 1982), 89.

40. Mallarmé, *Oeuvres complètes*, 307, 308.

41. Ibid., 307.

42. Ibid., 309.

43. McCarren, "Stephen Mallarmé," 225.

44. Gail Weiss, *Body Images: Embodiment as Intercorporeality* (New York: Routledge, 1999), 72.

45. Julie Ann Townsend, "Alchemic Visions and Technological Advances: Sexual Morphology in Loïe Fuller's Dance," in *Dancing Desires*, ed. Jane Desmond (Madison: University of Wisconsin Press, 2001), 84.

46. Ibid., 96.

47. Susan Manning, "The Female Dancer and

the Male Gaze," in *Meaning in Motion*, ed. Jane Desmond (Durham, NC: Duke University Press, 1997), 163.

48. Fuller, *Fifteen Years*, 265–66.

49. Peggy Phelan, "'I Never See You as You Are': Invitations and Displacements in Dance Writing," in *Dancing Desires*, ed. Jane Desmond (Madison: University of Wisconsin Press, 2001), 419.

50. Fuller, *Fifteen Years*, 264–65.

Notes to Chapter 2

1. "Li and Loïe Fuller," *Sketch*, December 30, 1896; Theatre Museum Archives, London.

2. Roger Marx, "Loïe Fuller," *Les arts et la vie* (January–June 1905): 270.

3. Gosta Bergman, *Lighting in the Theatre* (Totowa, NJ: Rowman & Littlefield, 1977), 225.

4. See http://wps.com/dead-media/notes/1/010.html (accessed October 23, 2006). I want to thank Jen Groseth for finding this site for me.

5. See http://www.magiclanternshows.com/history.htm (accessed October 23, 2006).

6. Quoted in Bergman, *Lighting*, 232.

7. David Belasco, *Theatre through the Stage Door* (New York: Harper & Bros., 1919), 56.

8. Ibid., 175.

9. Arsène Alexandre, "Le théâtre de la Loïe Fuller," *Le Théâtre* 40 (August 11, 1900): 23–25.

10. Current and Current, *Goddess of Light*, 96.

11. Bergman, *Lighting*, 279–80.

12. Georges Moynet, *La machinerie théâtrale: Trucs et décors* (Paris: Éditions Librairie Illustré, 1893); trans. Charles Robert Paul as "An Annotated Translation: *Theatrical Machinery: Stage Scenery and Devices*, by Georges Moynet" (Ph.D. diss., University of Southern California, 1970), 341.

13. Nozière, "Une fée," *Gil Blas*, January 5, 1907; clipping, Ro 12123, Rondel Collection, Bibliothèque de l'Arsenal.

14. "Loïe Fuller: Fait de beaux rêves"; clipping, Ro 12118, Rondel Collection, Bibliothèque de l'Arsenal.

15. Deborah Jowitt, *Time and the Dancing Image* (New York: William Morrow, 1988), 90–91.

16. Doris Humphrey, *The Art of Making Dances* (Princeton, NJ: Princeton Book, 1987), 75.

17. Arsène Alexandre, "L'art de Loïe Fuller," *La vie de Paris* (n.d.); Ro 12115, Rondel Collection, Bibliothèque de l'Arsenal.

18. Goethe, quoted in Bernard Howells, "The Problem with Colour: Three Theorists; Goethe, Schopenhauer, Chevreul," in *Artistic Relations*, ed. Peter Collier and Robert Lethbridge (New Haven, CT: Yale University Press, 1994), 83.

19. Howells, "Colour," 77.

20. Alexandre, "L'art de Loïe Fuller."

21. Howells, "Problem with Colour," 78.

22. Valerian Svetloff, "Lights That Dance," *Dance* (July 1929): 57.

23. Bergman, *Lighting*, 366.

24. Jean Lorrain, quoted in Gaston Vuillier, *La danse* (Paris: Hachette, 1898), 371.

25. Alexandre, "Théâtre," 24.

26. See the Dance Film Archive at Ohio State University for ordering information for this educational video: http://psweb.sbs.ohio-state.edu/faculty/jmueller/Dfa.htm (accessed December 1, 2006).

27. Fuller, *Fifteen Years*, 69.

28. Ibid., 62, 68.

29. Ibid., 63.

30. Ibid., 62–63.

31. Ibid., 70.

32. Ibid., 71.

33. Stephen Kern, *The Culture of Time and Space, 1880–1918* (Cambridge, MA: Harvard University Press, 1983), 132.

34. Ibid., 160.

35. Quoted in Kern, *Culture*, 142.

36. Henry Lyonnet, "Loïe Fuller," *Larousse mensuel illustré* (July 1928): 757–58.

37. Bergman, *Lighting*, 312, 325.

38. Felicia McCarren, *Dance Pathologies: Per-*

30. Ibid., 273.
31. Zeynap Celik and Leila Kinney, "Ethnography and Exhibitionism at the Expositions Universelles," *Assemblage 13* (1990): 39.
32. Ibid., 41.
33. Ibid., 43.
34. Ibid., 55.
35. Ibid.
36. For an interesting theorization of the serpentine line, see Emily Apter, "Figura Serpentinata: Visual Seduction and the Colonial Gaze," in *Spectacles of Realism: Body, Gender, Genre*, ed. Margaret Cohen and Christopher Prendergast (Minneapolis: University of Minnesota Press, 1995), 163–78.
37. Harris, *Magician of Light*, 22. Also included in Harris's book is a caricature of Fuller dressed in a silly peacock headdress and tail dressing from *La vie parisienne*, November 16, 1907.
38. *Théâtre des Arts*, vol. 1 (1837–1920), 469–70.
39. Current and Current, *Goddess of Light*, 182.
40. Quoted in Fuller, *Fifteen Years*, 282.
41. Ibid., 287–88.
42. Emily Apter, "Acting Out Orientalism: Sapphic Theatricality in Turn-of-the-Century Paris," in *Performance and Cultural Politics*, ed. Elin Diamond (London and New York: Routledge, 1996), 17, 19.
43. Ibid., 23, 24.
44. Camille Mauclair, "Loïe Fuller et Salomé," "Actualités" folder on Loïe Fuller, Bibliothèque de la Ville de Paris.
45. Loïe Fuller Papers (1872–1913), folder 215, p. 15, Dance Research Collection, New York Public Library for the Performing Arts.
46. Terry Castle, *The Apparitional Lesbian: Female Homosexuality and Modern Culture* (New York: Columbia University Press, 1993), 65.
47. Ibid., 199.

Notes to Chapter 5

1. Bentley, *Sisters of Salome*, 172, 12.
2. Townsend, "Choreography of Modernism," 112.
3. Colette, *The Vagabond*, trans. Enid McLeod (New York: Farrar, Straus, and Giroux, 1955), 13–14.
4. Judith Thurman, *Secrets of the Flesh* (New York: Alfred A. Knopf, 1999), 163.
5. Throughout her life, Colette's past career as a music-hall entertainer drew protests from an older generation whenever her name was suggested as the possible recipient of a literary prize. See Thurman, introduction to *Secrets of the Flesh*, xiii.
6. Nancy Miller, *Subject to Change* (New York: Columbia University Press, 1988), 60, 17, 61.
7. Colette, *Vagabond*, 42–43.
8. Ibid., 45–47.
9. Ibid., 47.
10. Thurman, *Secrets*, 195.
11. Colette describes this moment in *My Apprenticeships and Music-Hall Sidelights* (New York: Penguin, 1957), 113.
12. In 2004 the Musée Colette in Burgundy, France, published a pamphlet entitled "Colette au music-hall" that documents Colette's career. See the museum's Web site at http://www.yonne-89.net/Musee Colette.htm (accessed December 3, 2006) for more details and availability.
13. Colette, *Vagabond*, 8.
14. Thurman, *Secrets*, 210.
15. Colette, *My Apprenticeships*, 104.
16. Robert Phelps, *Belle Saisons: A Colette Scrapbook* (New York: Farrar, Straus and Giroux, 1978), 62.
17. Thurman, *Secrets*, 133.
18. Colette, *Vagabond*, 32.
19. Colette, *Oeuvres*, vol. 1 (Paris: Éditions Gallimard, 1984), 994, 997.
20. Thurman, *Secrets*, 109.
21. *Album Colette* (Paris: Éditions Gallimard, 1984), 114.
22. Colette, *My Apprenticeships*, 110.

23. Miller, *Subject to Change*, 232.

24. Colette, *Vagabond*, 28.

25. Loïe Fuller Papers (1872–1913), folder 255, Dance Research Collection, New York Public Library for the Performing Arts.

26. Fuller, *Fifteen Years*, 50.

27. Isadora Duncan, *My Life* (New York: Liveright, 1927), 323.

28. Ibid., 3.

29. Ibid., 75. See also my discussion of Duncan in chapter 1.

30. So have her racist remarks about African American popular culture, evident in both *My Life* and *The Art of Dance*. See Ann Daly, *Done into Dance* (Bloomington: Indiana University Press, 1995), and Franko, *Dancing Modernism*, for critiques of her ideology, including the ways in which "Greek" came to symbolize whiteness for Duncan.

31. Duncan, *My Life*, 213.

32. Daly, *Done into Dance*, 6–7.

33. Franko, *Dancing Modernism*, 8.

34. Isadora Duncan, "The Dancer and Nature," in *The Art of the Dance*, ed. Sheldon Cheney (New York: Theatre Arts Books, 1969), 69.

35. Gordon Craig, *Gordon Craig on Movement and Dance*, ed. Arnold Rood (New York: Dance Horizons, 1977), 249.

36. Franko, *Dancing Modernism*, 2.

37. Ibid., 11.

38. Daly, *Done into Dance*, 38.

39. Duncan, *My Life*, 75.

40. Lista, *Danseuse de la belle époque*, 417; Current and Current, *Goddess of Light*, 210.

41. Fuller, *Fifteen Years*, 223.

42. Duncan, *My Life*, 94.

43. Duncan, *My Life*, 95–97 passim.

44. Claude-Roger Marx, "Les danses de Loïe Fuller et d'Isadora Duncan," *Comœdia illustré*, February 1, 1912, 320.

45. Duncan, "Dancer and Nature," 66.

46. Ibid., 68.

47. Daly, *Done into Dance*, 89.

48. Colette, *Paysages et portraits* (Paris: Flammarion Éditeur, 1958), 153–54; translated in Thurman, *Secrets*, 133.

49. Colette, *Paysages*, 150; translation mine.

50. Duncan, quoted in Daly, *Done into Dance*, 101.

51. Duncan, *My Life*, 116–35.

52. My first full introduction to Eva Palmer-Sikelianos came during a workshop on her life and work organized by Artemis Leontis and Yopie Prins at the University of Michigan in January 2005.

53. Duncan, *Art of Dance*, 87.

54. Eva Palmer-Sikelianos, *Upward Panic: The Autobiography of Eva Palmer Sikelianos*, ed. John Anton (Philadelphia: Harwood Academic, 1993), 32, 25–26.

55. Ibid., 105–6.

56. Ibid., 57.

57. Ibid., 46.

58. Ibid., 50.

59. Ibid., xii.

60. Ibid., 106.

61. Ibid., 26–27.

62. Ibid., 181–82.

63. Duncan, *My Life*, 340.

64. Palmer-Sikelianos, *Upward Panic*, 182.

65. Robert Payne, *The Splendor of Greece* (New York: Harper & Row, 1960), 102.

66. Maurice Emmanuel, *The Antique Greek Dance*, trans. Harriet Jean Beauley (New York: John Lane, 1916), 25.

67. Palmer-Sikelianos, *Upward Panic*, 113–14.

68. Ibid., 109, 78.

69. Ibid., 114–15.

70. A number of these photographs are housed in the Princeton University Library Department of Rare Books and Special Collections. Several are reproduced in Gonda Van Steen, "The World's a Circular Stage: Aeschylean Tragedy through the Eyes of Eva Palmer-Sikelianou," *International Journal of the Classical Tradition* 8, no. 3 (Winter 2002): 375–93.

71. Eva Palmer-Sikelianos, "What Is Great Theater?," *Eos* 103–7 (1967): 301.

72. Van Steen, "The World's a Circular Stage," 379.

73. Fuller, *Fifteen Years*, x.

74. Flitch, *Modern Dancing*, 88.

75. Fuller, quoted in Current and Current, *Goddess of Light*, 196.

76. Claude-Roger Marx, "Loïe Fuller et son école," *Comœdia illustré*, May 1914, 739–41.

77. Current and Current, *Goddess of Light*, 202.

78. Ibid., 199–203.

79. Lista, *Danseuse de la belle époque*, 468.

80. Harris, *Magician of Light*, 28.

81. Quoted in the program for "Loïe Fuller et son école de danse," May 1914, Théâtre Municipal du Châtelet.

82. Lista, *Danseuse de la belle époque*, 489.

83. Jean d'Orliac, "Madame Loïe Fuller et son école de danse," *Le Théâtre* 377 (September 1914); clipping, Bibliothèque de l'Opéra.

84. Fuller, quoted in Clare de Morinni, "Loïe Fuller: The Fairy of Light," in *Chronicles of the American Dance*, ed. Paul Magriel (New York: DaCapo Press, 1978), 216.

Notes to Chapter 6

1. Garelick, *Rising Star*, 99.

2. Ibid., 101.

3. Felicia McCarren, *Dancing Machines: Choreographies in the Age of Mechanical Reproduction* (Stanford, CA: Stanford University Press, 2003). For a fascinating discussion of the instantaneous photographs of Eadweard Muybridge as a precursor to film, see Tom Gunning, "Never Seen This Picture Before: Muybridge in Multiplicity," in *Time Stands Still: Muybridge and the Instantaneous Photography Movement*, ed. Phillip Prodger (New York: Oxford University Press, 2003), 223–56.

4. McCarren, *Dancing Machines*, 62.

5. Philip Auslander, "Liveness," in *Performance and Cultural Politics*, ed. Elin Diamond (London and New York: Routledge, 1996), 198.

6. Ibid., 199.

7. Martin Heidegger, *The Question Concerning Technology and Other Essays* (New York: Harper & Row, 1977), 13.

8. Harris, *Magician of Light*, 28.

9. These patents can be easily accessed by going to the U.S. Patent and Trademark Office Web site and typing in Fuller's name or the patent numbers.

10. Gunning, "Art of Motion," 83.

11. McCarren, *Dancing Machines*, 62.

12. Ibid., 62–63.

13. Excerpts of this dance can be seen on the Wesleyan University Press Web site, http://www.wesleyan.edu/wespress/tracesoflight.

14. Current and Current, *Goddess of Light*, 208.

15. Raymond Charpentier, "Représentations de la Loïe Fuller et son école de danse," March 3, 1921; clipping, Département des Arts de Spectacle, Bibliothèque de l'Arsenal.

16. Sommer, "Loïe Fuller," 65.

17. Anonymous critic quoted in Current and Current, *Goddess of Light*, 213.

18. Lista, *Danseuse de la belle époque*, 553.

19. Sommer, "Loïe Fuller," 65.

20. Lista, *Danseuse de la belle époque*, 541.

21. Townsend, "Choreography of Modernism," 152, 154.

22. Gustave Fréjaville; clipping, Département des Arts de Spectacle, Bibliothèque de l'Arsenal.

23. Jean Faltier-Boissière; clipping, Département des Arts de Spectacle, Bibliothèque de l'Arsenal.

24. M. Borie; clipping, Département des Arts de Spectacle, Bibliothèque de l'Arsenal.

25. Germaine Dulac, *Écrits sur le cinéma, 1919–1937* (Paris: Éditions Paris Expérimental, 1994), 16, 14.

26. Ibid., 17.

27. Townsend, "Choreography of Modernism," 183.

28. *Interagir*, special issue, *Nouvelles de danse* 52 (2004).

29. Paul Kaiser, "Steps," in *Ghostcatching* [ex-

hibition catalog], ed. Ann Holcomb (New York: Cooper Union School of Art, 1999), 7.

30. Danielle Goldman, "*Ghostcatching*: An Intersection of Technology, Labor and Race," *Dance Research Journal* 35, no. 2, and 36, no. 2 (Winter 2003 and Summer 2004): 71.

31. Kent De Spain, "Dance and Technology: A Pas de Deux for Post-Humans," *Dance Research Journal* 32, no. 1 (Summer 2000): 11.

32. Ann Dils, "Absent/Presence," in *Moving History/Dancing Cultures*, ed. Ann Dils and Ann Cooper Albright (Middletown, CT: Wesleyan University Press, 2001), 468.

BIBLIOGRAPHY

*Archival Collections With Primary
Source Materials*

Bibliothèque de l'Opéra, Paris.
Cinémathèque de la Danse, Paris.
Loïe Fuller Archive. Musée Rodin, Paris.
Loïe Fuller Papers (1872–1913). Dance
     Research Collection, New York Pub-
     lic Library for the Performing Arts.
Rondel Collection for Loïe Fuller.
     Département des Arts de Spectacle,
     Bibliothèque de l'Arsenal, Paris.
Theatre Museum Archives, London.

Other Sources

Adshead-Lansdale, Janet. "The Concept
     of Intertextuality and Its Application
     in Dance Research." In *Proceedings
     of the Twenty-second Annual Society
     of Dance History Scholars Conference*,
     comp. Juliette Willis. Stoughton, WI:
     The Society, 1999. 109–15.
Albright, Ann Cooper. "Matters of Tact:
     Writing History from the Inside
     Out." *Dance Research Journal* 35, no. 2
     (Spring 2004): 11–26.
Album Colette. Bibliothèque de la Pléiade.
     Paris: Éditions Gallimard, 1984.
Alexandre, Arsène. "L'art de Loïe
     Fuller." *La vie de Paris* (n.d.).
     Ro 12115. Rondel Collection for
     Loïe Fuller at the Bibliothèque de
     l'Arsenal, Département des Arts de
     Spectacle, Paris.
———. "Le théâtre de la Loïe Fuller."
     Le Théatre 40 (August 11, 1900): 23–25.

Allan, Maud. *My Life and Dancing by
     Maud Allan*. London: Everett, 1908.
Apter, Emily. "Figura Serpentinata:
     Visual Seduction and the Colonial
     Gaze." In *Spectacles of Realism: Body,
     Gender, Genre*, edited by Margaret
     Cohen and Christopher Prenderghast.
     Minneapolis: University of Minnesota
     Press, 1995. 163–78.
———. "Acting Out Orientalism:
     Sapphic Theatricality in Turn-of-
     the-Century Paris." In *Performance
     and Cultural Politics*, edited by Elin
     Diamond. London and New York:
     Routledge, 1996. 15–34.
Auslander, Philip. "Liveness." In *Perfor-
     mance and Cultural Politics*, edited by
     Elin Diamond. London: Routledge,
     1996. 196–213.
Banes, Sally. *Dancing Women: Female
     Bodies on Stage*. London and New
     York: Routledge, 1998.
Belasco, David. *Theatre through the Stage
     Door*. New York: Harper & Bros.,
     1919.
Benjamin, Walter. *The Arcades Project*.
     Cambridge, MA: Belknap Press of
     Harvard University Press, 1999.
Benstock, Shari. *Women of the Left Bank*.
     Austin: University of Texas Press,
     1986.
Bentley, Toni. *Sisters of Salome*. New
     Haven, CT: Yale University Press,
     2002.
Berg, Shelley. "Sada Yacco: The Ameri-
     can Tour, 1899–1900." *Dance Chronicle*
     (1993): 147–96.
Bergman, Gosta. *Lighting in the Theatre*.

Totowa, NJ: Rowman and Littlefield, 1977.

Castle, Terry. *The Apparitional Lesbian: Female Homosexuality and Modern Culture*. New York: Columbia University Press, 1993.

Celik, Zeynap, and Lelia Kinney. "Ethnography and Exhibitionism at the Expositions Universelles." *Assemblage* 13 (1990): 35–39.

Chessman, Harriet. *The Public Is Invited to Dance*. Stanford, CA: Stanford University Press, 1989.

Clarétie, Jules. "La vie à Paris." *Le temps*, November 8, 1907. Clipping file. Bibliothèque de l'Opéra, Paris.

Clarétie, Léo. "Loïe Fuller matérialise l'insaisissable." Program notes, May 1914. Théâtre municipal du Châtelet, Paris.

Colette. *My Apprenticeships and Music-Hall Sidelights*. New York: Penguin Books, 1957.

———. *Paysages et portraits*. Paris: Flammarion Éditeur, 1958.

———. *The Vagabond*. Translated by Enid McLeod. New York: Farrar, Straus, and Giroux, 1955. Originally published as *La vagabonde* (Paris: La Vie Parisienne, 1910).

———. *Oeuvres*. Vol. 1. Paris: Éditions Gallimard, 1984.

Craig, Gordon. *Gordon Craig on Movement and Dance*. New York: Dance Horizons, 1977.

Crary, Jonathan, and Sanford Kwinter, eds. *Zone 6 (Incorporations)*. New York: Urzone, 1992.

Current, Richard, and Marcia Ewing Current. *Loïe Fuller: Goddess of Light*. Boston: Northeastern University Press, 1997.

Daly, Ann. *Done into Dance*. Bloomington: Indiana University Press, 1995.

Deleuze, Gilles. "Mediators." In Crary and Kwinter, eds., *Zone 6 (Incorporations)*, 281–94.

de Morinni, Clare. "Loïe Fuller: The Fairy of Light." In *Chronicles of the American Dance*, edited by Paul Magriel. New York: Da Capo Press, 1978. 203–20.

Desmond, Jane, ed. *Dancing Desires*. Madison: University of Wisconsin Press, 2001.

———, ed. *Meaning in Motion*. Durham, NC: Duke University Press, 1997.

De Spain, Kent. "Dance and Technology: A Pas de Deux for Post-Humans." *Dance Research Journal* 32, no. 1 (Summer 2000): 2–17.

Dijkstra, Bram. *Idols of Perversity*. New York: Oxford University Press, 1986.

Dils, Ann. "Absent/Presence." In *Moving History/Dancing Cultures*, edited by Ann Cooper Albright and Ann Dils. Middletown, CT: Wesleyan University Press, 2001. 462–71.

Dimond, Elin, ed. *Performance and Cultural Politics*. London and New York: Routledge, 1996.

d'Orliac, Jean. "Madame Loïe Fuller et son école de danse." *Le Théâtre* 377 (September 1914). Clipping file. Bibliothèque de l'Opèra, Paris.

Doughty, Heather. "The Choreographer in the Courtroom: Loïe Fuller and Leonide Massine." In *Proceedings of the Fifth Annual Conference of the Society of Dance History Scholars*. Cambridge, MA: Harvard University, 1982. 35–39.

Dulac, Germaine. *Écrits sur le cinéma, 1919–1937*. Edited by Prosper Hillairet. Paris: Èditions Paris Experimental, 1994.

Duncan, Isadora. *My Life*. New York: Liveright, 1927.

———. *The Art of Dance*. Edited by Sheldon Cheney. New York: Theater Arts, 1969.

———. "The Dancer and Nature." In Duncan, *Art of Dance*, 66–70.

Emmanuel, Maurice. *The Antique Greek Dance*. Translated by Harriet Lean Beauley. New York: John Lane, 1916.

Flitch, J. E. Crawford. *Modern Dancing and Dancers*. Philadelphia: J. B. Lippincott, 1912.

Foster, Susan. "Choreographing History." In *Choreographing History*, edited by Susan Foster. Bloomington: Indiana University Press, 1995. 3–21.

Franko, Mark. *Dancing Modernism/Performing Politics*. Bloomington: Indiana University Press, 1995.

Franko, Mark, and Annette Richards, eds. *Act-*

ing on the Past. Hanover, NH: Wesleyan University Press, 2000.

Fuller, Loïe. *Fifteen Years of a Dancer's Life*. Boston: Small, Maynard, 1913.

Garafola, Lynn. "The Travesty Dancer in Nineteenth-Century Ballet." In *Legacies of Twentieth-Century Dance*. Middletown, CT: Wesleyan University Press, 2005. 137–47.

Garelick, Rhonda K. "Electric Salome: Loïe Fuller at the Exposition Universelle of 1900." In *Imperialism and Theatre: Essays on World Theatre, Drama and Performance, 1795–1995*, edited by J. Ellen Gainor. London: Routledge, 1995. 85–103.

———. *Rising Star: Dandyism, Gender, and Performance in the Fin de Siècle*. Princeton, NJ: Princeton University Press, 1998.

Goldman, Danielle. "*Ghostcatching*: An Intersection of Technology, Labor, and Race." *Dance Research Journal* 35, no. 2, and 36, no. 2 (Winter 2003 and Summer 2004): 68–87.

Gunning, Tom. "Loïe Fuller and the Art of Motion." In *Camera Obscura, Camera Lucida: Essays in Honor of Annette Michelson*, edited by Richard Allen and Malcolm Turney. Amsterdam: Amsterdam University Press, 2003. 75–89.

———. "Never Seen This Picture Before: Muybridge in Multiplicity." In *Time Stands Still: Muybridge and the Instantaneous Photography Movement*, edited by Phillip Prodger. New York: Oxford University Press, 2003. 223–56.

Harris, Margaret Haile. *Loïe Fuller: Magician of Light*. Richmond: Virginia Museum Exhibition Catalogue, 1979.

Heidegger, Martin. *The Question Concerning Technology and Other Essays*. New York: Harper and Row, 1977.

Higgonet, Patrice. *Paris: Capital of the World*. Cambridge, MA: Belknap Press of Harvard University Press, 2002.

Howells, Bernard. "The Problem with Colour: Three Theorists; Goethe, Schopenhauer, Chevreul." In *Artistic Relations*, edited by Peter Collier and Robert Lethbridge. New

Haven, CT: Yale University Press, 1994. 76–93.

Humphrey, Doris. *The Art of Making Dances*. Princeton, NJ: Princeton Book, 1987.

Huysman, J.-K. *Parisian Sketches*. Translated by Brendan King. Sawtry, England: Dedalus, 2004.

Jackson, Anna. "Orient and Occident." In *Art Nouveau, 1890–1915*, edited by Paul Greenhalgh. London: V & A, 2000. 100–113.

Jowitt, Deborah. *Time and the Dancing Image*. New York: Willam Morrow, 1988.

Jullian, Philippe. *The Triumph of Art Nouveau: Paris Exhibition, 1900*. New York: Larousse, 1974.

Kaiser, Paul. "Steps." In *Ghostcatching* [exhibition catalog], edited by Ann Holcomb. New York: Cooper Union School of Art, 1999. 21–27.

Kermode, Frank. "Loïe Fuller and the Dance before Diaghilev." *Theatre Arts* (September 1962): 6–21.

Kern, Stephen. *The Culture of Time and Space, 1880–1918*. Cambridge, MA: Harvard University Press, 1983.

Koritz, Amy. "Dancing the Orient for England: Maud Allan's *The Vision of Salome*." In Desmond, ed., *Meaning in Motion*, 133–52.

———. *Gendering Bodies/Performing Art*. Ann Arbor: University of Michigan Press, 1995.

Latimer, Tirza True. "Butch-Femme Fatale." In *Proceedings of the Twenty-second Annual Society of Dance History Scholars Conference*, comp. Juliette Willis. Stoughton, WI: The Society, 1999. 83–87.

"The Length of a Petticoat." *Daily Graphic*. Friday, February 13, 1891.

Le livre d'or de l'Exposition de 1900. Book 2. Paris: Edouard Cornely, 1900.

Lista, Giovanni. *Loïe Fuller: Danseuse de la belle époque*. Paris: Éditions Stock, 1994.

"La Loïe Fuller and Her Artistic Achievements." *Poster* (February 1899): 69–74.

Lorrain, Jean. *Posssiéres de Paris*. Paris: Ollendorf, 1902.

————. *Une femme par jour*. Saint-Cyr-sur-Loire: Christian Pirot, 1983.

Mallarmé, Stéphane. *Oeuvres complètes*. Paris: Bibliothèque de la Pléiade, 1945.

————. *Selected Poetry and Prose*. Edited by Mary Ann Caws. New York: New Directions, 1982.

Manning, Susan. "The Female Dancer and the Male Gaze." In Desmond, ed., *Meaning in Motion*, 153–66.

Marx, Claude-Roger. "Les danses de Loïe Fuller et d'Isadora Duncan." *Comœdia illustré*, February 1, 1912, 320–21.

————. "Loïe Fuller et son école de danse." *Comœdia illustré*, May 20, 1914, 739–41.

Marx, Roger. "Loïe Fuller." *Les arts et la vie* (January–June 1905): 265–73, 352–57.

————. "Loïe Fuller." *Revue encyclopédique* 52 (February 1, 1893): 107–8.

Mauclair, Camille. "Loïe Fuller." *Revue encyclopédique* 52 (February 1893): 106–7.

————. "Sada Yacco et Loïe Fuller." In *Idées vivantes*. Paris: Librairie de l'Art Ancien et Moderne, 1904. 93–107.

————. "Loïe Fuller as Salomé." "Actualités" Folder on Loïe Fuller [clipping file]. Bibliothèque de la Ville de Paris.

McCarren, Felicia. "Stephen Mallarmé, Loïe Fuller, and the Theater of Femininity." In *Bodies of the Text*, edited by Ellen Goellner and Jacqueline Shea Murphy. New Brunswick, NJ: Rutgers University Press, 1995. 217–30.

————. *Dance Pathologies: Performance, Poetics, Medicine*. Stanford, CA: Stanford University Press, 1998.

————. *Dancing Machines: Choreographies in the Age of Mechanical Reproduction*. Stanford, CA: Stanford University Press, 2003.

Meltzer, Françoise. *Salome and the Dance of Writing*. Chicago: University of Chicago Press, 1987.

Miller, Nancy. *Subject to Change*. New York: Columbia University Press, 1988.

————. "Rereading as a Woman: The Body in Practice." In *French Dressing*. New York: Routledge, 1995. 45–52.

Morand, Paul. *1900 A.D.* Translated by Romilly Fedden. New York: William Farquahr Payson, 1931.

Moynet, Georges. *La machinerie théâtrale: Trucs et décors*. Paris: Éditions Librairie Illustré, 1893. Translated by Charles Robert Paul as "An Annotated Translation: *Theatrical Machinery; Stage Scenery and Devices*, by Georges Moynet." Ph.D. diss., University of Southern California, 1970.

Musée de l'École de Nancy. *Loïe Fuller: Danseuse de l'art nouveau*. Paris: Éditions de la Réunion des musées nationaux, 2002.

Nancy, Jean-Luc. "Corpus." In *Thinking Bodies*, edited by Juliet Flower MacConnell and Laura Zakarin. Stanford: Stanford University Press, 1994. 17–31.

Nye, David. *Electrifying America: Social Meanings of a New Technology, 1880–1940*. Cambridge, MA: MIT Press, 1990.

Palmer-Sikelianos, Eva. "What Is Great Theater?" *Eos* 103–7 (1967): 300–305.

————. *Upward Panic: The Autobiography of Eva Palmer Sikelianos*. Edited by John Anton. Philadelphia: Harwood Academic, 1993.

Payne, Robert. *The Splendor of Greece*. New York: Harper & Row, 1960.

Pinet, Hélène. *Ornement de la durée* [exhibition catalog]. Paris: Musée Rodin, 1987.

Phelan, Peggy. "'I Never See You as You Are': Invitations and Displacements in Dance Writing." In Desmond, ed., *Dancing Desires*, 415–22.

Phelps, Robert. *Belle Saisons: A Colette Scrapbook*. New York: Farrar, Straus and Giroux, 1978.

Rearick, Charles. *Pleasures of the Belle Epoque: Entertainment and Festivity in Turn-of-the-Century France*. New Haven, CT: Yale University Press, 1985.

Rudorff, Raymond. *The Belle Epoque: Paris in the Nineties*. New York: Saturday Review Press, 1992.

Russo, Mary. "Female Grotesques: Carnival and Theory." In *Feminist Studies/Critical Studies*, edited by Teresa deLauretis. Bloomington: Indiana University Press, 1986. 213–29.

Said, Edward. *Orientalism*. New York: Random House, 1978.

Schwartz, Hillel. "Torque: The New Kinesthetic of the Twentieth Century." In Crary and Kwinter, eds., *Zone 6 (Incorporations)*, 70–126.

Showalter, Elaine. *Sexual Anarchy: Gender and Culture at the Fin de Siècle*. New York: Viking, 1990.

Silverman, Deborah. *Art Nouveau in Fin-de-Siècle France*. Berkeley and Los Angeles: University of California Press, 1989.

Sommer, Sally. "Loïe Fuller." *The Drama Review* 19, no.1 (March 1975): 53–67.

Sperling, Jody. "Loïe Fuller's Serpentine Dance: A Discussion of Its Origins in Skirt Dancing and a Creative Reconstruction." In *Proceedings of the Twenty-second Annual Society of Dance History Scholars Conference*, comp. Juliette Willis. Stoughton, WI: The Society, 1999. 53–56.

Stone, Herbert Stuart. "Mr. Bradley's Drawings." *Chap-Book* 2, no. 2 (December 1, 1894): 55–62.

Svetloff, Valerie. "Lights That Dance." *The Dance* (July 1929). Clipping file. Theatre Museum Archives, London.

Thurman, Judith. *Secrets of the Flesh*. New York: Alfred A. Knopf, 1999.

Townsend, Julie Ann. "Alchemic Visions and Technological Advances: Sexual Morphology in Loïe Fuller's Dance." In Desmond, ed., *Dancing Desires*, 73–96.

———. "The Choreography of Modernism in France: The Female Dancer in Artistic Production and Aesthetic Consumption, 1830–1925." Ph.D. diss., University of California, Los Angeles, 2001.

Tschudin, Jean-Jacques. "The French Discovery of Traditional Japanese Theater." In *Japanese Theatre and the International Stage*, edited by Stanca Scholz-Cionca and Samuel L. Leiter. Leiden and Boston: Brill, 2001. 43–58.

Van Steen, Gonda. "The World's a Circular Stage: Aeschylan Tragedy through the Eyes of Eva Palmer-Sikelioanos." *International Journal of the Classical Tradition* 8, no. 3 (Winter 2002): 375–93.

Vuillier, Gaston. *La Danse*. Paris: Hachette, 1898.

Weiss, Gail. *Body Images: Embodiment as Intercorporeality*. New York: Routledge, 1999.

Wilde, Oscar. *Salome: A Tragedy in One Act*. Translated by Lord Alfred Douglas. Illustrated by Aubrey Beardsley. New York: Dover, 1967.

Worth, Katherine. *Oscar Wilde*. London: Macmillan, 1983.

Index

About the Author

Performer, choreographer, and feminist scholar, Ann Cooper Albright is a professor of dance and chair of the Gender and Women's Studies program at Oberlin College. She has received a National Endowment for the Humanities Fellowship for her work on Loïe Fuller and is currently head of the editorial board of the Society of Dance History Scholars, which produces the series Studies in Dance History. Albright has presented papers on Loïe Fuller at the Congress on Research in Dance, the Society of Dance History Scholars, and the International Federation for Theatre Research. She is the author of *Choreographing Difference: The Body and Identity in Contemporary Dance*, and the co-editor of *Taken by Surprise: Improvisations in Dance and Mind* as well as *Moving History/Dancing Cultures: A Dance History Reader*, all published by Wesleyan University Press.